W9-AOG-821

Canada and War

A Military and Political History

Desmond Morton
Professor of History
University of Toronto

Butterworths
Toronto

Bluffton College Library

Canada and War
© 1981 Butterworth & Co. (Canada) Ltd.

All rights reserved. No part of this publication may be reproduced, stored in a retrieval system, or transmitted, in any form or by any means, photocopying, electronic, mechanical, recording, or otherwise, without the prior written permission of the copyright holder.

Printed and bound in Canada

The Butterworth Group of Companies

Canada:
Butterworth & Co. (Canada) Ltd., Toronto and Vancouver

United Kingdom:
Butterworth & Co. (Publishers) Ltd., London

Australia:
Butterworths Pty. Ltd., Sydney

New Zealand:
Butterworths of New Zealand Ltd., Wellington

South Africa:
Butterworth & Co. (South Africa) Ltd., Durban

United States:
Butterworth (Publishers) Inc., Boston
Butterworth (Legal Publishers) Inc., Seattle
Mason Publishing Company, St. Paul

Canadian Cataloguing in Publication Data

Morton, Desmond, 1937-
   Canada and war

(Canadian political issues in their historical perspective)
Bibliography: p.
Includes index.
ISBN 0-409-85240-6

1. Canada-History, Military-To 1900.*
2. Canada-History, Military-20th century.*
3. Canada-Politics and government-1867-
I. Title. II. Series.
FC226.M67   971.06   C81-094074-4
F1028.M67

Cover design by Brant Cowie

110218

*To all who have served
in the Fort Garry Horse
and to those, like them,
who have served Canada
in war and peace by
deeds, not words.*

Canadian Political Issues in Their Historical Perspective Series

Editors

Bruce Hodgins, Trent University
George Rawlyk, Queen's University

This series attempts to deal with a variety of contemporary Canadian issues within a historical framework. Most volumes, it is expected, will be specifically oriented towards political problems. Emphasis will be placed not only on a sophisticated analysis of the present but also on how the past has impinged on the contemporary world. The volumes in the series will be original and sometimes controversial syntheses of existing literature and will raise, we hope, issues of fundamental importance regarding the essential nature of the Canadian experience. All the books in the series are written by acknowledged authorities and special emphasis is being placed upon sound scholarship, imaginative insight and clear and cogent writing.

FORTHCOMING TITLES IN SERIES

Peter Gillis: *Lost Initiatives: Canadian Forestry Policy*

William Godfrey: *Canadian Political Cultures*

Robert Paehlke: *Canadian Energy Policy in Historical Perspective*

Bryan Palmer: *Working Class Culture in Canada*

Bernard Vigod: *French Canada*

Keith Walden: *Canadian Mounties in Popular Culture*

Contents

Acknowledgements

Though the invitation to write this book came from an old friend, George Rawlyk, the inspiration came from classes at the St. George and Erindale campuses of the University of Toronto who have endured years of a course called Canada and War. Attracted by whiffs of gunpowder, hints of pacifism or perhaps the convenience of the hour, students have stayed to discover how profoundly war has influenced the politics, economics and social pattern of Canada and how, in turn, those influences have shaped our military role in war and peace.

In turn, this book is my small return to teachers and colleagues who have left their imprint on my thinking, from George Stanley, Richard Preston and Don Schurman at the Royal Military College, Norman Gibb and his extraordinary political-military seminar at Oxford, and Kenneth Bourne at the London School of Economics, to my colleagues in the old Army Historical Section and at the University of Toronto. Like so many others, I have been influenced, in their contrasting fashions, by Charles Stacey, the most demanding and generous of colleagues, by Jack Granatstein, a friend and inspiration for many years, and by Bruce White, an Erindale colleague of rare insight and broad knowledge.

A broad survey, stretching hard to reach close to the present, involves even a conscientious historian in many leaps of faith, misleading generalizations and ill-informed assumptions. In a realm where Freedom of Information has yet to cast its feeble light, I have been left to sources which historians usually revise: newspapers and published reports. If I have not erred farther from the truth, my gratitude belongs to Dr. Alec Douglas, Director of History at National Defence Headquarters, whose advice and knowledge have generously been placed at my disposal. For errors and misconceptions which survive, of course, only the author bears full responsibility.

Books remain a team enterprise. As so often before Clara Stewart and my wife, Jan, have typed and corrected manuscripts and preserved me from purveying even worse confusion. Their efforts have been seconded by David Hogg and Bruce Reeve, the editors at Butterworths, a team whose professionalism has not displaced charm and consideration.

Introduction

Canadians may be surprised to learn how important a formative influence war has been in their history. It was the experience of two world wars that fostered Canada's system of social security. It was the need for industrial peace that established the Canadian system of industrial relations in 1944. Wartime demand for munitions inspired the first really large-scale manufacturing in Canada. In turn, the munitions industry confirmed Canada's derivative, branch-plant industrial economy. The need to protect the Canadian West rather than an inherent devotion to law and order sent the North West Mounted Police on their historic march in 1874.

Canadians have been fond of describing themselves as an "unmilitary people" living in "the peaceable kingdom." Disdain for military institutions has been a thin connecting thread in the national fabric. French Canadians, it has been argued, detested and evaded conscription as much under the *Ancien Régime* as they did in two world wars. Canadians of British descent were taught to denounce standing armies and militarism as threats to liberal parliamentary institutions. The immigrant ships before 1914 were filled with men escaping service for themselves or their sons in the armies of the Tsar or the Hapsburg emperors.

On the whole, Canadians have set no very high value on the military virtues of discipline, subordination and sacrifice except, perhaps, for the very young. In few countries have military and naval leaders enjoyed less prestige in peace or war. During the Second World War, C. D. Howe deliberately managed defence production so that Canadian generals and admirals would have less influence over his department than their American or British counterparts. Civil supremacy has always been a lofty argument for playing politics with the defence budget, from the bread contracts at early militia camps to the purchase of multi-million dollar fighter aircraft. Senior officers who have complained have generally done so in vain: public opinion has both scorned and supported the politicians.

Being "unmilitary" has become a matter of self-congratulation. Like most people, Canadians have a high opinion of their military prowess. Part of the pleasing self-image has been confidence that Canadians do not need the tedious, costly preparations demanded of lesser folk. Professional historians regularly demolish the myth that raw Canadian militiamen vanquished American invaders in the War of 1812. The myth merely reappears in other versions like the legend of Canadian success at the Second Battle of Ypres or the seasick but triumphant sailors of Canada's corvette navy in the Battle of the Atlantic.

1

Most nations possess military myths. So long as Canada was geographically remote from potential invaders, had reached a friendly accommodation with her powerful American neighbour and could depend on allies to bear the brunt of major wars, the myth of amateur military prowess did no lasting harm. By spending far less per capita than did other countries in the nineteenth and twentieth centuries, Canadians have been allowed to devote their resources to presumably more productive purposes. If defence and foreign policies should be designed to keep war away from one's shores, Canadians have been well served.

Canadian unmilitarism was not without cost. In two world wars, Canadian soldiers, sailors and airmen have died because of ill-trained and inexperienced leaders. The simple, costly tactics of 1914-18 were not due simply to the stupidity of British generals; they were often all that could be expected of raw citizen armies. The impasse of trench warfare was broken not simply by tanks but by a bitterly learned professionalism integrating a multitude of technical advances. Given time, as they were in the First World War and in some aspects of the Second, Canadians developed a high degree of professionalism. When they did, the emphasis was on winning victories by careful training, painstaking preparation and rehearsal, and a careful use of every possible supporting arm and service. These were not the military traits of wild colonial boys.

In wartime, Canadians and their governments have consistently sought to establish a national military identity. Canadians, with the conspicuous exception of flyers in two world wars, have insisted on holding their forces together under Canadian command. This wartime preoccupation has not been matched by any peacetime concern for military independence. Officers of the tiny regular forces have had to learn their business from the British and, more recently, from the Americans. This has by no means always been a misfortune. The Royal Navy was an impressive professional model for Canadian sailors. After the First World War, British soldiers carefully digested the lesson that victories could be won without squandering lives. The Americans, unaffected by the bloodbaths of Passchendaele and the Somme, had no such doctrine. In some respects, Canada's dependence has bred misfortune. Canadians paid a heavy price for the British doctrines of airpower that led to the bomber offensives over Germany in the Second World War. The air defence confusion of the 1950s might have been reduced if Canadian service chiefs had been less mesmerized by the preaching of the American strategic establishment.

In wars beyond their shores, Canadians have fought as minor allies, a modest contingent in forces commanded by British or American generals or admirals, pursuing strategic goals in which Canadian governments have had little or no influence. That has often made it difficult for many Canadians to feel personally involved in their country's wars. Henri Bourassa, Armand Lavergne or Frank Underhill could never accept that Canada had any obligation to the British Empire; their latter-day counterparts would reject, with comparable fervour, a Canadian responsibility to North American or North Atlantic defence. To avoid the issue, governments since Confederation have made military service a voluntary choice in peace and, barring two traumatic conscription crises, in war as well.

Yet anyone who seriously assesses Canada's defence problems knows that even the heavily armed neutrality of Sweden and Switzerland is impossible. With her own resources, Canada always has been and remains indefensible. It could not be protected by 3,463,000 Canadians in 1867 when its area was only 384,595 square miles; it cannot be defended now by 23 million people in an area ten times as large. A less fortunate country might have felt compelled to bankrupt itself and to frighten its neighbours by making the effort. Instead, Canadians made peace with the United States and turned to the collective security offered by the British Empire, the North Atlantic Treaty Organization and, with more idealism than conviction, the League of Nations and the United Nations.

Disagreement about alliances or neutralism is a persistent theme in the history of Canada and war. Almost all use of military force in Canadian experience, from the young Dominion's first expedition to the Red River in 1870, has cracked the national consensus. War, as the French historian, Ernest Renan, claimed, is one of the central nation-building experiences. The American Civil War, the wars of liberation of Poland or Rumania, the Australian landing at Gallipoli, stand at the centre of those countries' sense of nationhood. Canadians have had just enough share of that experience to know what they have missed. The young Robert Borden, watching militia leave Halifax for the Northwest in 1885, felt his first small stirring of Canadianism. The news of Paardeberg in 1900 sent the Canadian House of Commons to its feet, cheering. The names of Vimy, Dieppe or Kapyong have their own echoes of glory or defeat.

In the fuller context of the Canadian experience, pride in Canadian military achievements seems almost incompatible with loyalty to the Canadian heterogeneity. When, as her contribution to the 1980 Quebec referendum campaign, an Ontario cabinet minister recalled childhood friends who had died for Canada, her speech drew sneers from those she had most hoped to impress. The two world wars have been depicted as crusades primarily for Canadians of British descent. Canada's armed forces have, until recently, been overwhelmingly English-speaking and led, predominantly, by Canadians of British ancestry.

That does not mean, of course, that Canada fought as a British dependency nor that her armed forces were merely colonial institutions. The British appearance of the volunteer militia or of the pre-unification navy, army or air force was deceptive. As an institution and as individuals, the Canadian military forces were among the clearest expressions of that phenomenon Carl Berger has christened "imperial nationalism." From the era of Colonel George Taylor Denison to the men of Canada's Special Force in Korea, Canadians in uniform have insisted on their separate identity and, frequently, on their own superior military merits. The Empire and Commonwealth were the league in which Canadians were determined to excel, confident that, for all their faults, they were better than any rival.

Since 1945, Canada and most other Commonwealth countries have become the military clients of another empire. The green uniforms and the American-style rank badges decreed in 1967 were merely the belated symbols of a change which began with the Ogdensburg agreement of 1940. Still, it was in a Commonwealth setting and against the enemies of the British Commonwealth that Canada's armed forces established their fighting traditions. It was in the uniforms and under the discipline of that tradition that millions of Canadian men and women experienced war. That influence was not always benign. The aping of British manners in the post-Confederation militia or in the post-1945 Royal Canadian Navy could become absurd and divisive. The gap between officers and other ranks, adapted from another social setting, could become indefensible particularly when raw officers understood their privileges more clearly than their responsibilities.

This study of Canada and war remains painfully incomplete. Much has been excluded by the constraints of length and more by subconscious personal preference. Some vital parts of the story have yet to be drawn from the records, notably the impact of war on Canadian veterans and their own impact on civil society. Recent biographies of Sir Joseph Flavelle, Donald Gordon and C. D. Howe have only begun to establish the extent (and the limits) of wartime policies on Canada's social and economic development. Quantitative techniques, illustrated in the newest Canadian official military histories and in the work of Jean-Pierre Gagnon, should soon be able to tell us much more about the men and women of Canada's armed forces and even more about the society which bred them.

Our knowledge of Canadian attitudes to war and to military institutions remains fragmentary and impressionistic. We have only begun to look at the reserve forces in peacetime as community organizations and to trace the political and economic connections of militia officers. Military organizations and values have a strangely symbiotic relationship with their parent societies. Does the transformation of military rank structure from the familiar pyramid of a few leaders and many followers to an egg-shaped profile in which officers now almost outnumber the privates reflect the transformation from an agrarian to a technological society—or merely confusion in the pay scales?

Like military weapons, books like this are obsolete as soon as they appear. Their value is their capacity to inspire improvements. This book claims to be a synthesis of much, though by no means all, that can now be said of the Canadian experience of war. It has been written in the conviction that the experience remains vital for a country trying to understand itself and its place in a dangerous world.

Defence
and
the New Dominion

It was no confession of old age or fatigue for Sir George-Etienne Cartier to choose the portfolio of Militia and Defence in the new government that took office on July 1, 1867. As a former prime minister of the United Provinces of Canada East and West, as a leading figure in the Confederation negotiations, Cartier could name his post. The seeds of his fatal illness were already planted but the big, bullish Cartier yearned for challenge. In the militia, Cartier knew, he could build a vital institution of the new state. As a man who had already codified the legal system of Lower Canada, ended the seigneurial system and drawn his French-Canadian people into the union of the British North American colonies, Cartier would crown his long career by creating what he would proclaim as "the triumphal arch of the new nation," its military system.

Such grandiose concern for the importance of defence had certainly not been characteristic of Cartier's generation. War placed very low on the scale of Canadian preoccupations. There would be time enough, it was widely felt, to prepare when danger finally approached. The militia, so legend proclaimed, had saved the country in the past; it would do so again. By their very nature, Canadians were a virile, courageous people, bred by rural life to make natural soldiers. Moreover (and more realistically), the country's security was someone else's concern. If Canada were attacked by her traditional enemy, the United States, it would be because of her loyalty to the British connection. It was up to Britain to shoulder the burden of Canadian defence. It was up to Canadians to prosper in civil pursuits.

For generations, the British grudgingly accepted their responsibility. The old experience with the American colonies left a painful reminder of the danger of taxing colonists for their own defence. The War of 1812 had shown that a small army of British regulars, backed by well-drilled troops raised in British North America, could throw back an American invasion. In the years of the long peace after 1815, British soldiers continued to garrison the North American colonies in numbers roughly comparable to the regular army of the United States. At Kingston, Quebec and Halifax and in the mosquito-infested swamps on the route of the Rideau Canal, British military engineers struggled to make the colonies ready for any renewal of the War of 1812.

For all their efforts, the British engineers and strategists could not escape the pessimism which had paralyzed all but Sir Isaac Brock in 1812. Defence plans for Canada all bore a family resemblance to the events of 1759-60 and 1775-76. Nova Scotia and, to a lesser extent, New Brunswick, might be safe behind the power of the Royal Navy. Upper and Lower Canada would just as surely be invaded. Holding Quebec through the first winter of the war was the key to any counterattack. If the Union Jack still flew from the battlements in the spring, a relieving British fleet and army might still drive back the Americans. This was, of course, a forlorn and defeatist view. In 1812, Sir George Prevost had mustered troops and militia to save Montreal as well. In a wholly unforeseen miracle, even Upper Canada had survived the first year of the war. Brock's victories at Detroit and Queenston Heights, purchased at the cost of his own life, compelled Prevost to reinforce the upper province and it was there that most of the land fighting in the war took place. By war's end, the British had been driven from Lake Erie and the "peninsula" of present-day southwestern Ontario, but a strenuous naval and military struggle had saved Lake Ontario and the territory around it. Early capture of Michilimackinac gave Britain renewed dominance of the vast fur-trading interior.

The War of 1812 had dramatic consequences for Canada's military tradition. The struggle gave the Upper Canadians a heroic national myth. It was no longer possible for military planners merely to abandon the region. Instead, its significance grew. The grudging allegiance of "late Loyalists" and American settlers was transformed by a flood of British immigration. William Lyon Mackenzie's rebellion of 1837 was, in large part, a final attempt by the American element of the population to assert their influence against the newcomers. Those who rallied in their thousands to defeat Mackenzie inherited the conviction that they, too, had saved the colony for the Crown. They could also believe that any threat could be met by citizens in arms.

The political transformation of Upper Canada only made the military problems of North American defence more difficult. Across the lakes, the American population surged into the millions. It was a carefully guarded secret that even in 1814 the Americans had been close to a military and naval preponderance in the region. Thanks to the Rush–Bagot agreement of 1817, both sides could dismantle their rotting battle fleets, but it was no secret that the United States could easily replace its warships. In the same year, construction began on the Erie Canal, linking New York and Buffalo. The logistical problems which had bedevilled American generals and commodores would vanish. There was no comparable improvement on the British side.

Sir James Carmichael-Smyth, the Duke of Wellington's chief engineer, brought his master's great prestige to the problem. If Upper Canada must be defended, there must be a strong garrison, a secure naval base at Kingston and a safe route from Montreal. Action followed: Fort Henry's only casemented redoubt was built in 1832 to guard the terminus of the Ottawa and Rideau canal system, finished by 1834. The huge, million-pounds-sterling Rideau undertaking had significant consequences. Colonel John By may be renowned as the man who located Canada's future capital and as an engineer constitutionally incapable of building cheaply, but the cost of his work outraged the British Treasury and undermined the prestige of the Ordnance Department. Whether or not soldiers could make the Canadas safe from the United States, the cost was intolerable to one of the richest governments in the world. British garrisons remained in Canada, sometimes growing in times of tension, like the aftermath of the 1837 rebellions, more often dwindling when soldiers were needed elsewhere. Canada, on the whole, was a healthy and popular garrison post, marred only by the ease with which troops could desert to the United States. However, in London, seeds of doubt had been scattered. They would sprout and grow.

Undoubtedly, the main impetus for British misgivings about colonial policy was economic. The self-confident demand for free trade among British industrialists, culminating in repeal of the historic tariff on wheat in 1847, went hand in hand with a determination to cut taxes and public spending. The same British principle that allowed Canadians, by mid-century, to manage most of their own affairs also removed the security of a protected market for Canadian wheat and timber. Sooner or later, British politicians would follow the lead of Benjamin Disraeli and demand to know why a colony which would not let Britain govern her should also insist that Britain defend her.

Of course, British North Americans might insist that they were engaged in their own defence too. From Prince Edward Island to Upper Canada, roughly comparable systems provided for a sedentary militia embracing every able-bodied male save judges, Quakers and lunatics. On paper, the militia could be an elaborate and impressive organization. In 1840, the rolls for Upper and Lower Canada claimed 426 battalions with 235,000 men. In the Oregon crisis of 1845, New Brunswick boasted a potential enrolment of 27,532; Nova Scotia had muster rolls for 1,455 officers and 39,542 other ranks. However, no informed person took the sedentary militia seriously. Militia commissions were modest rewards for social standing or political allegiance. The men were unarmed, unequipped and untrained. Legislatures avoided voting the modest sum required for annual musters; in Prince Edward Island, suspicion of discontented tenant farmers discouraged any attempt to discover whether the estimated strength of 8,000 had any relation to reality. Surviving records of militia administration would be useful to a social historian exploring local squabbles; they have no military significance. When armed, trained men were needed, as in the aftermath of 1837, units might be embodied with the aid of a lottery or "ballot" (with the time-honoured right to hire substitutes). More often, it was only the soldiers of the British garrison who could be depended upon to suppress riots or even to fight major fires.

By the late 1840s, British exasperation at costly North American defence commitments was already apparent. When American politicians asserted their "Manifest Destiny" to absorb the whole of North America and blustered about "54.40 or fight" as a policy for marking the western boundary, the British authorities refused to respond with troops. Instead, the garrison fell in strength. War with Russia in 1854 left barely 3,000 British regulars stretched from Newfoundland to Fort Garry in present-day Manitoba. In the United Canadas, Britain offered a bargain: an exchange of the valuable reserve of Ordnance lands in return for an efficient militia. The chance was too good to miss. In 1855, the provincial government cautiously appointed a commission ". . . for the purpose of investigating the state of the Militia of Canada, or reorganizing the said Militia, and of providing an efficient and economic system of public defence." The report was soon delivered and promptly enacted.

Speed was possible because most of the reforms were overdue and widely-accepted improvements of the traditional sedentary militia. Yet hidden in the report and the resulting Militia Act was a revolutionary idea. By tradition, the word militia had always implied universal, compulsory service. So it had meant since the *milice* of the *Ancien Régime*. However, the 1855 Commission had visited the United States. There, too, the traditional system was in decay but states like Connecticut, New York and Massachusetts had supplanted it with officially approved and publicly financed organizations of volunteers. Enthusiasts were apparently willing to drill, buy uniforms and hold themselves in readiness for the demands of state and nation. The Canadian commissioners were impressed. However splendid it might be to make military service a universal obligation of citizenship, politically it did not wash. The Militia Act of 1855 provided for an "Active Militia" of 5,000 volunteers, to be enlisted for a three-year term, to be armed and equipped at public expense and to be paid to train for ten days a year (twenty for the artillery).

Volunteering had some faint precedents. A desperate Brock had sought volunteers from the militia in 1812. Some embodied militia on the frontier from 1838 to 1850 (including companies of black Canadians) had been recruited from volunteers. Beginning in 1855, military service in Canada became essentially a matter of personal choice. Attempts to impose compulsion in the two world wars of the twentieth century would provoke nation-rending explosions.

Volunteering worked when military enthusiasm was in fashion. The distant Crimean War and the ensuing Indian Mutiny awoke many Canadians to a pitch of military enthusiasm. Prosperity helped. There was money for uniforms and employers could afford to be indulgent when clerks and workers wasted an occasional Saturday on drill. In 1856, the provincial government of the Canadas doubled the volunteer force to 10,000 though it insisted that the extra men must serve without pay. Some of the oldest units of the Canadian Armed Forces can trace their ancestry to the companies, batteries and cavalry troops formed in 1855-56. Montreal companies became the forebears of the present-day Canadian Grenadier Guards while Toronto companies formed the Queen's Own Rifles in 1860. In Nova Scotia and New Brunswick, a weaker volunteer movement followed the British example rather than the American. Units formed at the time of a war scare with France in 1859 flourished the following year when a North American visit by the Prince of Wales led to a widespread need for guards of honour.

Not even a volunteer militia could absorb all the military excitement of the mid-1850s in the Canadas. Hard-pressed for recruits for its Crimean expedition, the British War Office turned to North America. A patriotic colonial government had neither the right nor the desire to prevent Her Majesty from recruiting a regiment in Canada. By dint of the time-honoured device of allowing would-be officers to earn their commissions by recruiting their own soldiers, 1,027 Canadians had enlisted within three months. The new 100th Regiment (Royal Canadians) was too late for the actual fighting when it left Canada in the summer of 1858 but some of its officers would eventually return to lend their experience to Canada's militia.

The trouble with volunteering is that it depends on enthusiasm. By 1858, when the initial enlistments ran out, central Canada was in the midst of a severe depression. Employers were no longer indulgent. Ordinary Canadians were hunting for work. The provincial government was too short of revenue to waste money on mere soldiering. Then, when all the gains of 1855 seemed lost, along came the Prince of Wales and a new thirst for uniforms, martial music and glory. Nova Scotia's Militia Act finally recognized volunteers in 1861. Even Prince Edward Island boasted ten volunteer companies.

From the outset, volunteer militia units were social as much as military organizations. For example when young Will Otter, a future general, wanted to enter a Toronto company, other members rejected him on the claim that his origins were too humble. Otter's father, down on his luck but the son of an Anglican bishop, intervened. The early volunteers elected their own officers, a practice suppressed as "un-British." Officers and even soldiers needed money to buy an array of dress uniforms and accoutrements. By designing themselves elaborate uniforms, companies like Halifax's Chebucto Greys could guarantee their social exclusiveness. City corps could attract wealthy officers who cheerfully financed bands and excursions. In turn, they looked scornfully on the less well-endowed militia corps, particularly those formed in the rural counties.

These were the results of a voluntary system. In time, they would shape the military institutions of the new Dominion and Canadian attitudes to them. However, in the 1860s, the future could look after itself. British North America faced the most serious threat since the War of 1812. The decade would have historic consequences.

Rumours of war with the United States had rumbled in the background throughout the half-century after 1814. None was more serious than the *Trent* affair of 1861. William Seward, Abraham Lincoln's new Secretary of State, openly pondered whether Americans might forget their differences over slavery and secession in a war against Britain. Others mused that Britain's American colonies might be willing replacements for the departing slave states. Such notions had already drawn some British reinforcements to North America when the news burst that an American warship had forcibly removed two Confederate agents from a British steamer, the *Trent*. It was a grave provocation. To Seward and to Britain's bellicose prime minister, Lord Palmerston, it might easily be cause for war. Only Queen Victoria's husband, Prince Albert, had the influence and the presence of mind to soften Palmerston's policy and thus prevent war. His exertions hastened his death; they also obliged the Americans to fight each other.

The *Trent* crisis drew more British reinforcements to Canada. Too late to beat the freeze-up of the St. Lawrence, the troops travelled overland by sleigh through the New Brunswick woods. Canada's future security obviously depended on a railway to the Atlantic. Only a union of the colonies would make it possible. The American threat also spurred serious militia reform in the Canadas as well as in the maritime colonies. Both Nova Scotia and New Brunswick adopted new militia legislation, with the latter province concentrating on its small volunteer organization while the former adopted a more ambitious and costly scheme to revive and train the sedentary militia. In the threatened Canadas, the well-worn government of Cartier and Macdonald proposed a dramatic gesture to warn the Americans and capitalize on patriotic emotions. A new Militia Bill proposed a force of 50,000 men, raised from the volunteers and the old sedentary force, to train for twenty-eight days a year at an annual cost of $1,100,000. Macdonald, as architect of the proposal, misjudged badly. By the time the bill came to a debate, the border was quiet and patriotic fervour had ebbed. George Brown, his old enemy, led the Liberals in an assault on extravagant militarism. The government trimmed its proposal to only 30,000 men and fourteen days of training. The fury redoubled. Brown discovered that volunteer officers, furious at being lumped in with the sedentary militia, hated the bill. A. A. Dorion, Brown's *Rouge* ally, warned that French Canadians would be torn from their farms to fight in British wars. The government collapsed. Its feeble Liberal successor increased militia spending to a mere $250,000 and allowed the volunteer force to grow to 10,000 men.

It was easy enough for Canadians to explain that the Militia Bill was merely a pretext for defeating a bad government. Knowing Canadian opinion, not even the Tories had defended their scheme very vigorously. Brown's *Globe* probably spoke for most voters when it warned: "If the Ministry think that they can induce the people of Canada to lie upon their oars for the next ten years, waiting for a war which will never come, they are greatly mistaken." The British were not willing to make allowances. They were furious. Just the cost of sending troops to Canada after the *Trent* affair was four times more than even Macdonald would have spent. Early estimates indicated that it would take 150,000 men and $8,000,000 merely to make Canada partially defensible. Why bother, if Canadians were too foolish to defend themselves?

By 1863, it seemed clear that the North would win the Civil War. Most Canadians were pleased. Thousands had left to serve in the Union armies. They were also alarmed. War, claimed Thomas D'Arcy McGee, was an appetite that grew from feeding. Would the victorious federal armies turn northward? Canada's volunteer force grew to 35,000. By 1865, Nova Scotia had enrolled 59,379 men and trained 45,600 of them. Prince Edward Island's 730 volunteers were interrupted in their drill when their commander, Colonel John Hamilton Gray, had to turn his attention to organizing the Charlottetown Conference in the summer of 1864. On the Canadian-American border, Southern raiders invaded Vermont to rob a bank; furious American authorities closed the frontier, demanded passports for the first time in history and prepared to end the ten-year Reciprocity Treaty which many Canadians credited with their prosperity.

The American threat was not only real; it now had an excuse. The huge Northern armies might be short of polish and surfeited with political generals, but no one scorned American military power any more. Colonel W.F.D. Jervois of the Royal Engineers came to Canada, hurriedly inspected the defences, and concluded, in effect, that resistance against a major American assault was virtually hopeless. Some Canadians might be more sanguine but they now believed that if British North America was to be preserved and if Canada's own "manifest destiny" as a nation extending from ocean to ocean was to be assured, a union of the scattered British colonies must come. The British now fervently agreed. How could they better escape their hopeless military commitment in North America than by helping the colonists to organize themselves? Colonel Jervois's arguments were unanswerable but they might be redesigned for colonial consumption.

Canadians forget how much their Confederation was the result of military threats and strategic debate. For so unmilitary a nation, Canada had an exceptionally warlike conception. When the Fathers of Confederation met at Quebec late in 1864, Colonel Jervois was on hand with a suddenly optimistic version of his report. For $6,000,000 worth of fortifications, he assured the Canadians and their Maritime guests, the country could be defended. Moreover, others added, if the Confederacy, with roughly Canada's population, had resisted the North for four long years, so could Canada. It was a comforting illusion, particularly for militia officers like George T. Denison, whose hearts were with the South.

After Appomattox, the Northern armies dissolved with quite astonishing speed. They left a new threat. Irish-American veterans hunted for jobs and debated a new idea. Instead of rescuing their long-suffering homeland, why not invade British North America and hold it hostage. A Fenian Brotherhood burst into existence to give the idea substance. With obvious misgivings, Britain once again sent troops, while Canada and New Brunswick posted militia on their borders.

Politically, the Fenians were a secret blessing: dangerous enough to cause alarm, weak enough to avoid panic, foolish enough to do little harm. Their Irishness offended French Canadians; their Catholicism aroused Protestants. Even Irish Canadians grumbled at their folly. D'Arcy McGee was their sworn enemy and his murder in 1868 was one of their few successful coups. Their least successful was a comic opera attempt in 1866 to invade Campobello Island in the Bay of Fundy. The resulting shock and alarm helped to rush reluctant New Brunswickers into the arms of Confederation.

The most dramatic Fenian incursion occurred on a few hot days in early June, 1866, when about 800 crossed to Fort Erie from Buffalo. At Ridgeway, a hard-fought battle with raw Canadian militia ended in sudden defeat when the Canadians, ill-led and undisciplined, suddenly fled in confusion. Panting down the sunken road in a tangle of panic-stricken militiamen was young Will Otter of the Queen's Own Rifles. Whatever others concluded from the brief battle, Otter was an instant convert to the need for relentless training and strict discipline. Among his brother officers, it was a rare enthusiasm. As for the Fenians, they recoiled from their own triumph and fled back to Fort Erie, demolishing another, much smaller Canadian force on their arrival. All but a handful escaped across the river to be interned by the suddenly vigilant American authorities. Another Fenian invasion into Missisquoi county in present-day Quebec ended more rapidly and bloodlessly. They did not try again until 1870 when Fenians returned to Missisquoi to meet even better led Canadian militia. Again the invaders fled, this time abandoning a small cannon.

The Fenian experience undoubtedly added to the efficiency and (perhaps dangerously) to the self-confidence of the Canadian volunteers. Ridgeway would remain a source of jibes and recrimination but the five years of Fenian threats justified a great deal of drilling, re-equipment (at British expense) with the breech-loading Snider-Enfield rifle, summer camps and training courses. Ridgeway showed the British that the militia must be stiffened by regular troops. Joint service with the regulars taught the volunteers how professional soldiers looked and acted.

Such memories would become faded and distorted. The days of British garrisons in central Canada were numbered. When the Confederation negotiators visited England in the spring of 1865, they brought not only a draft of what would become the British North America Act but a commitment to spend a million dollars that year on militia and defence purposes. Even George Brown, a member of the Confederation coalition, now preached preparedness: "there is no better mode of warding off war when it is threatened," he had told an astonished Canadian provincial parliament, "than to be prepared for it if it comes." Edward Cardwell, the British colonial secretary, was less impressed by such belated military-mindedness than his Canadian visitors would have wished. However, the game had to be played. The Canadians sought a maximum of guarantees for a minimum of commitment; Cardwell's response was as vague as he could make it. In a formal despatch to the Governor-General in Ottawa, Lord Monck, Cardwell reported that the Canadian ministers had "expressed unreservedly the desire of Canada to devote her whole resources, both in men and money, for the maintenance of the connection with the mother country." For its part, the imperial government "fully acknowledged the reciprocal obligation of defending every portion of the Empire with all the resources at its command." The Cardwell commitment of 1865 was the basis of Canadian defence policy until the eve of the First World War. In Ottawa, Canada's "whole resources" were translated into a million dollars a year for defence, spent as and how the Dominion government chose. Britain's commitment might be reciprocal but it would be exercised at Whitehall's discretion. As a first instalment, the British made it clear that they had no intention of even guaranteeing a loan for the fortifications Colonel Jervois had deemed indispensable.

In 1865, not even Cardwell could have anticipated the revolution in imperial defence he was personally to initiate when he returned to office in 1868 as Secretary of State for War. Britain's determination to cut its costs in North America was, of course, bipartisan and of long standing. Canadians did nothing to allay the mood. There were no more devastating affronts to British feeling like the defeat of the 1862 Militia bill but there was endless niggling about small bills for the transportation and accommodation of the troops sent to Canada to meet the Fenian threat. There was absurd haggling about who would pay to repair the Enfield muskets obviously abused and battered by the Canadian volunteers. Most Canadians were oblivious to growing British resentment. Voters had always rewarded politicians who were sturdily independent of British authority. In the new Dominion government, Cartier and his colleagues regarded the British taxpayer as a dependable source of funds. Besides, Canada had fulfilled her share of the 1865 agreement.

Cartier's Militia bill, introduced in the 1868 session, effectively extended the Province of Canada's militia system to the entire country. An "Active Militia" of 40,000 could be recruited by ballot as a "Regular Militia" but everyone understood that it would really be based on the volunteer corps. Militia would be armed, clothed and equipped at public expense and drilled from eight to sixteen days a year. Nine military districts (four in Ontario, two French-speaking and one English-speaking in Quebec, and one each in New Brunswick and Nova Scotia) formed a basis for drilling the Active Militia and enrolling a Reserve Militia of every able-bodied male from eighteen to sixty. Except in Nova Scotia, where the volunteer system had been weakest and where anti-Confederation sentiment was strongest, Cartier's legislation was a success. New units were soon added to the force and even in Nova Scotia a volunteer organization slowly developed. The first militia enrolment in February, 1869, found 37,170 volunteers and 618,896 members of the Reserve Militia. When Manitoba, British Columbia and Prince Edward Island entered Confederation, each became a military district and gained a small allotment of volunteers. Tiny district staffs, with a deputy adjutant-general, brigade majors, storekeepers and paymasters, provided some welcome government patronage, particularly for that inexhaustible category of place-seekers, gentlemen down on their luck.

Cartier's militia organization was not really a balanced army. It was a collection of infantry battalions, artillery batteries and cavalry troops fitted for the role the Canadian militia had always played: an auxiliary to regular army garrison. In war or crisis, it was the British who would provide trained staff officers, a supply and transport organization, hospitals and, above all, an example of discipline and efficiency. However, the framework on which the militia organization was spread was suddenly dismantled. The reasons had something to do with Britain's financial resentments and a great deal to do with the alarming rise of Prussia as a military power in the 1860s. As Secretary of State for War in a reforming Gladstone government, Edward Cardwell found that Britain had virtually no field army. Regiments scattered across the world in the wake of the Napoleonic wars had to be called home. An army composed of life-service soldiers had too few recruits and no reserves. Cardwell's answer was a much shorter term of enlistment but an army of short-service soldiers must have at least half its strength in Britain to train recruits and feed them as drafts to overseas garrisons. Since the British taxpayer would never allow the army's strength to grow, the garrisons must shrink—drastically. Canada was an obvious place to start.

Cartier and his colleague, William McDougall, in London in 1868 to negotiate the transfer of the North-Western Territory to Canada and to haggle over some small military transactions, seem to have been wholly unaware of the impending changes (or of the bad impression they created). It hardly mattered. They could have behaved like angels. Cardwell and most of his colleagues in Britain's new Liberal government had hardened their hearts to colonial politicians. A military presence of 110 years was to be liquidated within two years. The haste owed something to Cardwell's determination and something to a panicky defeatism that gripped some British generals. "The worst that could happen to Canada," moaned Sir John Michel, the commander-in-chief in North America, "would be annexation to a free and prosperous country. To England, pecuniary ruin and loss of prestige." Even if the Americans had not attacked, what if the Fenians managed to seize and humiliate some small remnant of the British garrison? By the summer of 1870, British soldiers had left Ontario and Montreal and a single battalion remained at the Citadel in Quebec during the winter of 1870-71.

The withdrawal was not free of backward glances. British commanders like Sir Charles Windham and his successor, Sir James Lindsay, pleaded with the Dominion authorities to fill the military vacuum. Veterans of the Royal Canadian Rifles, a garrison unit, could transfer to the Canadian service. Mounted rifle troops should be organized to patrol the Quebec frontier. Fortifications must be taken over or dismantled. Ottawa ignored the appeals. By acting, it might legitimize the shocking British abandonment; by inaction, it might panic the British into at least a partial resumption of their responsibilities. Canadians had never taken defence problems seriously as long as Britain provided most of the troops and paid most of the bills, and Sir John A. Macdonald's government was in no hurry to change. Only at the end of 1871, on the eve of the departure of the last British troops from Quebec did the Militia Department authorize the organization of two artillery batteries to serve as caretakers of the fortifications at Quebec and Kingston and to train militia gunners. When Canada refused to buy surplus British arms and stores, Whitehall shipped them home to England. The unwanted blankets were contributed to victims of the great Chicago fire.

The Northwest demanded more than a backward glance. Cartier and McDougall had returned triumphant from their negotiations with the Hudson's Bay Company and the British government; neither side had bothered to consult the ten thousand people of the Red River colony at the heart of the Company's trading empire. In the transitional period, the Company's feeble authority collapsed before the indignation of the French-speaking Metis and their ambitious young spokesman, Louis Riel. The *de facto* authority of a provisional government under Riel was strengthened when, on December 1, 1869, McDougall crossed the border from the United States, proclaimed the Canadian takeover of the territory and then waited pathetically while the few Canadians in the colony tried to make his authority stick. Instead, most of them were rounded up by Riel's tough buffalo hunters. The same fate befell another mismanaged attempt in early 1870. Desperate to show his authority, Riel commanded that one of his new prisoners, Thomas Scott, be put to death. It was an act of savage folly, mitigated by generations of Canadian historians on the grounds of Scott's alleged bad manners.

The killing of Scott complicated and poisoned an already difficult situation. As in most of the crises of their Confederation, Canadians were divided in their interpretation of the issues at Fort Garry. French Canadians believed that Riel was a guardian of French and Catholic interests in the West. Ontario Protestants suspected that the Quebeckers might be right and were outraged at the thought. Ottawa, less bothered by sectional prejudices, feared mainly that Riel was a tool of the Fenians and of American agents. Macdonald cursed McDougall for fumbling the first stage of the long and delicate Canadian campaign to guarantee its sovereignty all the way to the Pacific. He also insisted that the British had an obligation to ensure Canada quiet possession of its $1.5 million purchase. With obvious reluctance, the British government agreed. The result was a joint military expedition across the Great Lakes and along a rugged canoe route from present-day Thunder Bay to Fort Garry.

The undertaking had most of the defects of joint ventures. As Minister of Militia, Cartier did his best to ensure a balance of English and French by recruiting one militia battalion for the expedition in Ontario and the other in

Quebec. Since any fighting would have painful political consequences in French Canada, Cartier did nothing to hurry preparations. The British officer chosen to command the expedition, Colonel Garnet Wolseley, was driven to fury. However, his energy and foresight and the skill of Indian and *Canadien* boatmen delivered the 1,044 men of the expedition to Fort Garry without a single casualty and at the modest cost of $500,000. No sooner had they arrived, to find Riel and his government in flight, than Wolseley and his British troops obeyed strict orders to return to Quebec. The Canadian militiamen remained for the winter of 1870-71, making a nuisance of themselves by persecuting the real and fancied murderers of Tom Scott. Wolseley, on the strength of his achievement and of brilliant press relations, went on to become the military hero of late Victorian England and the inspiration for Major General Stanley in *The Pirates of Penzance.*

Wolseley's troops, the 60th Rifles, remained at Quebec for most of 1871. They were delayed by a final Whitehall concession that the garrison not leave central Canada while British and American negotiators (with Macdonald among them) sought a settlement of a long list of mutual grievances, from the Fenian Raids to the depredations of a British-built Confederate commerce raider, the *Alabama.* The resulting Treaty of Washington of 1871 was a bitter disappointment to Canadians and an embarrassment for Macdonald. His British colleagues simply traded American for Canadian claims and went home happy. Perhaps it was fair retribution for Britain's long, costly chore of defending Canada; it was certainly clear notice that Britain would no longer risk war or perhaps even bad feelings with the United States for Canada's sake.

Perhaps that was also Britain's best advice to Canada. The slate had been wiped clean and it would be wiped again before the First World War. The benefits were incalculable. If Canadians wished to avoid a huge defence burden or endless insecurity, they must live in peace with their powerful neighbour to the south. Indeed, as the British had privately conceded in the 1860s, not even a major military effort could save most of Canada. The undefended border and the century of peace did not really date, as Canadians and Americans would later pretend, from 1814 but it certainly began in 1871. Perhaps it should be dated from November 11 of that year, the day when men of the 60th Rifles marched out of the Citadel and down through the narrow streets of Quebec City for the last time.

It seems almost obligatory, even for commentators of almost pacifist sympathies, to denounce the Macdonald government and its Liberal successors for a neglect of defence and an indifference to the militia. Conscious or not, their policy was entirely logical. Canada had only one potentially dangerous enemy: the United States. There was no prospect of successful resistance to her. Even an attempt at preparation would have seemed provocative to Washington and its anglophobe congressmen. Canadian security depended on eliminating any possible cause of serious conflict. That could sometimes be costly and humiliating. The reward was that defence would cost Canadians only a few cents a head. Military duties could safely be left to the few enthusiasts who wanted a military hobby or some extra spending money. Canadians, as their politicians and businessmen insisted, could get on with nation-building or cultivating their own gardens.

The second line of defence remained Cardwell's 1865 commitment. Some defence expenditure, defined in the first quarter-century of Confederation as the original million dollars a year, served as an insurance premium for that remote day of crisis when Britain might be called upon for "all the resources at its command." From time to time, it was desirable to pretend to Britain that Canadians really were in earnest about their defences. The appointment of a senior British officer to be general officer commanding the militia in 1874 seemed a useful step at the time although it would produce great friction when such officers took their duties seriously. Opening the Royal Military College at the old naval dockyard at Kingston in 1876 was premature for Canada's real military needs but it was a highly public gesture. The trickle of graduates who secured British army commissions after 1880 was a useful reminder to Whitehall that Canadians had not wholly submerged their military spirit. A Liberal minister of militia in 1878 confessed that he had "always felt that the amount we paid annually for military purposes was more to show the Horse Guards our willingness as far as possible to take upon ourselves a fair share of our own defences than for any other purpose."

Both the British general and the military college were Liberal reforms introduced after the government of Alexander Mackenzie took office in 1873. A former militia major, Mackenzie lacked the instinctive anti-militarism of many members of his party but even he could not spare the Department of Militia and Defence from the ruthless economies imposed as the depression of the 1870s ravaged Canada. For the volunteer movement, cost-cutting was only a second blow. Even during the exciting 1860s, some employers had fired workers for attending militia drills, but excitement and public approval had buoyed up morale and brought recruits. The final repulse of the Fenians in 1870 allowed public enthusiasm to languish. Except in Toronto and central Ontario, where patriotic fervour always seemed a little more intense than elsewhere, militia officers struggled in vain to fill their ranks. By 1872, many officers denounced Cartier for failing to invoke the compulsory features of his 1868 legislation. The lack of volunteers was particularly acute in French Canada, and the senior French-speaking battalion, the 4th Chasseurs Canadiens, collapsed. Soon however, the manpower crisis was overshadowed by financial constraints. Between 1871 and 1876, militia spending fell by two-thirds, to only $650,000. Gradually, the annual total struggled back to the target of $1 million a year but by then a peacetime pattern had been imposed on the Canadian militia.

Lieutenant-Colonel Henry Fletcher, military secretary to Lord Dufferin, the Governor-General from 1872 to 1878, argued in a memorandum to the Canadian government, that there were three elements in determining its military policy. The government could decide how much it wanted to spend, how many men it wished to have in uniform and how efficient its soldiers should be. By answering two of the questions, the government automatically settled the third. It was a shrewd if overly simple observation. No one ever dreamed of setting peacetime defence policy simply on the basis of numbers and efficiency, leaving the taxpayers to meet the bill. Military advisers, including successive British generals commanding the militia, pleaded for a reduction of units and numbers to a level that could be properly armed and efficiently trained. Instead, political considerations insisted that Canada must have a large, ill-equipped and lightly trained volunteer organization. The reasons were eminently political and practical. Whatever its military limitations, a large force could look impressive on paper. Canada's insurance premium approach to defence was always more show than tell. Reductions in militia manpower from 45,000 in 1872 to 37,000 in 1880 were achieved by eliminating privates, not by disbanding battalions. A major economy slashed drill pay by allowing rural units to meet only every other year. Rural colonels might be furious that their city cousins drilled annually but they at least held their rank and status. When militia officers pleaded for compulsion in 1872, Cartier had understood that their demand could kill the militia: only voluntary enthusiasm could carry it through. A militia with too many officers, too little training and obsolete equipment had little fighting value. No professional soldier could believe that the ceremonial review or the mock battle that climaxed a twelve-day summer camp was any preparation for war. Indeed, they pandered to the illusions of politicians and militiamen. To be fair, Canada's military organization in the thirty years after Confederation was not preparing for an enemy or a war. It was a device to allow a military structure to survive for the as yet unforeseeable circumstances when it might be needed.

Other countries in the nineteenth century developed a professional military staff, eager to make or invent a case for military preparedness. Canada's militia staff had neither expertise nor prestige. Some were British half-pay officers who had settled in Canada; others were militia officers of limited experience. Almost all owed their appointment and promotions to political influence. The senior Canadian-born officer, Colonel Walker Powell, entered the Militia Department in 1863 as a Liberal appointee. By careful attention to politicians from both parties and a devotion to military minutiae, Powell held his post as Adjutant-General until 1895. If Powell was generally popular, his fellow staff officers were not. Politicians and militia colonels regularly denounced them as idle and overpaid—at $1,700 a year for the deputy adjutant-general of each military district or $1,200 for a brigade major. The appointment of a senior British officer to command the force should have guaranteed the professional expertise other armies developed. Certainly the first of the generals, Sir Edward Selby-Smyth, filled his annual reports with endless advice. It was politely ignored. When successors followed his example with less tact, their careers in Canada ended prematurely. Much of the advice was sensible. British officers urged bilingualism for the staff, simpler, cheaper uniforms for the militia, more target practice and less ceremonial drill. In the face of an instinctive Canadian prejudice at being patronized by experts from the mother country, the advice went unheard.

British generals had some difficulty in realizing that they commanded not so much a military force as a social and political institution. A militia officer on parade might be a powerful politician off duty. In the first seven parliaments after Confederation, between a sixth and a quarter of the members were militia officers. The annual debate on the militia estimates was known as "Colonel's Day" and non-military MPs usually stayed away. In 1868 the militia lobby made minor constitutional history by defeating the government during the Militia Bill debate. Its grievance—that Cartier had proposed the same pay for officers as for their men—was soon remedied. Most of the colonels were professional politicians but amateur soldiers. Their military connection was a means of commanding the support of several hundred local volunteers and their families. Officers like Major Mackenzie Bowell and Colonel Arthur Williams used their parliamentary status to avenge themselves on military superiors. Colonel Patrick MacDougall, the first and ablest Adjutant-General, and the second of the British generals, Major-General R. G. A. Luard, both left Canada after losing battles with these militia politicians.

There was much that the militia could gain by political influence. Officers could lobby for fresh issues of uniform, an extra turn at camp or the transfer of an unpopular staff officer. They could argue successfully for an increase in their battalion despite the official view that the militia organization was already too large. On the eve of the 1891 election, the 10th Royal Grenadiers were granted two extra companies on the colonel's claim that "you can always rely on the Grenadiers being a good Conservative Regiment." When Toronto had demonstrated its Tory loyalty, the city was also granted a brand new regiment, the 48th Highlanders. Politicians could favour their friends by locating a camp in their community and by issuing contracts for messing, canteens, forage and haulage as patronage. In the circumstances, there was much to be said for limiting militia spending. When Macdonald died in 1891, General Ivor Herbert commented shrewdly to the Duke of Cambridge:

> He looked upon money voted for militia purposes, only as a means of gaining political ends, but he was honest enough to keep that use of it within strict limits, and consequently cut down the militia estimates to the lowest possible figure. He knew that at any time he could obtain an

increased vote but he also knew that any money so voted would not yield any corresponding efficiency, but merely add to the party claims which would have to be satisfied from that source.

Going to a militia summer camp was an important part of Canada's social heritage. Between 1875 and 1896, about twenty thousand men attended each summer; thereafter the numbers rose sharply. Militiamen enlisted for a three-year term but since their battalion might only go to camp every other year and sometimes even less frequently, a great many volunteers attended only a single camp. Chances are that a great many of our ancestors experienced at least one summer camp but only a devoted nucleus persevered. In rural corps, captains recruited their forty-man companies in the spring. The attractions seem small: fifty cents a day for a twelve-day camp; a uniform which was usually second-hand and, before the era of dry-cleaning, very much as its previous wearer had left it; the honour of representing the county at Niagara or Sussex or Laprairie. Probably the boredom of farm life and the chance to pass some of the familiar tests of young manhood were enough. Camps were always scheduled between seeding time and harvest to encourage farmers to attend.

The battalion would muster on a warm June morning to travel by train, steamer and occasionally on foot to Barriefield, Levis, Aldershot or wherever civic or party pressure had located the district camp. Some colonels would veer the route through one of the larger cities to fill up the ranks with the unemployed. It was notorious that battalions at Niagara-on-the-Lake were prone to enlist Americans eager for fun and a little money. At camp, soldiers lived in long lines of bell tents, sleeping on the ground in their own greatcoats and one of the notoriously shoddy militia blankets. Food was based on the traditional British army ration of a pound of bread and a pound of beef a day, supplemented by a few ounces of vegetables, coffee, sugar, tea, salt and whatever the colonel had the foresight to purchase from regimental funds. The canteen concession, wet or dry, was an obvious prize for a politically influential contractor. Training in camp was simple and repetitive: drill, beginning with the squad and culminating in a grand review on the final day; firing thirty rounds from the Snider-Enfield, with minimal damage to one's shoulder and the target; guard-mounting and sometimes a sham battle. Afterwards, the volunteers would be free to sample the attractions of the nearby town and to bring indignation to the souls of temperance reformers and many fathers. Militia officers provided more comfortably for themselves, often handing over their messing arrangements to a contractor and carefully imitating what they knew or fancied of British mess etiquette. On the final day, tents were struck, camp equipment returned to store and the battalions wended their way home, handing in uniforms, rifles and equipment wherever their captain had rented storage space. For many it would be their only military experience.

Three years later, they would be "in Manitoba, the States or otherwise occupied."

For officers, the commitment was more durable. In a society acutely conscious of social status, the militia commission was a badge of respectability. Officers had to spend three months at a military school to qualify for their rank. Rural candidates were embarrassed by the emphasis placed on elaborate mess etiquette. Would-be officers usually had to pay an entry fee, hand over their pay to the regimental fund and buy increasingly expensive uniforms on which, if imported from Britain, they also paid a handsome duty. Militia rank was not a perfect guarantee of bourgeois gentility but it was the best available. As Governor-General, Lord Minto decided that officers who might not otherwise be socially acceptable for Government House would be received in uniform. In Canada, noted the *Montreal Herald,* "an officer is useful to his regiment because he has the means to spend and the will to spend it; the regiment is useful to him because the paths toward social distinction are smoothed for the militia officer."

British visitors to Canada frequently deplored the Americanization of manners and morals in the Dominion. Their hearts would have been warmed by the militia. The government found little money to modernize the arms contributed by Britain in the 1860s but private subscriptions purchased helmets, busbies, kilts, feather bonnets and any available British military finery. Minute changes in the British drill book were promptly adopted in Canada. Officers and politicians regularly reiterated British doctrines on the subordination of military to civil authority or the immunity of the army from political interference. In most respects, British influences were harmless or even beneficial. Canadian militiamen needed a model and the British regimental tradition was a valuable heritage. Militia officers who denounced political interference while seeking it privately would eventually be caught in the hypocrisy of a double standard. Even the social snobbery of the city battalions was not a total bar to ability as William Otter proved by rising without private means to command the Queen's Own Rifles. Of course, the Britishness of the Canadian militia had few charms for most French Canadians. Fewer French Canadians than English possessed wealth or the will to lavish it on a militia battalion and, without private means, the volunteer movement was enfeebled. Only in Quebec City, where uniforms and rank "faisait la pluie et le beau temps" during the social season, were there rewards of prestige.

In 1868, Cartier had been acutely conscious that his "national institution" must be both French and English, yet it was symptomatic of a coming problem that one of his two French-speaking deputy adjutants-general was a surplus politician who cheerfully confessed that he knew no drill. In the ensuing decades, intermittent efforts were made to translate drill books and manuals into French. Half of the permanent artillery battery at Quebec was recruited from French-speaking volunteers. In Sir John A. Macdonald's cabinets, the militia portfolio was normally assigned to a French Canadian, notably from 1880 to 1892 Sir Adolphe Caron. Such ministers guaranteed that French Canada never lost its quota of appointments; it did little to ensure that those appointed were equal to their responsibilities. Cartier had identified a critical and specifically Canadian military problem; neither he nor his successors, however, worked very hard on a solution.

Nor was the problem concealed in the future. In 1870, despite current and subsequent claims that French Canadians would always leap to the defence of their own country, Sir James Lindsay had warned Cartier that French-speaking units had mustered barely a third of their strength against the Fenians. Militia staff complained that Quebec battalions filled their ranks with the elderly, the unfit or Montreal slum-dwellers. Though the Quebec battalion in Wolseley's Red River expedition had French-speaking officers, most of the men in the ranks were English-speaking Ontarians, frustrating Cartier's desire for a racially balanced force. In 1879, attempts to revive the Chasseurs Canadiens were frustrated by official objections to clothing the regiment in Zouave costume. The uniform, recalling the French Canadians who had volunteered to serve the Pope in 1868, was contemptuously dismissed as "foreign fancy dress." Nobody questioned the suitability of Highland kilts.

Yet, for all its limitations, Canada's militia was equal to its modest responsibilities. Of these, the most frequent was aid to the civil power. In a country where police forces were small, ill-trained and limited to the major towns and cities, it was easy enough for a religious argument or a drunken brawl to get out of hand. The very first duty of the volunteer militia, after its formation in 1855, had been to cope with an Orange-Catholic battle in Guelph. Between 1867 and 1914, the militia was called out on at least 120 occasions. Volunteers guarded a hanging, broke up illegal boxing matches, deterred election violence and protected innumerable strike-breakers. In Montreal, militia infantry, cavalry and artillery escorted the body of Joseph Guibord to his court-ordered burial in consecrated ground in 1875. In Quebec, gunners from the permanent battery confronted furious mobs of Irish longshoremen and French Canadian shipbuilders, battling for jobs in the declining port. Nova Scotia militia went to the Cape Breton coal mines at least three times before the end of the century. In Toronto, Montreal, Saint John and Charlottetown, volunteers turned out to restrain Orange and Catholic tensions during the 1870s.

Since aid to the civil power had been a brutal strain on the discipline of even regular troops, one might imagine that the Militia Act would at least attempt to make such duty attractive to militiamen. On the contrary, though it was easy enough to call out troops (any two magistrates could sign a requisition) the volunteers had to collect their pay from the municipality, not Ottawa. Local politicians could easily find reasons to refuse or postpone payment. The act compelled militia officers to sue for the money and to face the risks and costs of litigation while their men waited as long as a year for reimbursement. Far from supporting the fabric of social order, employers dismissed workers who were absent on militia duty. Even the federal government docked civil servants who fell in with their units to suppress a riotous strike in Ottawa and Hull in 1891. Only in 1904 did Parliament choose to make the federal government, not a hapless militia officer, the claimant. Until then, Ottawa hid behind a federal arrangement that assigned the militia to the central power but maintenance of law and order to the provinces. In the circumstances, it is surprising that the volunteers turned out so faithfully and, evidently, so cheerfully. The middle-class composition of some city battalions was one explanation; so was the prospect of excitement in an otherwise drab existence. During the Grand Trunk strike of 1876-77, municipal and company officials at Belleville scorned the local troops and summoned the renowned Queen's Own Rifles from Toronto. To be fair, the local volunteers had not mustered for two years, lacked greatcoats against the bitter winter weather and, once mobilized, discovered that there was no riot to disperse.

There were some challenges to law and order which Ottawa could not possibly abandon to jurisdictional confusion. By 1872, a joint British and American expedition had delineated the international boundary westward along the 49th Parallel. Thereafter, any assertion of American expansionism into the Northwest would have challenged the feeble safeguards of international law. Nonetheless, Canada's destiny as a nation *a mare usque ad marem* was far from secure. To Macdonald and his colleagues, Riel's offence in 1870 was not his "rebellion" but the opportunity he had given to American troublemakers. By the summer of 1871, after most of the militiamen of Wolseley's expedition had returned to Toronto, there were rumours of a Fenian invasion of the tiny new province of Manitoba. Almost too late in the season, two hundred militia reinforcements raced overland to Manitoba. By the time they arrived, the threat had dissolved. To Ottawa's delight, Metis (including Riel) had formed militia units. Less pleasing was news that the Fenian invaders had been arrested on Canadian soil by American cavalry. That was alarming. Even an agreed boundary did not guarantee sovereignty. Canada must have enough strength on the spot to enforce her own laws.

Sir John A. Macdonald's original plans for the Canadian takeover of the Northwest had included a 250-man police Force. "It seems to me," he had written, "that the best Force would be *Mounted Riflemen*, trained to act as cavalry, but also instructed in the Rifle exercises. They should also be instructed, as certain of the Line are, in the use of artillery. This body should not be expressly Military but should be styled *Police* and have the military bearing of the Irish Constabulary." The notion was shelved by the Red River problems and by the decision to create a province of Manitoba where a federal police force would have had a very modest role. Instead, Macdonald agreed to a permanent militia garrison to show the flag, provide dependable aid to the local civil power and back Dominion officials in treaty negotiations with the native people. The 300-man Manitoba Force pre-empted the money Macdonald might otherwise have spent to realize his vision of a mounted police. Only in March, 1873, was Parliament asked to pass enabling legislation, and it took sensational reports of the Cypress Hills massacre later that year to jar the government into action. A first contingent of 150 police recruits left for Winnipeg in the autumn of 1873, to be billeted and trained by the Manitoba Force. The balance left in the spring of 1874 with the grudging approval of a new Liberal government. Alexander Mackenzie would frankly have preferred a military force; he was talked out of it by his Minister of Justice, A. A. Dorion. More dangerous was Mackenzie's desire for a joint expedition with the Americans. Lord Dufferin managed to talk his prime minister out of that notion as unbefitting the Dominion's new dignity. The result was the famous "March West" in the summer and fall of 1874, a near-disaster for the participants and a badly-needed national legend. The new North West Mounted Police, helped by sympathetic Indians and Metis, learned from its mistakes. It became a versatile and inexpensive means of maintaining both the law and Canadian sovereignty. Macdonald had every right to be proud and protective of his creation.

Though the mounted police came under the Militia Department estimates for only a brief period in the 1870s, it was a vital part of Canada's defence system. It had been created not merely because of murder and whiskey-trading in the Northwest—these were evils of long standing—but because a turbulent frontier would have been a standing invitation to American intervention. Nor could Canada afford the long and costly Indian wars which had punctuated American frontier expansion. By arriving after the fate of American Indian resistance was no longer in doubt but before the westward tide of Canadian settlement, the NWMP could give the Canadian prairies a foundation of order. Ottawa's inventiveness in creating the force was, unfortunately, unique. Canadian dealings with the Indians—the treaties, land surrenders, annuities, agents and reserve land—bore a sad resemblance to American methods, partly because they were the joint inheritance of a more paternal pre-revolutionary British practice. No government would have found it easy to help in the catastrophe which overtook the Indians and Metis with the failure of the buffalo, but the frigid Victorian charity of the Indian Department undermined the standing of the mounted police in native eyes. Critics of the policy have not, of course, been obliged to propose realistic alternatives beyond leaving the West as a huge empty reserve. It was on the luckless police that the task fell of converting nomadic hunters into passive agriculturalists within a single generation. The influence of the chiefs, artificially inflated by the police to fit their own image of authority, plummeted in the new era of starvation. By 1883, making an arrest required a small military operation. The Metis, who had welcomed the NWMP with polite resignation, grew as restless as the Indians when Ottawa, on well-intentioned advice, postponed any settlement of their shaky land claims. The police became local scapegoats.

When the explosion came in March, 1885, the uprising was a Metis rebellion, not an Indian war. Louis Riel, invited back from his Montana exile by both white settlers and Metis, tried but failed to create a wide Indian alliance. The attempt appalled potential white sympathizers and frightened many of the Metis. It also shaped the uncompromising response of Sir John A. Macdonald's government in Ottawa.

The Northwest Campaign of 1885 was essentially an operation in aid of the civil power. It became necessary when Riel and his lieutenant, Gabriel Dumont, defeated a force of mounted police and special constables at Duck Lake on March 26; it ended for most purposes on May 15, when Riel surrendered to Major-General Fred Middleton three days after the fall of Batoche and the dispersal of his few hundred Metis and Indian supporters. Almost 8,000 Canadian militia took part; 26 died and 103 were wounded. The government absorbed the cost: $4,451,584, with $3 million more in civil claims.

To Canadians at the time, short of lustrous national achievements, the 1885 campaign took on epic proportions. Newspaper coverage was intense. The crisis united the country. Haligonians joined Quebeckers and Ontarians in the West; New Brunswickers complained that there had been no time to get their battalion to the front. French Canadians were appalled by Riel's anti-Catholic apostasy and by the murder of two Catholic missionaries at Frog Lake. French-speaking battalions from Quebec and Montreal joined the 3,500 militiamen from eastern Canada who struggled along the unfinished line of the CPR. Rather more volunteers were assembled in the West. The successful completion of the campaign long before realists in eastern Canada had expected was a dangerous confirmation of the militia myth. Raw volunteers, many of whom had never even pulled a trigger before, had triumphed over ferocious Indians and hawk-eyed Metis buffalo hunters. The militia could return in triumph and self-congratulation, grumbling only that their aged British commander, General Middleton, had not only held them back from an even more rapid triumph but had seized the credit, a promotion, a knighthood and $20,000.

The truth about 1885 was that the Canadians were extraordinarily lucky. The inexperience of officers and men had reduced the militia to nervous immobility when they came under fire at Fish Creek and Cut Knife Hill. The Canadians had really won only one battle; fortunately for them, it was the last. Despite their awesome reputations, the Metis were as nervous as their adversaries and even more badly armed. Riel had paralyzed Gabriel Dumont with his indecision and his mysticism and Dumont's own passive tactics had been no match for an experienced soldier like Middleton. Indian leaders like Poundmaker and Big Bear were anxious moderates, holding back their followers and, in the circumstances of war, impeding their effectiveness. General Middleton's planning was not impeccable, but he had launched the campaign when experts in east and west had counselled a delay, he had shepherded his raw soldiers against a dangerous enemy and he had done his utmost to avoid casualties. For a man of 65, his energy was impressive. His pomposity may be forgiven. His critics then and since have rarely considered the astonishing logistics problems Middleton had to overcome with a militia lacking any supply, transportation or medical organization of its own. Tradition has given enormous credit to the Canadian Pacific Railway for getting troops to the West so swiftly. This is absurd. Unlike 1870, when the Americans had done their utmost to impede Wolseley's expeditions, there would have been no obstacle to sending the Canadians through the United States without any of the misery or delay of the route north of Lake Superior. Middleton, some of the militia and all of the ammunition and supplies came through the United States. It was really the Hudson's Bay Company that was indispensable. Its far-flung organization provided the Canadian expedition with a ready-made supply and transport organization at, of course, a respectable profit.

Canadian reaction to the Northwest campaign foreshadowed much that would happen in future wars. The experience inspired an ebullient mood of national self-confidence. Militia officers were certain that they no longer needed the fussy tutelage of British generals. The initial good feeling between French and English eroded rapidly during the campaign as the two French-speaking battalions were shunted away from the main theatre to serve in Alberta. Alarmist telegrams from the political colonels in command of the two battalions were widely publicized; there was no comparable recognition for the dogged good spirits of the Montreal men, struggling through the swamps and mosquitoes along the North Saskatchewan river. French-Canadian soldiers returned with memories of sneers and prejudice, ready to share in Quebec's bitter response to the trial and execution of Louis Riel.

The 1885 campaign was the first great crisis of Confederation. It was also the first war that Canadians had managed almost wholly for themselves. The machinery, flawed and creaky, had worked. Much credit belonged to one man. Adolphe Caron was a lightweight in the Macdonald government, dismissed as one of the more venal of the *patroneux*. In the time of crisis, he had been energetic, inventive and efficient. He had galvanized the sleepy officials of his department and he had supported his commander in the field. Like Middleton, he deserved his knighthood for the campaign. That did not make Caron a reformer. The Canadian militia had met its first real test and it had passed with apparent brilliance. There were some, like Colonel William Otter, who drew some sour lessons from their experience. Otter had commanded the column that had raced to rescue Battleford—a needless diversion since the police and settlers in the fort far outnumbered the Indians outside. Against his better judgement, Otter had taken his men to Cut Knife Hill to punish the marauding Crees and, as at Ridgeway nineteen years before, he watched helplessly as raw, undisciplined soldiers threw away the chance of an easy victory. Only the forebearance of Otter's opponent,

Poundmaker, allowed the militia column to escape without punishing losses. Otter had fresh evidence of the desperate need for discipline and training. His conclusions were exceptional. Far more typical was Colonel George Denison, the self-taught Canadian cavalry expert whose ego had been battered in a struggle to make British officers accept his expertise. In 1866, Denison had also seen the Fenians, but in retreat. In 1885, he and his Toronto cavalry squadron fretted in idleness at Humboldt while Middleton recruited western settlers and their rough prairie ponies to do his scouting. Indignation turned to a conviction that Canadians no longer needed British military leadership.

It seemed a long time since 1871.

Imperialism and Nationalism

Britain's military withdrawal from central Canada and from other historic colonial garrisons around the world reflected a crisis of confidence about her own strength and also a pervasive disillusionment about the value of colonies to her economy. Almost as soon as the deed was done, the mood shifted. In 1874, Benjamin Disraeli led his Conservatives to a majority over Gladstone's Liberals partly on the basis of an appeal to British imperial sentiment. Yet there was more in common between the two philosophies than might appear. To Gladstone, England was too weak to bear her worldwide burden; to Disraeli, the colonies must become a source of economic and even military strength.

The British position in the European world was certainly deteriorating. Prussia's military power, demonstrated in her shattering triumph over France in 1870, was based on an industrial strength that rivalled and would soon surpass that of the self-proclaimed "workshop of the world." More and more at odds with her old German allies, deeply resented by her old enemies of France and Russia, an isolated Britain could look only to her navy for security. However, naval technology, racing faster than ever before in history, regularly undermined Britain's naval advantage by offering revolutionary innovations in propulsion, gunnery and armour plate. Moreover, a steam-powered fleet depended on coaling stations and drydocks as the sail-powered wooden walls of Nelson's navy never had. Having left her self-governing colonies to their own devices, Britain now found need of them. She needed their ports and she might soon need their financial and military resources as well.

A later age might wonder why Canada or Canadians would feel obliged to answer such a call. Confederation had united three self-governing colonies but collectively they remained a colony. No one yet imagined that the sovereignty of Queen Victoria or her successors could be divided. Through her ministers in Whitehall she spoke to the world for an entire empire. If war must be waged against the Queen's enemies, every colony and each remote dependency was as much at war as Britain herself. At the same time, it was also apparent that self-governing colonies would determine their contributions to such wars. For all the patriotic euphoria and the loyal resolutions, the North American colonies had sent no contingents to the Crimean War, and when the 100th Regiment was raised in 1858, it was on the initiative and at the expense of Britain. Individual Canadians had gone to the Crimea. One of them, Lieutenant Alexander Dunn, had joined in the famous charge of the Light Brigade and had won a Victoria Cross. In the Indian Mutiny, a black Nova Scotian, William Hall, also won the gallantry award. However, such Canadians were volunteers, like the thousands who served in the American Civil War or the 800 devout Catholics who left Montreal in 1868 to serve in the Pontifical Zouaves. Their "ninth crusade" did not save the Papal States from a newly united Italy but it did give French Canada a military tradition of its very own.

In the wake of Confederation, some Canadians were painfully aware of their subordination to British foreign policy but their response was not to seek independence. Not even the ardent young men of "Canada First," with their talk of "Canada for the Canadians," could dream of leaving the Empire. Edward Blake, the future Liberal leader and their hero, aired a sentiment in his famous speech at Aurora in 1874 which would have many echoes: "Tomorrow, by the policy of England, in which you have no voice or control, this country might be plunged into the horrors of war." Yet Blake's answer was some form of imperial federation in which Canadians would have a voice in British foreign policy. However, Blake's Aurora speech only confirmed his reputation in Canadian eyes as a quirky theorist. Most Canadians, it seems safe to say, thought nothing at all of such matters and waited patiently for the future to unfold, as they still do.

In 1878, the "horrors of war" seemed suddenly very close. Disraeli's government intervened dramatically to save an ailing Turkish empire from Russia. In advance, the Russians had chartered the *Cimbria*, loaded her with sailors and cannon, and detached the vessel to Eastport, Maine, to fit out privateers. Ottawa politicians, accustomed to think only of war with the United States, were suddenly reminded that a "dominion from sea to sea" also had two vulnerable coasts, merchant fleets and some very anxious voters. Halifax, fortified and still garrisoned by British troops, was secure from any Russian raider; Saint John, Sydney and a bevy of smaller Maritime ports were not. Neither was Britain's only naval drydock in the Pacific, at Esquimalt. A Canadian plea to London for a squadron of fast cruisers was ignored. Sir Edward Selby-Smyth, commanding the militia, discovered that the only coast artillery Canada could mount were ancient smoothbores, abandoned by the British and virtually useless against armoured ships. A Montreal firm offered to cut rifling into the barrels of the old guns, a cheap expedient the government gratefully welcomed. However, by the time approval was granted, the war scare had dissolved, the company was bankrupt and the Conservatives had returned to power in Ottawa. The physical vestiges of the 1878 Russian threat were a few guns mounted on earthworks at Esquimalt and a contingent of British Columbia militia drilled briefly by an artillery officer from the East.

Mackenzie's Liberal government felt sorely disappointed in the British. After all, Ottawa had voted a whole $10,000 for coast defences. Then a committee of British officers insisted that Canada spend at least $250,000 merely to defend Saint John and Sydney. It would be cheaper, the Canadian politicians angrily concluded, to let the Russians destroy everything. For their part, the British were also displeased by the state of affairs revealed by the 1878 crisis. An interdepartmental committee grew into a Royal Commission headed by Disraeli's former colonial secretary, Lord Carnarvon, empowered to take the first coherent look at colonial defence. The Royal Commission's work was blighted by Gladstone's return to power in 1880 and its full report was never published. Nevertheless, the Carnarvon Commission was important: vital data had been collected and the concept of imperial defence was firmly established. Parliament and successive British governments refused to allow the Admiralty or the War Office the kind of planning and intelligence agencies other late nineteenth-century European powers had evolved but the problem of imperial defence gradually forced the evolution of naval and military versions of a general staff. By insisting that self-governing colonies must assume responsibility for defending their own commercial ports, Carnarvon also began to rationalize the distribution of defence tasks in time of war.

Coast defence problems may have launched the Carnarvon Commission but no serious examination of British military problems could stop short of manpower. By European standards, Britain's army was tiny; it was also chronically short of men. Short service, voluntary recruiting, low pay, hard conditions and world-wide commitments all contributed to the problem. In 1878, a desperate War Office had even summoned Indian troops to Malta. It was depicted as a splendid imperial gesture but officials were privately appalled at the prospect of using non-white troops in a European war. The self-governing colonies offered a better answer. Though the former 100th Regiment had long since lost touch with Canada and recruited its men in Ireland, its memory remained green. At the height of the 1878 crisis, Selby-Smyth had talked of raising a Canadian division of 10,000 men, though nothing official had been done. At Halifax, where the former Adjutant-General, Sir Patrick MacDougall, was now commander-in-chief, fresh schemes were concocted for attracting Canadian recruits to the British army. If the Carnarvon Commission wanted to feed on such notions, it got a cool response from one of its star witnesses, Sir John A. Macdonald. It would be wise, the Canadian prime minister suggested, not to try to negotiate for colonial contingents before the danger was apparent. "I think if war were imminent the spirit of the people themselves would force on the Legislature and the Government of the day the necessity for taking an active part in it." Macdonald and anyone else who understood Canada knew that peacetime recruiting for the British army in the Dominion would be hopeless. A shilling a day was miserable even by the standard of the worst-paid Canadian day labourer and no Canadian government would be keen on any scheme that took able-bodied men out of the country. Canada's manpower contribution was limited to the four and sometimes more graduates of the Royal Military College who were granted British army commissions each year. Since prospects for military employment in Canada were dismal, the commissions usually attracted the best in the class and some influential Canadian families soon had sons in the British army. Canadian officers were also eager for active service. In 1881, when a British army occupied Egypt, a French Canadian, Major P. O. J. Hebert, accompanied Sir Garnet Wolseley. He died of fever in Cairo, the first of many Canadians who gave their lives in the imperial cause.

Sir John A. Macdonald was clear on one point: there was no legal and certainly no moral bar to British recruiting in Canada even if common sense and experience advised against it. Section 61 of the Militia Act provided that "Her Majesty may call out the Militia or any part thereof for actual service, either within or without the Dominion, at any time, whenever it appears advisable to do so by reason of war, invasion, or danger of any of them. . . ." To Macdonald, that was a contingency plainly designed for war with the United States. Neither the volunteer force nor the tiny permanent schools for the infantry and cavalry, finally authorized in 1883, was intended for imperial wars. The permanent units—three infantry companies and a cavalry troop, joining the two earlier artillery batteries, were designed as schools and as models for the militia, not as a standing army. Only on that proviso had the colonels of the Militia Lobby grudgingly accepted their creation. Overworked, paid a mere forty cents a day, rife with desertion and indiscipline, the new Cavalry and Infantry School Corps were ill-equipped to do their assigned work, much less to dream of foreign wars.

The distinction between British and Canadian responsibilities seemed to be clarified by the 1884-85 crisis over the fate of Major-General Charles Gordon, the quintessential Victorian hero besieged by the Mahdist forces at Khartoum. A British relief expedition under Lord Wolseley was belatedly authorized by Gladstone, whose orders Gordon had deliberately defied. To help his troops navigate up the cataracts of the Nile, Wolseley remembered the Indian and *Canadien* voyageurs of his 1870 expedition. With Ottawa's agreement but wholly at British expense, a contingent of 386 voyageurs was assembled and despatched. Though most of the Canadians won high praise for their efforts (the exceptions were mere adventure-seeking youths), Khartoum had fallen and Gordon was dead by the time the expedition drew close to its goal. It withdrew, crestfallen. However, the Sudan excitement and a simultaneous Russian thrust on the Russian-Afghan border at Pendjeh produced near-hysteria in London and a flurry of volunteering by Canadian militia officers. Against its better judgement, the War Office accepted a contingent of cavalry from New South Wales, and the unfortunate Australians spent the ensuing months at Suakin on the Red Sea, training under a broiling sun. Sir Charles Tupper, Canada's High Commissioner in London, pleaded with Macdonald for Canada to show the same imperial enthusiasm. The prime minister showed the blunt realism which underlay his occasional platform patriotism:

Why should we waste money and men in this wretched business? England is not at war but merely helping the Khedive to put down an insurrection and now that Gordon is gone the motive of aiding in the rescue of our Countrymen is gone with him—Our men and money would therefore be sacrificed to get Gladstone & Co. out of the hole they have plunged themselves into by their own imbecillity [sic].

In 1885, Macdonald had Canadian public opinion on his side. He could afford to be indignant that "the spasmodic offers of our Militia Colonels anxious for excitement or notoriety" had aroused false expectations in England. In any case, within a month, the colonels could satisfy their military ardour in the Northwest. For the rest of Macdonald's career, his government took almost no interest in imperial defence matters. Despatches and inquiries on military matters went unanswered. Two attempts to prod the cabinet into making policy failed. In 1884, Lord Melgund, the governor-general's military secretary, persuaded Adolphe Caron to allow him to form a defence committee, but he too, was distracted by the 1885 campaign. In 1887, after Canadian representatives at the first Colonial Conference had parried criticisms of Canada's military efforts, Caron himself launched an elaborate "Commission on the Defences." It met only once and adjourned forever to await its terms of reference. Even British interest was languid: it took several years before anyone in Whitehall noticed that the Canadian committee had never functioned.

In 1890, in the wake of a long and politically motivated inquiry into looting during the Northwest campaign, Sir Fred Middleton returned to England. Not for the first time, Canadian politicians found it easier to sacrifice a British military adviser who had become a political liability. The Queen, offering her own eloquent comment on Canadian charges that Middleton was a thief, made him Keeper of the Crown Jewels. More important for Canadian defence and politics, Middleton's successor was a very different officer. The Canadian command had been a modest prize for officers near the end of their careers; Colonel Ivor Herbert was a highly qualified young man on his way up—energetic, fluent in French, a Catholic and a man of ideas. He also reflected a new policy: henceforth colonial militias would figure, however lightly, in the scales of British military strength. Herbert was the first of a succession of British officers who would wrestle with suspicious politicians, dubious subordinates and unmilitary populations to draw colonial forces into the great imperial cause.

With tact and an infectious enthusiasm, Herbert tackled the major weaknesses of the militia. He persuaded Caron to publish unit establishments, revealing the absurd proportion of officers, non-commissioned officers, buglers and bandsmen to privates—1 to 2.24 in 1894. Herbert enforced penalties against officers who brought unfit recruits to camp. He persuaded the government to appoint a quartermaster-general and filled the post with Major Percy Lake, a brilliant British officer with Canadian connections. Nowhere was Herbert more successful than in Quebec where he involved the Catholic hierarchy in militia camps, sponsored choral competitions between battalions and openly praised the Zouave tradition—provoking outrage from Orange stalwarts like Major Sam Hughes MP, an outspoken Ontario Tory.

Herbert's main focus for reform was the permanent force, more demoralized, ill-disciplined and disregarded than ever. As soon as he could, he amalgamated the scattered units into regiments. The four infantry schools, at London, Toronto, St-Jean and Fredericton became companies of the Royal Regiment of Canadian Infantry. The cavalry school at Toronto and a mounted infantry school started by Middleton at Winnipeg in 1885 became the Royal Canadian Dragoons. The artillery was organized into two field batteries and two companies of garrison artillery. Since 1887, a third artillery school, "C" Battery, had struggled to man fortifications and provide instruction at Esquimalt. Conditions were dreary—the unit spent its first years in a drafty barn at the local exhibition grounds—and desertion was easy. After ingenious, protracted negotiations, Herbert persuaded Ottawa to pay for a small British garrison at Esquimalt. "C" Battery became one of the garrison artillery companies at Quebec. Driven to provide adequate defences for a strategic drydock, the British felt obliged to increase their garrison and found themselves paying most of the bill. For his part, Herbert was quietly creating a tiny Canadian regular army, potentially capable of serving with British troops. To promote the idea, he even won permission to exchange individual permanent force units with companies from the British garrison at Halifax.

Herbert's reforms undoubtedly made the permanent corps more useful to the militia as a whole. What volunteers needed, as much as actual training, was to see and model themselves on efficient professional soldiers. Of course, anything that built the self-esteem of the permanent troops offended the militia. They, after all, were the front-line defenders of Canada; the "school corps" were their servants. Jealousy found a focus in 1894 when Herbert and Lake negotiated a deal to purchase the Martini-Metford rifle, a weapon whose chief virtue was that it was too robust for militiamen to damage. To meet the cost, summer camps were cancelled at short notice. "We can't have both camps and rifles," the minister told Parliament, "and the Militia would rather get the rifles and go without camps for one season." That proved debatable. In militia circles, outrage was intensified when funds were found to assemble the entire Royal Regiment of Canadian Infantry at Levis to train as a unit. Herbert was so proud of his men that he even persuaded his minister, J. C. Patterson, to offer the regiment to fill a vacancy in the British garrison at Hong Kong. With that, he had overreached himself.

Herbert's success owed a lot to the political turmoil that followed Macdonald's death. Caron, under fire for a host of scandals, retired. His successor, Sir Mackenzie Bowell, dutifully accepted a year of Herbert's instruction before moving on. Patterson, Herbert confessed, was "the laziest man I ever knew." That made him easy to manage but it also meant that Patterson would not protect his general in cabinet or Parliament. After the Hong Kong offer had been hastily withdrawn, Patterson withdrew to become lieutenant-governor of Manitoba. Herbert went to England and did not return. The purchase of the Martini-Metfords was abruptly cancelled, the permanent force was sharply reduced in strength and firmly put in its place and the stalwarts of the Militia Lobby could feel vindicated.

Even General Herbert's best efforts left Canada unprepared when, quite suddenly in December, 1895, Canadians found themselves closer to war with the United States than at any time since the *Trent* affair of 1861. The situation was frankly absurd. Intervening in an obscure, long-drawn border dispute between Venezuela and British Guiana, the American Secretary of State issued a thunderous warning to London: "To-day the United States is practically sovereign on this continent and its fiat is law upon the subjects to which it confines its interpretation." Unrepentant but slow, Lord Salisbury replied for Britain in December, 1895. President Grover Cleveland despatched a warlike message to Congress. The popular press exploded in excitement and patriots roared in ecstasy. North of the border, Canadians felt appalled and vulnerable. Colonel Lake left for England to buy what he could: 40,000 Lee-Enfield rifles, twenty-four modern field guns and a few machine guns. Since Colonel Walker Powell had finally retired in dudgeon at the end of 1895, Herbert's successor, Major-General W. J. Gascoigne, had no staff in Ottawa at all. He prevailed on an able young instructor at the Royal Military College, Captain Arthur Lee (later Lord Lee of Fareham), to draft a sketchy mobilization order and campaign plan, and waited anxiously for Lake's weapons to arrive.

What really worried Gascoigne was the discovery that, after a first flurry, no one else in Ottawa seemed to be worried about impending war. His political superiors were engrossed in a more immediate battle—trying to depose Sir Mackenzie Bowell, the prime minister, and wrangling over solutions to the Manitoba schools question. Perhaps they were better informed than their general. The crisis passed as quickly as it had come. Cleveland's warlike glee was dampened when the New York stock exchange plummeted, when the powerful Pulitzer papers did not echo the general jingoism and when General Nelson A. Miles confessed that the United States had only three modern guns to defend its shores. In Britain, the new colonial secretary, Joseph Chamberlain, used his moderating influence on Lord Salisbury and British public opinion was diverted by news of the Jameson raid, a bungled attempt to overthrow the Transvaal government in South Africa. The settlement of the crisis confirmed once again that no interest in the Western Hemisphere would persuade Britain to risk war with the United States. Canadians, facing their own disputes with an increasingly belligerent United States, could take due note. Americans, for their part, moved on to find a pretext for war with a weaker and even more congenial enemy, Spain.

In a number of ways, 1896 was a decisive year for Canadians and for their military history. In the aftermath of the Venezuela crisis, both the British and the Canadians did some of the planning and building they should have done before. The British army, determined not to lose its forces in the interior of North America, planned instead to land an expeditionary force at New York or Boston "and make a vigorous offensive gesture." It soon discovered that the Royal Navy had no intention of convoying any expedition until it had completed the difficult and by no means certain task of disposing of the growing United States Navy. Together, the army and navy fitfully worked around to the conclusion that a war with the United States was not merely diplomatically, but militarily, unthinkable. That gloomy message was not, however, conveyed to Canada. Instead, discreet efforts were renewed to make the Canadian militia equal to its impossible task. With some ingenuity, Canada was persuaded to pay for a new defence review, conducted by Major-General E. P. Leach of the Royal Engineers. Completed in 1898, two parts of his report enumerated a long and costly list of reforms needed by the Canadian force as well as a strategic plan similar to, if far more sophisticated than, that concocted by Captain Lee. A third, highly secret part of Leach's report went straight to the British War Office. It warned the British army to avoid any involvement in Canadian defence at least until all the reforms had been completed.

For most Canadians, the main events of 1896 were not military but political. In June, the Conservatives went down to their first federal defeat since 1874; in July, Wilfrid Laurier led the Liberals into office. With occasional interruptions, Canada would be ruled by Liberals for most of the next century. One reason was that the depression which had hung over North America since the early 1870s began to lift. Prosperity might have nothing to do with Liberal leadership or policies but it would hang on the party like a good luck charm. For General Gascoigne and perhaps for many conscientious militiamen, the change was welcome. "I do respectfully implore you Sir," the general had written to Laurier; "to send me a Minister who will take a real broad interest in the Militia and, above all, one who is likely to stay." Laurier obliged. The militia portfolio went to a Nova Scotia country doctor and veteran backbencher, Frederick W. Borden. The new minister had been surgeon of his county militia battalion, a *bon vivant*, capable of playing the fiddle and step-dancing on the table at mess dinners. Borden also wanted to reform the force although he also understood the rules of political patronage and he knew that his influence in the Liberal caucus and cabinet depended on applying them. If Gascoigne wanted stability, he got it. Borden was minister until the Laurier government was defeated in September, 1911. He was perhaps the most important peacetime defence minister Canada has had.

Dr. Borden's mettle was soon tested. In the election campaign, both parties had repeated the familiar promise of annual camps for all the militia. Once in office, the Liberals found that the Tories had made no financial provision to keep their promise. Borden's colleagues decided that they, too, would renege. The new minister fought back so ferociously that his colleagues reconsidered. All the militia went to camp in September. Next, Borden upheld General Gascoigne's settlement of two of the bitter regimental disputes endemic to a volunteer force. Both decisions had appeared to favour Tory officers and Liberals had expected an election victory to reverse the judgement. The new minister went over the facts, hesitated and then stood firmly by Gascoigne. Just before the change of government, Borden's Conservative predecessor had finally approved regulations limiting the term of command of a militia regiment. Borden decided to enforce the rules even when a violent-tempered fellow Liberal, Colonel James Domville of the 8th New Brunswick Hussars, threatened physical violence. Borden wrestled money from his reluctant colleagues for a long series of projects, beginning with rifle ranges. Purchase of the Lee-Enfield, with its high velocity bullet, meant that almost every range in the country was unsafe. Finally, the new minister had his own agenda of reforms, beginning with a militia medical service. A quarter of a century after the British departure, the Canadian militia still lacked even an embryo of a supply, transport, medical, ordnance, signalling, or intelligence organization. Beginning with Borden's medical service, the rest would slowly follow.

In the summer of 1898, Borden acquired a new general officer commanding. Colonel Edward Hutton should have been a powerful ally. He was as able and well-connected as Herbert and he was even more experienced. He had been a leader of the mounted infantry movement in the British army and he came to Canada fresh from comparable experience in New South Wales. He was also a close personal friend of the new Governor-General, Lord Minto who, as Lord Melgund, had been involved in Canadian defence fifteen years before. Hutton, however, had no intention of being merely the servant of the colonial government that paid his salary. In Australia, he had pursued his own reforming policy and established his own popularity. He had, he boasted, brought down a colonial government, and he had obviously enjoyed the experience. Before leaving London, he visited a variety of influential patrons, from the venerable Duke of Cambridge to the colonial secretary, Joseph Chamberlain, announced his plans and discounted any warnings. Once in Canada, Hutton toured his new command, delivered speeches in every major centre and assured his militia audiences that the force was safe in his hands. Armed with a sound instinct for public relations and a taste for self-advertisement, the new general found an avid audience among reporters, particularly from the more imperial-minded and Conservative newspapers. In his section of the Militia Department's annual report for 1898, Hutton deliberately published his own version of the Leach commission report, citing only the criticisms and proposals he personally supported. The result was a harsh indictment of Canada's defences and a costly programme for their reform.

The Minister of Militia regarded his new general with growing concern. Obviously most of the faults of the militia dated from Tory times, but after three years of Laurier's government, the Conservatives felt free to condemn the Liberals for Canada's defencelessness. For his part, Hutton grew equally contemptuous of both political parties. He was indignant at the tolerance Borden showed for Colonel Domville. Hutton's own patience with the bumptious and insubordinate Tory, Colonel Sam Hughes, was soon exhausted. Everywhere, Hutton preached the slogan of a "National Army" for Canada. By this, he meant two things. Like his minister, he wanted a balanced army, complete in every department and able to take the field on its own as, indeed, British policy now dictated. Hutton also meant that the militia must become immune from partisan political influences. "A good army, a national army," he told the Military Institute in Toronto, "must be one which is apart from party, and which sinks all individual views, be they political or religious, in the general welfare of the country." In principle, no one disagreed. In practice, officers continued to carry their wishes and grievances through political channels. Staff officers discovered often that their orders had "run against a snag." Hutton was horrified to find that the Militia Stores, the engineering branch and the pay department were all under the deputy minister and managed under the full rigours of the patronage system. When the ancient Colonel Charles Panet died in 1898, his successor as deputy minister, Major L. F. Pinault, proved a redoubtable adversary in departmental power struggles.

Borden really had no quarrel with most of Hutton's reforms. Improving the artillery, less drill and more field work at the summer militia camps, even a central training camp for the permanent corps in the spring of 1899, brought no protest. Hutton's directive to staff and instructors to learn French for the sake of the Quebec militia produced predictable grumbling and a warm glow of appreciation from French-Canadian officers. However, the minister would not have been in politics if he had not wondered what damage Hutton was doing to the Liberals by his public speeches. Separating the militia from politics meant, in practice, that the general and not the minister would be the dominant power. That, in plain language, was unconstitutional.

Unlike Herbert, Hutton's priority was to improve the Canadian militia—mainly on the widely admired Swiss model—not to help with imperial manpower needs. While he encouraged the use of Nova Scotia militia to reinforce the British fortress garrison at Halifax, he cancelled any further exchanges of permanent force units with their British counterparts. His pretext was a decision to rush 200 Canadian regulars to the Yukon in the summer of 1898 to reassert Canadian sovereignty and to back the hard-pressed North West Mounted Police during the Klondike Gold Rush. In fact, the major preoccupation of Hutton's career in Canada was the approaching war in South Africa. The Jameson Raid, which had helped divert attention from the "Christmas crisis" over Venezuela, was only one step in the deteriorating relations between the British self-governing colonies of the Cape and Natal and the neighbouring Boer republics of the Transvaal and the Orange Free State. The issues, as usual, were complex and, to most Canadians, remote. Nevertheless, Canada would be involved. Searching for expedients to bring pressure on the Boers, Joseph Chamberlain decided to overawe them with the united diplomatic and military strength of the Empire. Laurier's government co-operated. On July 31, 1899, the Canadian House of Commons unanimously supported the British case in South Africa. Even French-Canadian MPs could be persuaded to make common cause with the oppressed *Uitlanders* rather than with their Dutch Protestant oppressors.

Would Canada do more? Chamberlain hoped so. Through Lord Minto, Britain's official representative in Canada as well as the titular head of state, and through his friend, General Hutton, the colonial secretary's wishes would not go unheeded. By July 3, 1899, Hutton had drafted a proposed organization for a small Canadian contingent of infantry, mounted rifles and artillery numbering about 1,200 men. Lieutenant-Colonel William Otter, commanding the military district at Toronto, was pencilled in as an appropriate commander. His two assistants would be Lieutenant-Colonel Sam Hughes, the Tory imperialist and Lieutenant-Colonel Oscar Pelletier, the son of a Liberal senator. Hutton's scheme was kept strictly secret, however, and Dr. Borden learned of it only in September when the South African situation had grown far more serious.

How would the Laurier government respond? Minto was uncertain. He personally recalled Macdonald's blunt response in 1885. Yet in 1898, when Britain and France had drifted close to war over the Fashoda incident, Minto had been astonished to learn that Laurier would have no objection if Britain used Canadian militia to occupy the tiny French islands of St. Pierre and Miquelon in the Gulf of St. Lawrence. Was Laurier more loyal than Macdonald? The real distinction was in who took the initiative. Neither Macdonald nor Laurier could object if it was Britain that ordered out Canadian militia; it was a wholly different matter for Canada to do so herself. Yet, in the South African crisis, it was an enthusiastic colonial initiative that Chamberlain wanted. Neither the War Office nor Chamberlain believed that colonial troops would actually be needed. Experience with the Australian cavalry in 1885 had taught British officers how long it took to train colonials to regular army standards—and incidentally explained why the War Office would ask for infantry, not the harder-to-train mounted troops. What the Colonial Office wanted was a clear, symbolic and official colonial demonstration of support.

The Laurier government would not oblige. The prime minister's letter to a Liberal editor in London, Ontario, might well have been written by Macdonald:

> We have a great deal to do in this country to develop it to its legitimate expansion. Military expenditure is of such a character that you never know where it will end. I am not disposed to favour it. We have done

more in favour of Imperial defence in building the Intercolonial and the Canadian Pacific, than if we maintained an army in the field in those last twenty years.

Yet many Canadians now disagreed. Prosperity had given Canadians optimism, self-confidence and a new desire to cut a figure in the world. Professor Goldwin Smith, the venerable scholar who wrote so trenchantly of his adopted country, had denounced the Americans' "splendid little war" against Spain; his fellow Torontonians and perhaps most Canadians were merely envious. Newspapers like the *Montreal Star* or the *Toronto Mail & Empire* portrayed the South African problem as a clear case of British right against Boer wrong. Unaware of his possible role in an official contingent, Sam Hughes spent the summer of 1899 publicizing his plan to raise a private contingent to fight for Britain. Thousands of offers, he boasted to Hutton, had poured in.

Both Minto and Hutton were appalled. A privately-raised contingent was not at all what Chamberlain wanted but it would be precisely the excuse Laurier needed to do nothing. When Hutton clamped down military regulations to curb Hughes's plans, the Tory colonel exploded in a torrent of furious letters and nasty innuendo. How dare a British general interfere with a Canadian member of Parliament and a citizen of the Empire exercising his rights. At the outset of the crisis, two like-minded but outsized egos had collided. Soon there were more complications. On October 3, the Colonial Office despatched telegrams to each self-governing colony, thanking it for its patriotic spirit and spelling out the conditions for any contingents: 125-man units, "infantry most, cavalry least, serviceable," to be fully equipped and embarked for Cape Town by October 31. By foolish oversight, Canada, which had made no offer, received thanks and approval for four such units. Moreover, the text of the telegrams was released to the British press. If that was not enough, Hutton's plan for a 1,200 man contingent appeared in the October issue of the *Canadian Military Gazette*, a magazine for militia enthusiasts. The government, which had declared that it had no plans for a contingent, was acutely embarrassed. On October 7 Laurier left for a speaking engagement in Chicago, confident that the agitation would subside. He returned on October 9 to frenzied excitement, reports of a Boer ultimatum, and a private warning from the editor of the major Liberal organ, *The Globe*, that "he would either send troops or get out of office."

Publicly, *The Globe* insisted that rumours of cabinet division were "wholly unfounded." In fact, as C. P. Stacey has observed, "Never since 1899 has the outbreak of a war found the national government so deeply and gravely divided." Differences long postponed or muffled were now exposed. William Mulock and other Ontario ministers who insisted that Canada send a contingent and pay for it could point to the clamour of public opinion. J. Israel Tarte, urged on and briefed by a brilliant young backbencher named Henri Bourassa, protested that Canada should not contribute soldiers when she had had no voice in the imperial decisions which led to the conflict. Tarte's logic concealed a much more real French-Canadian objection which Laurier knew very well: Canada had no business risking her men in England's wars. At different times, both Mulock and Tarte threatened resignation. The compromise, painfully and angrily accepted, was found in the terms of Chamberlain's message: Canada would organize, equip and despatch a contingent, but Britain would pay for it in South Africa and guarantee pensions to widows and those who returned disabled. By ingenious argument, Parliament need not be summoned for so modest a commitment and the bitter debate within the cabinet need not be repeated in a public forum. On October 14 the announcement was made:

> The Prime Minister, in view of the well known desire of a great many Canadians who are ready to take service under such conditions, is of opinion that the moderate expenditure which would thus be involved for the equipment and transportation of such volunteers may readily be undertaken by the Government of Canada without summoning Parliament, especially as such expenditure under such circumstances cannot be regarded as a departure from the well-known principles of constitutional government and colonial practice, nor construed as a precedent for future action.

Next, Laurier's ministers sought scapegoats for their humiliation. Hutton was the prime suspect though (having satisfied himself that Hugh Graham, owner of the *Montreal Star,* and other imperialists would manage an agitation) he had ostentatiously departed for western Canada. Lord Minto was obliged to divide his time between defending his tactless friend and pressing for a more dignified Canadian contingent than Chamberlain's little units. In large measure, he was successful. Though Laurier would have preferred to create an impression in French Canada that he had done no more than help some rabid imperialists go off to a distant war, the governor-general's pressure in Ottawa and London worked. Canada would be represented by the 2nd (Special Service) Battalion of the Royal Canadian Regiment, a thousand men commanded by Colonel Otter. Because of Hughes's public insubordination, Hutton barred the Tory colonel from the expedition. Only united pressure from Laurier and Minto persuaded the general to allow Hughes to travel with the contingent "in an unofficial capacity."

In a remarkable organizing feat, the contingent was recruited at eight centres across Canada, assembled in Quebec City and embarked on the S.S. *Sardinian* within seventeen days. Summer uniforms were manufactured, volunteers enlisted and officers selected amidst a barrage of patriotic excitement and political pressure. A month-long voyage in the overcrowded ship (renamed the "Sardine") convinced Otter that most of his men were excellent and many of his officers were not. Once in South Africa, he had two months to drill, discipline and harden his men into a fair replica of a British line regiment. His men grew to hate their big, greying colonel, whose ideas were so completely at odds with the militia spirit, but when they joined a British regular infantry brigade for the brutally punishing march to Pretoria, some of them began to understand Otter's ideas. In the week-long battle of Paardeberg, from February 18 to 27, the Canadians performed creditably. Confusion in a night attack on the last day of the battle sent most of them back to their trenches but a remnant held on to a position overlooking the Boer trenches. When dawn broke and the hungry, demoralized Boer army surrendered, journalists eagerly gave the Canadians the credit. It seemed marvellous imperial symbolism that on the anniversary of an earlier Boer triumph at Majuba Hill, soldiers from the colonies should avenge Britain's disgrace.

Back in Canada Laurier's government was sufficiently emboldened by the approval of English-speaking Canada and the lack of outrage in Quebec to offer a second contingent. The offer was politely declined and then, in the wake of severe British setbacks, accepted. This time, the cavalry and artillery, excluded from the earlier contingent, had their chance. Two battalions of mounted rifles, one raised in eastern Canada, the other in the West, and three batteries of field artillery were organized, equipped and, early in the new year, embarked at Halifax, 1,320 strong. As a further gesture, Canada agreed to replace the British infantry battalion at Halifax with men of its own. A 3rd Battalion of the Royal Canadian Regiment was enlisted for a year.

Though the Canadian mounted rifles shared in the march to Pretoria, their main fighting came in small actions later in the campaign. In a violent little battle at Liliefontein, three Canadians won the Victoria Cross for saving a gun from capture. Other contingents were also recruited in Canada but by the means Laurier might well have preferred in 1899. Lord Strathcona, fabulously wealthy thanks to the Canadian Pacific Railway, and serving as Canada's High Commissioner in London, used part of his fortune to raise a mounted rifle regiment of his own in western Canada. When Canada's two official contingents returned in December, 1900, after a one-year enlistment, Britain recruited twelve squadrons of South African Police in Canada and, late in the war, raised a few more battalions of mounted rifles. Although Parliament made up the difference between British and Canadian rates of pay for its official contingents (and Lord Strathcona did the same for his regiment) participation cost Canada relatively little—under $3,000,000, a quarter of which was spent for the battalion in Halifax. A total of 8,300 Canadians enlisted during the war, 3,499 of them at Canadian expense. Of these, eighty-nine were killed in action and 135 died of disease or accidents. Among them was the minister's own son, Harold Borden. A knighthood was no compensation for his two shattered parents. For Sir Frederick and Lady Borden, the price of careless patriotism was paid in full.

The vast majority of Canadians could be delighted by their war efforts. Reports from the front gave newspaper readers a colourful and flattering account of Canadian military exploits. Otter's friends kept most complaints of his martinet behaviour out of the press. Casualty reports were painful but the toll was small and war could still be portrayed as a glorious and manly adventure. Yet, even from the outset, there were critics. War fever was an English-speaking, urban phenomenon. No one seems to have noted it at the time, but rural western Ontario failed to find its quota of recruits for Otter's battalion. Neither did Quebec. One company of the first contingent and an artillery battery in the second contingent had French-speaking officers but very few of their men were French Canadians. When Parliament met in 1900, Henri Bourassa could speak for himself, not through Tarte. He insisted that British machinations had forced Canada to send troops, that the precedent had been set by the deed itself, regardless of the sophistry in Laurier's order-in-council, and that Canada's constitution had been overthrown. Bourassa, as usual, went farther than the facts, but he drew nine Quebec MPs with him in his protest, though not in his ensuing resignation from Parliament.

The truth in 1899, and subsequently, was that British machinations were either ineffective or non-existent. A majority had clamoured for action because of an intermingling of national and imperial sentiment which French Canadians, armed with a strong but very different national sentiment, could never share nor fully understand. Sam Hughes was a fervent imperialist who had financed his own journey around the world in 1898 to promote his version of the idea, but he still despised Englishmen like General Hutton and he looked forward confidently to the day when Canadians would show the British how to run the empire properly. He also sought a chance to fight in South Africa as a personal outlet for his energy. Left behind in Cape Town, he finally succeeded in attaching himself to smaller British columns and he vindicated his Canadian critics by publishing boastful accounts of his exploits. When some of his letters, critical of his British superiors, reached the Cape Town papers, Lord Roberts, the commander-in-chief, sent him home. Hughes returned unrepentant and unfulfilled. There would be much for him to do.

A Canadian soldier like Otter was no less a nationalist though his pride was to prove that Canadian soldiers could match the discipline and courage of the finest British military organization, its infantry line battalions. Otter, as a Canadian, felt humiliated by the conduct of men like Hughes, George Denison or Colonel G. S. Ryerson, the Canadian Red Cross Commissioner in South Africa. "We are a great nation of carpet knights," he complained to his wife. Otter was obliged to be more than a mere battalion commander; he was also a pioneer in the double duties of a Canadian contingent commander, compelled to serve two masters. Minto's insistence that Canadians serve together and not be scattered in small detachments was a precedent Canadians would later defend jealously, but no one had prepared Otter for the task nor furnished him with a staff. Seated under a wagon in the pouring rain, his feet in a mud puddle, armed with a pencil and a message pad, Otter and a dependable staff sergeant were the forerunners of the huge Canadian overseas bureaucracies in two world wars.

Canada did not know it in 1900 but Bourassa was right. A precedent had been set. Canadian military planning for a few years more would continue to contemplate war with the United States. After South Africa, however, any British involvement in war would automatically raise the possibility of a Canadian expeditionary force. Other precedents, good and bad, were established by the South African experience. Canadians would be kept in identifiable units under their own commanders. Senior Canadian officers would face a dual responsibility to Ottawa and to their British superiors in the field. Ottawa would use its forces in the field, as it already used the militia, to demonstrate Canada's capacity to produce uniforms, equipment and a growing array of military stores. The results would often be painful. In South Africa, Canadians had found that their canvas duck uniforms chafed when new and rotted when old. Heavy western-made stock saddles were comfortable for the rider but exhausting for the horse. The Canadian water bottle was too small and the Canadian-made Oliver equipment, already rejected by the War Office, proved to be painfully uncomfortable and awkward. An emergency ration sold to Borden by the son of a former Liberal MP, was so worthless that it provoked a parliamentary scandal. Canadian soldiers also criticized their officers, not merely Otter or Colonel Lawrence Herchmer, removed from the command of the Canadian Mounted Rifles after a nervous breakdown, but junior officers who were ignorant of their duties and incapable of commanding respect. These, too, were precedents for future wars.

Such complaints were not taken seriously at the time. Canadian soldiers came home from South Africa in a mood of high self-confidence and national pride. They had embarked as soldiers of the Queen; they returned, for the most part, as self-conscious Canadians. War was and would remain a nation-building experience; it was all the more painfully significant that French Canada shared in it so slightly. Confidence raised questions about Canada's own dependence on British military expertise. The appointment of British generals had seemed appropriate because only they could claim active service experience and a professional education. In South Africa, Canadians had commanded battalions and regiments in battle. Defeats and setbacks had greatly discounted British military competence. In the summer of 1899, Hutton and Hughes had traded insults about the military potential of the Boers "on their old plugs of horses." Brutal experience had confirmed Hughes's faith in the tough Afrikaner farmers with their mobility and marksmanship.

General Hutton, himself, was a victim of British setbacks in South Africa. Strained relations between Borden and the general reached breaking point with the despatch of the first contingent in October, 1899. Minto's peacemaking and Laurier's fear of political embarrassment prevented an open breach but Hutton was unrepentant. Invited by Lord Strathcona to help organize his regiment, Hutton had to be bluntly reminded that he was a government employee, not a free agent. The general seethed. In January, Borden cancelled permission for two prominent Tory officers to attend a militia staff course: one of them had openly advocated war with French Canada because of its disloyalty. Hutton used the episode to embarrass the government. The outcome, for all that Lord Minto could do, was Hutton's dismissal, barely camouflaged as a summons to serve in South Africa. In an election year, Borden's well-publicized quarrel with his general did the Liberals little good. It was also easy to claim, as Norman Penlington has, that Borden used high constitutional principles to justify low partisan dealings. It was up to Canadians to reform themselves.

Canadian nationalism made allies of Borden and Sam Hughes. An alliance of a Liberal minister and his chief opposition critic was an obvious convenience. One result was the Ross Rifle. When Sir Charles Ross, a Scottish sportsman and promoter, appeared with his design, Sir Frederick Borden was a frustrated man. He had tried and failed to arrange for the British service rifle, the Lee-Enfield, to be manufactured in Canada. The British, he suspected, wanted to keep the jobs and profits at home. Ross's rifle design offered Canada a superior weapon and a new industry. Appointed to a committee to evaluate the rifle, Sam Hughes promptly became its most ardent promoter. Certainly the Ross was a fine target rifle, but it had some well-known defects that made it impossible as a service weapon. It was delicate, heavy and easily jammed by dirt or the heat of rapid firing. Attempts to remedy the faults made the Ross heavier, longer and far more costly than the Lee-Enfield. However, its critics had to face two formidable politicians, Hughes and Borden, and swelling Canadian pride in a rifle that won a long succession of marksmanship prizes.

Concern about marksmanship was a legitimate outcome of the South African war. Less plausible was a conviction that the Boers had shown Canada how to defend herself from the Americans. It was a proposition argued publicly when Lord Dundonald arrived to command the militia in 1902. The twelfth Earl of Dundonald was one of the few British generals to add to his reputation in South Africa. He was an energetic, inventive Scot whose Liberal leanings should have won him a welcome from Laurier. Certainly the prime minister was almost as friendly as the crowds who thronged to see a war hero, but his advice was cool. Dundonald should not take the militia seriously, "for though it is useful for suppressing internal disturbances, it will not be required for the defence of the country, as the Monroe doctrine protects us against enemy aggression." The Monroe Doctrine could not, of course, protect Canada from the United States. Perhaps nothing could. Lord Minto, among others, had argued that Canada's contribution in South Africa might be traded for British backing on Canada's Alaska boundary claims. In most parts, Canada's claim to the long panhandle along her Pacific coast was weak and it might hardly have mattered if gold had not been discovered in the Yukon in 1897. Canadians still counted on a compromise. That was not the style of President Theodore Roosevelt. When he grudgingly gave his consent to an arrangement the United States had demanded for years, an arbitration tribunal, he filled the American seats with three outspoken partisans of the American case. Canadians, frankly, did the same. Since Roosevelt bluntly proclaimed that he would fight if he did not get what he wanted, the stage was set for the most dangerous Anglo–American confrontation since 1895.

The British were impressed. Their nominee on the tribunal, Lord Alverstone, dutifully voted with the Americans even on the points where Canada had a good case. Britain promptly ratified the agreement and joined in the rejoicing. Canadians were furious, not only at the success of American bullying but at the British satisfaction. The realities were not hard to understand. In the South African war, only the United States among the major powers had sympathized with Britain's plight. In 1901, by surrendering her right to a Panama canal in the Hay-Pauncefote treaty, Britain had accepted American dominance in North American waters on both sides of the continent. There could be no war over an Alaska boundary and Canadians, if they thought about it, would be the last people to want one.

They were not thinking that way in 1903 and Lord Dundonald had some beguiling ideas for making Canada defensible. Amidst a welter of overdue reforms in pay, training, camp conditions, the organization of military engineers, map-making and military intelligence, the general promoted a common theme. For $5 million a year and a single investment of $12 million for arms and fortifications, Canada could have security. Even before he left England, Dundonald had propounded his theory of a "skeleton army" of well-trained officers and non-commissioned officers, with a cadre of privates. In an emergency, the skeleton would be fleshed out by thousands of men who had learned to shoot at rifle clubs and who had mastered drill and military routine through compulsory cadet training at school. The militia must be reorganized in peacetime for immediate mobilization in war. A big central camp was needed so that the officers and men of the "skeleton" force could train realistically.

Most of this was very much to Sir Frederick Borden's taste but in Lord Dundonald, the minister suspected, he had another Hutton. Like his predecessor, the new general had a zest for popularity and a flair for public relations. His public speeches attracted attention and alarmed Liberals like Bourassa by their warlike tone. When Dundonald used his annual report as a platform for his ideas, Borden edited them out. In the following year, when Dundonald tried again, the minister simply suppressed large sections of the report. At the same time, most of Dundonald's actual reforms were implemented with a determination no one could have predicted only five years before. Friction between the two men was personal and it grew faster when Dundonald set out, with effusive flattery, to win over Sam Hughes.

It was time for a new Militia Act. The last major revision in 1883 had merely allowed for the permanent corps. There was much to be done. Pay rates should be increased. Old problems of aid to the civil power could be cured. Moreover, some changes reflected Canada's military self-confidence. Henceforth, Borden proposed, Canadian officers would have the same seniority as British officers of the same rank instead of being automatically junior. Canadians would become eligible for the post of general officer commanding. A passage which delegated royal authority over the militia to the Governor-General would be omitted. Lord Minto and his successors would no longer have a legal claim to involve themselves in Canadian military affairs. Minto and Dundonald were horrified. As far as Minto was concerned, no Canadian could be fit to command the force and the post would go to "some utterly incompetent public favourite or political supporter." The Colonial Office must intervene.

The British did their best. Borden's bill was held over to 1904 so that he could attend the new Committee of Imperial Defence in London and be subjected to some eloquent flattery. Instead, the Canadian minister came home with a new idea. In Britain, badly-needed reforms in the wake of the South African War had led to the abolition of the historic appointment of commander-in-chief and the creation of an Army Council of senior political and military figures. To Borden, the idea might be a solution of his problems. Instead of depending on a single military commander, he could get advice directly from a number of senior officers and from his civil officials as well. A new post of inspector-general would dispose of Dundonald.

That proved unnecessary. Dundonald disposed of himself. Despite warnings from Lord Minto, the British general made himself more and more politically offensive to the government. On June 3, 1904, he chose a banquet of Montreal militia officers to denounce the Minister of Agriculture for meddling in the selection of officers for a new militia cavalry regiment. The officers managed to stop press reports but with Dundonald's help the news leaked out. In Parliament, government ministers disputed the charges. Laurier contributed to the Tory din when, in a slip of translation, he referred to the British general as a "foreigner" when he meant "stranger." By June 10 Dundonald was dismissed. For more than a month he stayed in Canada, hinting broadly that he might be a candidate in the forthcoming elections. A blunt message from the War Office brought him back to England. In Ottawa, huge crowds cheered when he cried: "Men of Canada, keep both hands on the Union Jack," but in Montreal driving rain drowned any attempt to repeat the demonstrations.

With Dundonald's departure, British influence could have vanished from the militia. It did not. Conservatives, led by Hughes, denounced the Militia Council idea with Dundonald's slogan that the militia department had become a "Military Tammany." Others, reviving an older theme, insisted that a huge military staff was beyond Canada's means. However, Borden neatly defused the opposition when he announced that Colonel Percy Lake, the popular former quartermaster-general, would return to Canada to fill the senior military appointment in the council, the Chief of General Staff. In 1908, when the post was filled by a Canadian, Brigadier-General William Otter, Lake remained as Inspector-General, continued in the Militia Council and kept the highest rank firmly in British control. Otter's two pre-1914 successors, Major-General Colin Mackenzie and Major-General Willoughby Gwatkin, were both British. It took fifteen more years and a world war before Canadian officers were trusted with all the appointments in their military organization.

To be fair, there was much to be done and officers like Lake and Gwatkin brought a skill and intelligence that would have been exceptional in any country. There was no precedent for the pace of military reform and militia expansion in Canada in the years between 1900 and 1914, and ability of any kind was at a premium. Under Borden, at least, the Militia Council was a success, with serious political-military consultation and a formality in recording decisions that allowed new members (and historians) to have some grasp of what transpired. In eastern Canada, the military districts were grouped as commands and later as divisions to allow administrative decentralization, stronger staffs and an organization suited to mobilization. In the West, military potential finally began to be exploited after the South African War. Funds and energy were applied to develop a military organization in the fastest growing region of the country. Strathcona's Horse was revived as a permanent force unit in the West in 1910. The Laurier government had balked at Dundonald's armament and fortifications proposals but from 1903, $1,300,000 a year was earmarked for new arms and equipment. If British manufacturers had met their delivery deadlines, Canada's active militia would have been reasonably well armed by 1914.

The logic of Britain's attitude to war in North America and the growth of German naval power in home waters rendered British garrisons at Halifax and Esquimalt useless. When Sir John Fisher became First Sea Lord at the Admiralty in 1902, his insistence on disposing of ships that could "neither fight nor run away" ended his old command, the North American and West Indies Squadron. The new Committee of Imperial Defence proved its value by a prompt decision to abandon both the remaining Canadian fortresses. The discovery that Sir Frederick Borden had already assumed that Canadians would take over the defences led to a tiresome delay while a transition was arranged. On July 1, 1905, the two fortresses became Canadian although some British troops remained until Canadian soldiers could be recruited and properly trained.

Militarily, the two fortresses were questionable assets. Esquimalt, in particular, had been judged indefensible. Canadian experience in garrisoning Halifax in 1900 gave ample warning of the difficulty of finding men at forty or even fifty cents a day to perform routine garrison duty. After 1905 manning the permanent force garrisons was only possible by recruiting British reservists in England. But, responsibility for the fortresses did provide Canadian officers with challenging professional and technical problems. The presence of more than a thousand Canadian regular soldiers at Halifax, serving in the artillery and engineers as well as in a battalion of infantry gave experience in handling significant administrative problems. The garrison required small permanent elements of army service corps, medical corps and other departmental organizations. Even women gained their first tiny foothold in the Canadian forces when nurses were recruited for the military hospitals. The Canadian occupation of the two fortresses also had political and economic significance. Sir Frederick Borden would not have been a Nova Scotia politician had he ignored the patronage benefits of maintaining a large garrison at Halifax or the economic loss for his region if the British troops had simply left. By the early twentieth century, Canadians no longer needed to be reminded that their country faced on two oceans and that what was done for the Atlantic must also be done, if on a more modest scale, for the Pacific.

British withdrawal from Halifax and Esquimalt completed a process that had begun in 1871. Militarily, Canada was now on her own in North America. That did not mean that Canada could be counted out of Britain's military calculations. Unlike Australia and New Zealand, acutely conscious of the new Asiatic power of Japan and of their own dependence on British naval and military power, Canada could have opted out of imperial defence. That was certainly what some Canadians and most *Canadiens* would have wished. However, as the British digested the lessons of South Africa and sought greater military standardization of all imperial forces, Canada went along. In her eyes, Halifax and Esquimalt remained imperial fortresses and their defence plans were regularly submitted for British criticism (though the British, on their own, would have abandoned them). Canada attended imperial conferences in 1907 and 1909 and went home with commitments to standardize training, organization and stores in the militia. Canadian officers passed British promotion examinations (oriented to warfare in Europe and on the northwest frontier of India) and after 1909 a few Canadians attended the British army's staff college at Camberley. At home, Canadians might still pretend that their national enemy remained the United States, and Sam Hughes, for one, prepared his own plan to invade the New England states. In practice, the Canadian militia was preparing to share in the great European war which, by 1909, seemed almost inevitable.

By no means all Canadians were appalled at such a prospect. In the first years of the century, militarist thinking in Canada asserted itself with quite unprecedented vehemence. As Carl Berger has indicated, enthusiasm for war as a form of human development and as a repudiation of materialism and self-indulgence was a prominent feature of the writing of men like Andrew Macphail or William Hamilton Merritt. Charles Mair, the poet, rejoiced that the South African war had rescued Britain from "the gangrene of wealth and luxury." The Canadian Defence League, founded in Toronto in 1909 by Merritt, Dr. J. T. Fotheringham and a number of local businessmen, professors and militia officers, called for universal military training on the Swiss model. The League looked for support to a galaxy of Protestant clergy and intellectuals, including Albert Carman of the Methodists, Principal Maurice Hutton of University College, Principal D. M. Gordon of Queen's University and Nathaniel Burwash of Victoria University. Money came from Edmund Walker of the Bank of Commerce, Henry Pellatt, the Toronto utilities magnate and militia colonel, and J. C. Eaton of the merchandising family.

If militarism was a state of mind or set of values which supported patriotism, discipline, subordination, order and a competitive view of human nature, it was amply reflected in the cadet movement in Canada. Cadet corps had existed in Canada since before Confederation. By the 1890s, Sam Hughes's brother J. L. Hughes, the superintendent of Toronto's schools, mustered the city's entire schoolboy population for annual military reviews. Moreover, the cadet movement was one military institution which appealed to French-speaking as well as English-speaking Canadians. The first official corps after Confederation had been organized in Quebec classical colleges. Armand Lavergne, Bourassa's military-minded lieutenant, assured a Toronto audience in 1910 that: "There is no doubt that compulsory cadet service in the schools or educational houses of our country is most beneficial as it teaches the young men the lesson of patriotism and citizenship and teaches them to have a sane mind in a sound body."

Naturally the cadet movement intensified or languished in tune to the level of warlike enthusiasm. It took Lord Dundonald to give cadet training a place in the country's defence system and it became a personal crusade of Sir Frederick Borden to implement the system officially. By September of 1908, he had extracted a comprehensive agreement with Nova Scotia. Henceforth, every teacher in the province would qualify in drill and physical training. In return, the militia department would provide instructors, arms, books, examinations and a bonus for the qualified. The catalyst was provided by Lord Strathcona: a gift eventually totalling half a million dollars, to be distributed widely in prizes. By 1911, six of the nine provinces and both the Catholic and Protestant education committees of Quebec had joined the federal scheme. Earl Grey, the governor-general, did his part by contributing a trophy for community participation. The first winner, in 1912, was Strathcona, Alberta, with 2.4 per cent of its population enrolled; in 1913, Joliet, Quebec won with 3.41 per cent. In 1908, 9,000 boys had enrolled in cadet corps; by 1913, the total exceeded 40,000, three times the number in the Boy Scout movement.

Militarism drew an indignant response. Farm organizations deplored the waste of time and money and the snobbishness of "gilded staff officers." The trade union movement noted the frequent use of militia to break strikes, particularly in the first decade of the new century, and commanded members not to join. Pacifist organizations pointed to the progress of humanitarian reform, illustrated by the Hague conferences of 1899 and 1907, and the spread of arbitration as a solution to human conflict. William Lyon Mackenzie King, Canada's youthful Minister of Labour after the 1908 election, a fervent promoter of peace in industrial disputes, argued for mediation in international as well as labour conflict. He was the natural choice, after his 1911 defeat, to plan celebrations in 1914 of the century of peace along the Canadian-American border. However, it was Sir Wilfrid Laurier himself who provided the definitive statement of Canada's opposition to war and to warlike preparations:

> There is a school abroad, there is a school in England and in Canada, a school which is perhaps represented on the floor of this parliament, a school which wants to bring Canada into the vortex of militarism which is the curse and blight of Europe. I am not prepared to endorse any such policy.

The ultimate act of Laurier's government in defence matters in the summer of 1911 was to assign a senior staff officer to prepare a mobilization plan for a contingent of one infantry division and a cavalry brigade to serve in a "civilized country." The European vortex was sucking Canada closer. It was really to escape its attraction that the Laurier government had embarked on its naval policy two years earlier. Despite her coasts and her substantial merchant and fishing fleets, the Dominion had never really considered a navy. The "marine militia" mentioned in the 1868 legislation soon vanished. An ill-fated attempt to acquire an aged British warship as a training vessel ended ignominiously when the *Charybdis* was towed around to Halifax in 1882 and returned to the Royal Navy. Its name remained for generations as a taunt to any Canadian who ever dreamed that the Dominion could match the efficiency and might of the British fleet. That was fine with the Royal Navy. Its doctrine decreed that the Empire's navy must be as indivisible as the seas themselves. In its eyes, intermittent efforts of the Australian colonies to develop their own navies proved the point. By the early twentieth century however, both the Royal Navy and the British taxpayer needed help. The naval building race with Germany, fed on mutual paranoia, gained pace. In 1909, the British government proposed to build four of the huge *Dreadnought* class battleships; the navy demanded six; public outcry gave it eight. A Liberal government, building the first frail stage of Britain's welfare state, found its naval expenditures intolerably high. The colonies must be invited to help.

New Zealand, ever the most loyal, was willing. Its contribution of the cost of a dreadnought embarrassed the others. Australia already had a navy and wanted more. What about Canada? Laurier's government was firmly opposed to purely financial contributions. Politically, the Admiralty's alternative proposal—to build a "fleet unit" of a battle cruiser and supporting warships on the Pacific coast—was unacceptable. Canada had two oceans and the only acceptable plan would be to have a small squadron on each coast. Though British admirals believed that such a force would be virtually useless for imperial defence, they reluctantly conceded the point. Better some help than none at all.

In early 1909, support for a Canadian navy appeared to be bipartisan and unanimous. The original motion on March 22, was offered by George E. Foster, a New Brunswick Conservative. A Laurier version passed without dissent. In fact, both the Liberals and Conservatives concealed deep internal divisions. In both parties, French-Canadian opinion sharply opposed any naval effort as a concession to imperialism. In Tory ranks, another faction dismissed a separate Canadian service, in a phrase popularized by a McGill economics professor Stephen Leacock, as a "tin-pot navy." Canada must contribute to Britain's dire need. Within a year, the apparent consensus dissolved as the Conservative party leader, Robert L. Borden, shifted toward his party's imperialist wing. When Laurier introduced his Naval Service Bill on January 12, 1910, party discipline was exerted to force the proposal through. By May 4, 1910, a Canadian naval service was apparently launched. Tenders were issued for four light cruisers and six destroyers, a Royal Canadian Naval College was opened at Halifax and two elderly British cruisers, the *Niobe* at Halifax and the *Rainbow* at Esquimalt arrived to serve as training vessels. Rear Admiral Charles Kingsmill, a Canadian who had made his career in the Royal Navy, agreed to become the service's first director.

In fact, the curse of the *Charybdis* pursued the Canadian navy. Despite some impressive Canadian recruits and the loan of some able British officers and ratings, the sneers of the Tory opposition and the hostility of French Canada pursued the new service. It was born at the same time that Henri Bourassa launched his newspaper, *Le Devoir,* as a passionate exponent of French-Canadian nationalism. Laurier's navy gave Bourassa his theme. While Tory imperialists raged that Laurier had turned his back on Britain's naval crisis, Bourassa insisted that Canada's new fleet bound her to participate in any imperial war. In vain had Laurier insisted that Canadian ships would be transferred to British command only by consent of Parliament. Their mere presence at sea, Bourassa argued, would make them objects of attack as much as any British warship. In 1900, Laurier had made his compromise on the South African contingent a strongpoint against extremists on either side; now older, tired and lumbered with all the failings of a worn-out government, Laurier proved an ineffective battler. With extraordinary opportunism, the Tory imperialists and Bourassa's *nationalistes* made common cause in Quebec constituencies. Conservatives provided funds for *Le Devoir* while Bourassa and able lieutenants like Armand Lavergne and Olivar Asselin stumped the rural counties, warning mothers that their sons might be conscripted for the imperial fleet. The naval issue cost the Liberals Laurier's old riding of Drummond-Arthabaska in a by-election on November 10, 1910 and the turmoil did not subside.

When the general election came in September, 1911, there was the usual host of issues and, outside Quebec, the navy issue hardly ranked with Reciprocity as the dominant question. In French Canada, though, Bourassa brilliantly exploited suspicion of the new navy and a vague but potent fear of conscription. Laurier went into the campaign with fifty of Quebec's sixty-five seats; he emerged with only thirty-seven. The absurd ironies of the naval question were not exhausted. Elsewhere in Canada the Conservatives also triumphed and even without Bourassa's *nationalistes,* Borden commanded a majority of five. Even then, to Bourassa's chagrin, most of the MPs he had helped to elect proved only a little less loyal to the new Conservative regime than Ontario or British Columbia Tories. Bourassa had helped to defeat Laurier for creating a Canadian navy; the government he had helped to bring to power set out in 1912 to contribute $35 million to Britain as the price of three new dreadnoughts. To force his policy through a Liberal filibuster, Borden was reduced to imposing closure on the House of Commons for the first time in Canada's history. Even then, the Liberal majority in the Senate defeated the naval aid bill and defied the Conservatives to call a general election. Thanks to Borden's policy, the infant Canadian naval service was left to waste away and there was no naval aid for Britain. When war came, the security of Canada's Pacific coast depended on the Imperial Japanese Navy.

It was very different for the Canadian militia. Sir Frederick Borden shared personally in the Liberal debacle of 1911, but when the new prime minister contemplated his choice for Minister of Militia, his Liberal cousin's nomination was decisive: Colonel Sam Hughes. Certainly Robert Borden had profound misgivings; they were balanced by his admiration for Hughes's energy and knowledge, and gratitude for his personal fidelity during the long opposition years. Hughes, repentant and tearful, swore solemnly to mend his ways. It was a promise he could not possibly keep.

Thanks to Sir Frederick, Hughes had risen to be the senior colonel in the militia. As minister he now behaved as both political master and as commander-in-chief. Never before or since has so devout a militarist held the defence portfolio. Hughes attended manoeuvres, camps and parades in full uniform and harangued officers and men like a drill sergeant. In his office, he took off his jacket, hoisted his feet on the desk and entertained old cronies. He delighted journalists with anecdotes, philosophy and occasional tasteless displays of his authority over frightened subordinates. Under the Liberals, the militia department budget had grown from $1.6 million in 1898 to $7 million in 1911. By 1914, Hughes had raised the total to $11 million in the midst of a severe depression. In 1904, 25,000 militiamen had trained with rural and city units; in 1913, 55,000 went to camp. As minister, Hughes could lend his full official prestige to James Hughes's crusade for universal cadet training. Senior militia officers, assembled at the end of 1911 for their first national conference, heard a minister almost wholly after their own hearts. Hughes promised drill halls, an issue of boots, more camps and the government's full moral backing for the force. They were delighted when the minister publicly scolded staff officers and the permanent force for pretending to displace the volunteers as Canada's true defenders. The officers differed on only one point: Hughes's absolute insistence that liquor be banished from militia camps. As on most points touching his judgement, the new minister was inflexible: the camps and drill halls of Canada must become the schools and community centres of the nation. Hughes's convictions, delivered to innumerable audiences across the country, were in stark contrast to the apologetic tone normally considered appropriate for a Canadian defence minister:

> To make the youth of Canada self-controlled, erect, decent and patriotic through military and physical training, instead of growing up, as under present conditions of no control, into young ruffians or young gadabouts; to ensure peace by national preparedness for war; to make the military camps and drill halls throughout Canada clean, wholesome, sober and attractive to boys and young men; to give that final touch to Imperial unity, and crown the arch of responsible government by an inter-Imperial Parliament dealing only with Imperial affairs.

Hughes's charm and energy captivated many militia officers. So did his policy of retiring older staff officers and replacing them with keen militiamen like Colonel E. A. Cruikshank, an able amateur military historian, or Colonel J. P. Landry, son of the new Conservative speaker of the Senate. Hughes also promoted Armand Lavergne to command a Quebec militia regiment but he soon made himself cordially detested in French Canada by forbidding French-Canadian regiments to carry arms in traditional religious processions. Hughes's enemies were not limited to Quebec. By 1914, a resurgent Liberal party found that the Conservative defence minister had become their best asset all over the country. In a depression mood, Canadians had little patience with the excesses of "Drill Hall Sam," with his enthusiasm for buying Ford cars and his extravagance in taking militia cronies and their wives on a prolonged excursion to the British, French and Swiss manoeuvres. As a fashion in thought, militarism ebbed rapidly away. By early 1914, the Canadian Defence League had given up the ghost. Universities which had promised to establish contingents of the new Canadian Officers Training Corps had second thoughts.

War might be unexpectedly close in 1914 but a great many Canadians had other matters on their minds.

The Great War

3

The war crisis in the summer of 1914 boiled up with incredible speed. So had many others in previous years, only to subside. In Canada, remote from the chancelleries and general headquarters of Europe, few took the threats very seriously. If war did come, surely Britain, with her Liberal government, would stay out. Such a possibility enraged Sam Hughes. Militia department officials only barely dissuaded him from hauling down the Union Jack in disgust. Within hours, the news improved. The sixty-one-year-old minister would have his war. At midnight, August 4, 1914, the British ultimatum to Berlin expired.

"When Britain is at war, Canada is at war," Laurier had declared in 1910, "There is no distinction." There was also no question. By all the evidence of speeches, cheering crowds and editorials, Canada was united during that first hot week of August. Even Henri Bourassa, who narrowly escaped German internment in Alsace, returned to Canada to add his blessing. Laurier promised a party truce for the duration of the war. When W. F. O'Connor, one of Sir Robert Borden's legal advisers, took on the task of drafting emergency legislation, a prominent opposition member insisted: "Make absolutely sure that you omit no power that the Government may need." O'Connor's War Measures Act certainly met that test. In 1899, Laurier had insisted that an overseas contingent was no precedent; in 1914, Canada's offer of 25,000 men was almost instantaneous and unchallenged anywhere. Offers poured into Ottawa. Even before the outbreak of war, wealthy Toronto ladies met to raise funds for a hospital ship.

Canadians, taking no interest in military matters themselves, presumed that the nation was unprepared and most historians have echoed that assumption. In fact, Canada was probably better prepared in 1914 than for any war before or since. Takeover of the Halifax defences promoted a new sophistication in Canada's mobilization arrangements. The fortress defence plan required a co-operation between the militia, the naval service and other government departments that never before had existed. A War Book of plans for each branch of government in the event of hostilities, was completed just in time. Precautions, for the most part, slipped quietly into place. Wireless stations, canal locks and vital points were placed under guard. Port defences and an examination service were mobilized at Halifax and Quebec. Men of the neglected navy became the first Canadians to risk their lives when HMCS

Rainbow set out from Esquimalt. If she had met the German cruiser *Leipzig*, her crew would have become Canada's first casualties.

Canada also had a detailed plan and most of the arms and equipment for an overseas contingent of one infantry division and a brigade of cavalry. By Hughes's command, the plan was scrapped. Instead, at his insistence, the telegraphic equivalent of bonfires on the mountain tops of Scotland summoned volunteers to a hastily improvised camp at Valcartier near Quebec City. As the minister personally pulled some kind of order out of the chaos he had deliberately created, most Canadians marvelled. They had no idea Colonel Willoughby Gwatkin's plan had offered a better arrangement than was possible from a sweating, swearing Sam Hughes on horseback, promoting cronies, damning critics and boasting incessantly of his accomplishments. One advantage of Hughes's preoccupation at Valcartier was that he could not interfere with other defence arrangements. There were many disadvantages.

Canada could certainly have been better prepared in 1914. She could have had more men in uniform, more qualified officers, more equipment and uniforms in storage. She would have had more guns if British factories had delivered them on schedule. The critical questions are whether more preparations would have made Canada more secure in 1914 and whether they could have altered the outcome of the war. Canada remained almost wholly immune from enemy action from the first day of the war to the last. No one would argue that an additional Canadian division or two on the Western Front in October of 1914 instead of March and September of 1915 could have tipped the balance. Instead, Canada's casualty toll would have been very much larger and her reinforcement crisis would have come even sooner.

No belligerent, not even Germany, was prepared for the kind of war that lay ahead. Ivan Bloch had written prophetically that war would become a merciless struggle between two impregnable trench lines, ended only by utter exhaustion. Polish-Jewish bankers were not considered experts in such matters. For a dozen excellent reasons, experts predicted that the war would be over by Christmas. Canada's contingent, increased to 32,000 before it sailed for England on October 3, was unlikely to see action. The incredible financial burden of the war, already half a million dollars a day by November, 1914, would soon be lifted. Hughes's insistence that the Canadian Expeditionary Force would never condescend to accept anyone but a volunteer—and only the best of them—seemed a safe promise. With a federal election impending, the party truce would soon end and the political wars could resume.

In fact, there was no way for the war to end quickly except by a German victory or a negotiated peace. On both sides, the atmosphere of a popular crusade, allegations of atrocities, denigrations of enemy leaders and entire peoples made compromise impossible and defeat intolerable. Only victory could justify the terrible sacrifices being made by the people of each warring nation. The mood and the energy mobilized by the likelihood of a short war made a long war inevitable. So did a military technology which, with the machine gun, massive artillery concentrations and huge conscript armies, gave the defence a decisive advantage over the offence until the final year of the war. Belligerents, including Canada, were caught in moods and with commitments they would never have adopted if they could have foreseen that the war would last for fifty-two months.

There were a few who, by temperament or forethought, glimpsed the dimensions of the struggle. Lord Kitchener, invited to take over the War Office at the outset of the war, stunned his new cabinet colleagues by predicting that he would need a million men. In fact, he would need far more. In Canada, General Gwatkin, newly promoted as Chief of the General Staff, tried to restrain Canada's overseas manpower commitments in 1915 because he could anticipate a recruiting crisis. Making his first significant critique of Canada's war effort in September, 1914, Bourassa urged the government to begin "by resolutely envisaging its real situation, to take exact account of what it can do, and to ensure our own internal security before starting or pursuing an effort that it will perhaps not be in a state to sustain until the end." It might have been wise advice but it came from someone already becoming indifferent to the struggle across the Atlantic. Canadians might explain their growing passion about the war as national pride or imperial loyalty but it was, and is, hard for a democracy to fight any war by half-measures. The United States would discover that when it entered the war in 1917.

There might be real benefits from the outpouring of enthusiasm at the outset of war in 1914. Men like Andrew Macphail or Stephen Leacock could find vindication for pre-war theories that only such a national struggle would drive out selfish materialism, petty politics and self-indulgence. Canadians not only exhorted sacrifices from others; many made them. In a nation of close to eight million people, only a few thousand had any direct experience of war but others tried to envisage the demands and, in the phrase instantly adopted at the time, "do their bit." The government was delighted. There was much to do and no precedent for a Canadian government doing it. The emergency session of Parliament in August, 1914, chartered the Canadian Patriotic Fund, a huge charitable venture that collected $6 million in its first three months, including a day's pay from employees of the CPR, the T. Eaton Co. and Dominion Textiles. The Fund was the main source of financial support for soldiers' families (at up to $30 a month in eastern Canada and $40 in the West). Until 1916, charity supported widows and the disabled. Almost every national or community organization, from the IODE to the Salvation Army, sought war work.

One form of voluntarism was discouraged by the government: persecuting the 100,000 German and Austro-Hungarian citizens in Canada or 400,000 more Canadians of German ancestry. By policy as much as neglect, German and Austrian reservists had little initial difficulty in escaping to the United States. When internment began in October, it was a reluctant response to public demand and a counter to German imprisonment of Henri

Beland, a Liberal MP, Ernest Macmillan, a future Toronto conductor and other Canadian civilians. Some communities, notably at the Lakehead and in western Canada, demanded internment camps as a way to make Ottawa pay relief costs for armies of jobless labourers of Austro-Hungarian origins.

The major reason why any major war had to be short was economic, not military. Bankers insisted that national economies would collapse because of financial strain and the disruption of trade. Pre-war radicals, including most of the officers of Canada's Trades and Labour Congress, placed their faith in a general strike of workers of the world as a way of paralyzing belligerent nations. Instead, the workers thronged the city squares to cheer the departing armies. National economies proved to be unexpectedly robust. Canada's was no exception. The war came at the end of a period of rapid capital creation. Three transcontinental railways—two of them in desperate financial trouble—were in place. If Canadians suffered from an economic depression in 1914, it was because her productive capacity was so far in excess of her peacetime needs. Initially, the war aggravated the problem. Massey-Harris, the huge farm implement manufacturer, had distributed its European exports but it had not collected the money when the war broke out. Everywhere buyers cancelled orders and employers laid off more workers. Many of the men at Valcartier and even more of the volunteers for the Second Contingent, authorized in October, were driven by unemployment as much as they were tugged by patriotism. Postwar estimates suggested that a fifth of the men in the Canadian Expeditionary Force came from long-term unemployment. Supplying Sam Hughes's soldiers became a vital stimulus for a sagging economy, with the hope of more business in England when Canadian soldiers showed off their new boots, uniforms and Bain wagons. In western Canada, where drought and poor prices had begun to budge some prairie farmers from their dangerous preoccupation with wheat, wartime demand reversed the trend. Wheat acreage grew from 10.3 million in 1914 to 15.1 million in 1915. Farm prices climbed faster than costs. Summer fallowing and other prudent techniques were widely abandoned to cash in on wartime markets.

A short war would have done little for Canadian manufacturing. Far from attracting orders, much of the clothing and equipment of the First Contingent was abandoned as unsuitable after a few months' experience in the mud of Salisbury Plain. Canadian promoters, even when armed with Sam Hughes's endorsement, attracted little business (though the War Office contracted for two million army boots in Canada). The United States, with its huge manufacturing potential, attracted most of the Allied orders. Sir Robert Borden complained of a "very painful and even bitter feeling" that some jobless Canadians went without food while orders were placed across the border. A partial answer, in the Hughes spirit of improvisation, was the Shell Committee, a chance consortium of militia friends and manufacturers from Canada's small metal manufacturing industry. By the end of 1914, the committee had contracted for $25 million in shells and casings and orders kept pouring in through the winter and spring of 1915. The Shell Committee was better at promises than production. It wrestled with inexperience, a clamorous host of small firms, most with more political than financial backing, and a tendency to cry foul if rejected. The problems were not limited to Canada. By the summer of 1915, a desperate shortage of artillery ammunition for the British army brought about a national scandal, a coalition and the appointment of David Lloyd George as British Minister of Munitions. Canada's Shell Committee was only part of the problem but with orders worth $170 million, it had delivered only $5.5 millions' worth, only two per cent on time. Out of the welter of confusion, back-biting and suspicion came a clear British policy: Canada would get no more munitions orders until its industry was reorganized.

The result was the Imperial Munitions Board, managed by a self-made Methodist millionaire from the bacon-exporting business, Joseph Flavelle. While Hughes and the Shell Committee sparred with a parliamentary committee and a Royal Commission, the IMB set out to create a munitions industry. Taking full advantage of efficient managers and using his British appointment to keep most patronage-seekers at bay, Flavelle put together a strong executive team, forced down prices in some of the more scandalous instances of profiteering and imposed quality control on manufacturers who descended to faking inspection stamps. The West, with high unemployment and little manufacturing industry, complained that Flavelle sent it little business. The IMB chairman replied that western contractors had been allowed specially high prices and had failed to perform. Trade unions demanded the "Fair Wages" clauses required by both British and Canadian government contracts. Flavelle refused: without IMB contracts, union members would be out of work. The Imperial Munitions Board was autocratic, powerful, increasingly efficient and utterly unloved. It was the biggest Canadian business yet created, with 600 factories, a quarter of a million workers (including 40,000 women) and a turnover of $2 million a day by 1917. By the end of the war, it had built boats, merchant ships, aircraft and flying boats. It produced chemicals and explosives, often in "National Factories" directly owned by the Board. Although artillery ammunition had been almost beyond Canada's manufacturing capacity in 1914, it was not a high technology product. Michael Bliss, Flavelle's biographer, is correct in deflating some of the bold claims made for Canada's wartime munitions industry. However, the IMB played an enormous role in a vital task: financing Canada's share of the war.

Unlike 1899, when the government accepted only a small part of the cost of participation, the mood of 1914 made Borden's proud undertaking to bear the full financial burden seem appropriate. Parliament, watchdog of the treasury, never barked. At the special 1914 session, a Liberal member queried the financial implications, hurried on to a question about post office patronage and never paused for an answer. As Minister of Finance, Sir Thomas White later confessed that the department lost control of expenditures. So did the auditor-general. White's role was to be a kind of quartermaster, bringing in the money for others like Hughes to spend. Few people seemed concerned about where he would find it. There were no precedents save Canada's past record of overseas borrowing for railways. However, the failing transcontinental railways, the Canadian Northern and the Grand Trunk Pacific, had already put Canada's credit at risk in foreign money markets. Apart from expanding the money supply dramatically at the onset of the war, White proved a timid, unimaginative financial manager. Tariffs remained the main government revenue source. Increases added to the cost of living but, White argued, gave everyone a chance to make wartime sacrifices. Direct taxes were avoided. Most provinces and some municipalities already occupied the income tax field. White turned to the international bond market, first in London and, when that was closed, to New York. "We are justified in placing upon posterity the greater portion of the financial burden of this war," he explained, "waged as it is in the interests of human freedom and their benefit. . . ." One source he was strangely reluctant to tap: Canadians' own savings. The country, he believed, could not finance its own needs. He was wrong. By 1915, prosperity was fast returning. War-generated spending, including the income from Flavelle's IMB, meant that when White cautiously sought $50 million in the Canadian market, he got $100 million. Again in 1916 and 1917, bond issues were over-subscribed. A first Victory Loan in 1917, designed for small savers and hitched to forceful patriotic appeals, sought $150 million and got $500 million. Further campaigns in 1918 and 1919 were almost as successful.

The biggest crisis in Canadian war finance came in 1917 when Britain, in a desperate financial position, concluded that she could no longer afford to buy the IMB's products. Flavelle, a pre-war associate of White at the National Trust, temporarily floated the Board's finances on the Canadian treasury, bank loans and the proceeds of the Victory Loan over-subscription while he hunted for a lasting solution. It came from the Americans. Faced with huge war production needs, Washington agreed to place orders with the Imperial Munitions Board on condition that Canadian prices were at least 7 per cent lower than American. Canadian manufacturers, already well-established and with their capital costs already covered by earlier profits, had no trouble meeting the condition. One result was a diversification in the Board's production to include ships, aero-engines and flying boats.

The war demanded food and munitions from Canada. It also demanded men. In March, 1915, after a winter of unexpected misery on Salisbury Plain, the 1st Canadian Division had gone to France. A second contingent spent the winter in Canada, somewhat better housed in exhibition halls, disused factories and militia drill halls, but suffering from a lack of equipment, winter clothing and competent instructors. More battalions were authorized during the winter of 1915 and twelve regiments of mounted rifles were organized, originally to defend the Suez Canal from the Turks. The initial 25,000 men authorized in August, 1914 expanded steadily. By July, 1915, the approved strength for the Canadian Expeditionary Force had reached 150,000; in October, after Sir Robert Borden returned from England, the total was pushed to 250,000. In his New Year's message for 1916, the prime minister declared that Canada would send half a million men to the war.

During 1914, the CEF attracted 59,144 officers, nursing sisters and other ranks. Recruiting in 1915 drew almost three times as many, 158,859. Most of the volunteers in the First Contingent and many in the Second had been born in the British Isles. Britain's crisis drew them home; so did experience of unemployment, seasonal layoffs and the weary frustrations of prairie homesteading. Most were recent arrivals. British army reservists were channelled into Princess Patricia's Canadian Light Infantry, a new regiment organized with a gift of $100,000 from a wealthy Montrealer, A. Hamilton Gault. With picked officers and well-trained men, the regiment reached the front line by the first week of 1915. It served for a year with a British regular army division before rejoining the Canadians. Its early casualties were replaced by university students who might better have been trained as officers.

No other millionaire was allowed to recruit his own battalion but the example of the PPCLI was influential. To find men for the CEF, Hughes accepted offers from businessmen, politicians and wealthy militia officers. The old regiments of the volunteer militia had been largely by-passed in organizing the First Contingent; they were ignored again. Hughes's newly minted CEF colonels sometimes used the old militia as a recruiting base. Others depended on city, county or regional loyalties, to the passion for wearing Scottish uniforms, or to the allegiance of Methodists, Orangemen or temperance enthusiasts as a basis for organizing the thousand men of a battalion. During 1915, not counting units of the Second Contingent, 141 different CEF battalions were approved by Militia Headquarters; 79 more were authorized in 1916. The Militia department never had assumed any responsibility in peacetime for recruiting; it saw no reason to start. Depots in major cities collected men for the artillery, army service corps and other supporting arms and services but the search for infantry soldiers was left to private initiative. Hughes's colonels devised their own recruiting messages and paid for them from their own pockets or from what they could collect from a sympathetic community.

The recruiting appeals ranged from the lofty to the crude. A Toronto colonel sought help from wives and mothers to drive cowardly men into the ranks. A Montreal regiment promised its recruits warm clothing for the winter and boasted that it would be "le dernier à partir et le premier à profiter de la victoire." Clergy and women were active recruiters. Hughes, an ardent pro-feminist, had insisted that married volunteers obtain written permission from their wives. Many women exercised their veto; others; on the contrary, distributed white feathers to young men in civilian clothes as a symbol of their apparent cowardice or wore badges declaring "Knit or Fight." J. S. Woodsworth, a Methodist clergyman and pacifist, was appalled when a prominent Montreal minister, C. A. Williams, used his sermon to demand that young men in the congregation enlist. He was utterly shocked when recruiting sergeants took up posts at the church doors. Clergymen who criticized Sunday recruiting meetings on Sabbatarian grounds found themselves in trouble with their congregations and communities.

Not all volunteers were acceptable. Many failed medical tests though standards dropped by 1915, allowing men of five foot, two inches to enlist. Urged by colonels, a fee system and a desire to be obliging, examining physicians tended to be tolerant. The result was a heavy toll of physical and mental breakdown by the time Canadian soldiers reached France and a costly burden of medical care for men who should never have been allowed to enlist. Medical standards were not the only barriers to enlistment. For racial reasons, offers by Japanese Canadians to form a battalion were rejected, although Japan was one of Britain's allies. Individual Japanese Canadians did enlist. Black Canadians, as individuals or collectively, faced more serious obstacles. Most colonels did their best to enforce a colour bar in their recruiting, and Militia Headquarters did nothing to discourage them. While a few black Canadians served in fighting battalions, most were segregated in units like the 2nd Canadian Construction Company. Canadian Indians, on the other hand, were generally welcomed as particularly ferocious fighting men, though there was some concern about whether the Germans would respect their rights as prisoners of war. Black and Japanese Canadians wanted to serve, if only to win respect in a society which had often treated them with contempt. Other Canadians were not eager to volunteer. The old German-Canadian community of Berlin in southwestern Ontario might be coerced into changing its name to Kitchener but the bullying tactics of the officers and men of the local 118th Battalion did not win eager recruits. In the West, foreign-language minorities unconsciously revenged themselves on their prejudiced Anglo-Saxon neighbours by quietly staying on their farms and prospering from high wartime prices. Not for them were the acute labour shortages of farmers who sent their sons to enlist.

The most important resistance to the war and enlistment came in French-speaking Quebec. Acadians in the Maritimes and French-speaking minorities in other provinces appear to have enlisted in roughly the same proportions as other Canadian-born citizens. Quebec was different. At the outset of the war, it had not seemed so. There are many obvious explanations for the rapid erosion of French-Canadian support for the war. For all his claims to French ancestry and his friendship for Armand Lavergne, Sam Hughes was utterly unfitted to appeal to French Canada. By his chaotic management at Valcartier, careful arrangements in Gwatkin's mobilization plan to ensure French Canadian representation in the First Contingent were ignored. Precedents from 1870, 1885 and 1889 were forgotten. By the time the 1st Division reached France, only one company of its twelve infantry battalions was French-speaking. The omission was only partly filled by including a French-speaking unit, the 22nd Battalion, in the Second Contingent and by appointing a French Canadian, Colonel J. P. Landry, as one of the brigadiers. Hopelessly inexperienced, Landry was removed before the 2nd Division reached France. A second French-speaking battalion, the 41st, was disbanded in England because of inefficiency, bad officers and two murders in its ranks. With a couple of exceptions such as the 163rd Battalion, raised by Olivar Asselin, and the 189th, recruited from tough Gaspesien fishermen, none of the twelve CEF battalions raised in French Canada in 1915 and 1916 was fit for service.

The blame lay with a militia organization which, in peacetime, had refused to address the special problems of French-speaking participation and had become an institution in which few French Canadians felt at home. In peace or war, the voluntary military spirit of Toronto or Winnipeg could not be found in Trois-Rivières or Victoriaville. If good officers could not be found, bad ones like Tancrède Pagnuelo or Onésime Readman had to be used. Both were court-martialled, not for disloyalty but for theft. When militia authorities sought the kind of business backing common in English Canada, they could turn only to Arthur Mignault, a wealthy pharmaceutical manufacturer who organized a medical unit for service in Paris and who returned in 1916 to direct French-language recruiting in Quebec. His was the only recruiting effort the militia department supported from its own funds. When military authorities wanted clergy to help with recruiting, they turned in Montreal to the Rev. C. A. Williams, the Methodist who had appalled Woodsworth. No Catholic priest volunteered.

These criticisms and more were highlighted by French-Canadian apologists for Quebec's recruiting record. Williams (who in fact was unusually tolerant of his French-Catholic neighbours) was portrayed as a bigoted Orangeman whom Hughes had appointed to control Quebec recruiting. Liberal politicians insisted that Laurier's speeches at recruiting rallies for the 22nd Battalion showed what might have been done. These were smoke screens. The fact was that few French Canadians had much interest in the war. It was, as Lavergne told Hughes, "a somewhat interesting adventure in a foreign country." French Canada was told that its enemies were much closer to home: the "'Boches" of Ontario, whose Regulation 17 had choked off French-language education for a tenth of the people in that province. The enemies of French civilization in Canada, Bourassa told readers of *Le Devoir,* were not the Germans but the "English-Canadian anglicisers, the Ontario intriguers, or Irish priests." If French Canada wanted a front line to defend, it was in Ottawa, not Flanders.

Sir Robert Borden desperately wanted to lead a united Canada into the national crusade for victory but he could not budge the Ontario backers of Regulation 17. Neither could Laurier. The Ontario Liberal leader, Newton

Rowell, was as opposed to French-speaking demands as the province's Tory government. The old issues of education and cultural survival took precedence over the war effort not merely in Quebec but in Ontario, too. In the West, where the dispute was even more recent, Manitoba and Saskatchewan responded to wartime nativism to annul the French and minority education rights grudgingly conceded years before.

How important was the Ontario school question to the war effort? How much did Bourassa's fiery speeches and editorials against British imperialism really influence ordinary French Canadians? The funds raised for Ontario's embattled French schools were meagre. Most French Canadians needed little persuading to stay out of uniform. Only a few, like the unpredictable and fiery Olivar Asselin, were moved by the threat to France. Others would enlist because of unemployment or because of an urge for adventure or escape. For most Quebeckers, however, there was well-paid work in the new munitions factories or the old textile mills. There was the comfortable familiarity of the farm or small town. If Quebec's leaders gave the *mot d'ordre* to stay home or not to exert themselves in an English war, that was reassuring but the decision had already been made.

If there would be no patriotic crusading in the towns and villages of Quebec, there was very little among Canadians overseas, either. Any glories of war were rapidly shredded away by the banalities of army life. British soldiers during the war complained of the gulf between their experiences at the front and the absurdly romantic and sometimes condescending attitude of people only a few miles away in England. People in Canada, buffered by an extra three thousand miles of ocean as well as strict censorship of war news, were even more remote from reality. Except for his visits to England and France and a single packet of secret despatches, Sir Robert Borden was as dependent on newspapers for his knowledge of the war as any other citizen. Even his visits to the front, sanitized by the precautions accorded to Very Important Persons, were remote from the trench warfare realities of mud, lice, excrement, exhaustion, hunger and imminent death.

So long as he was in Canada a soldier lived in a mitigated chaos of politics, discipline and inexperience. Generals and sergeants aped British mannerisms they had rarely seen. Officers behaved with the mixture of aloofness and overfamiliarity which British advisers had always noted in Canadian officers. Whether at Valcartier, at countless exhibition grounds or in the dust of the Angus Plains, where Hughes opened Camp Borden in 1916, the CEF volunteers could turn to politicians or journalists when military discipline weighed too harshly.

In England, it was very different. No matter how long Canadians had served in Canada, British instructors seldom rated them better than two-week recruits. Volunteers discovered that they had enlisted as "Imperials," troops raised in the colonies under the British Army Act. Not until 1916 did the CEF become formally part of the Canadian militia and until the end of the war,

Canadians were subjected to the stern British disciplinary code. The experience began when the First Contingent unloaded on Salisbury Plain in late October 1914. Amidst the coldest, wettest winter anyone could remember, the Canadians began to shed misfit officers and bad equipment. Hughes had proudly provided "his boys" with the Ross rifle, the Oliver equipment (condemned in South Africa), boots that dissolved in the mud and the MacAdam shield-shovel, named for his secretary, Ena MacAdam, an absurd contraption designed for protection and entrenching. Most of the Canadian-made equipment was promptly replaced by the regular British issue. Hughes never forgave Lieutenant-General Edwin Alderson, the British officer chosen to command the division, for the switch. The Ross, for all its defects, went to France. The British, in early 1915, would have been hard-pressed to replace it. By the time the 1st Canadian Division went to France in March, 1915, it was a credit to Canada and, above all, to itself.

Canadians who arrived later were spared Salisbury Plain but their encounter with the military organization in England could be almost as traumatic. Hughes's recruiting system was a confidence trick. Men enlisted on the promise that they would fight their way to Berlin in the CEF battalion they first joined. When it reached full strength in the summer of 1916, the Canadian Corps needed only forty-eight infantry battalions for its four divisions. While some units joined the Corps later when Quebec and British Columbia battalions were broken up for lack of recruits, 210 CEF battalions and six mounted rifle regiments never reached the front. Canadian camps and headquarters in England filled up with disgruntled surplus officers, qualified only in the political skills which had won them their commissions. Their men were thrown into the brutal anonymity of reinforcement depots. Veterans, contemptuous as ever of newcomers, had little sympathy for bewildered newcomers.

The CEF veterans had had their own grim experiences. Tradition, even among anti-military historians, has celebrated the "tough and terrifyingly efficient Canadian Corps." The success of the 1st Division in holding the line in the Second Battle of Ypres in April, 1915, against massed German assaults and the first use of chlorine gas, down to the triumphant final days in 1918, legitimized the legend of a Corps that never lost a trench nor ever failed to win an objective. The efficiency was real but it was hard-won. The notion of Canadians as natural soldiers, inherent in the militia myth, was as absurd in 1914-18 as it had been in the War of 1812. Each new Canadian division learned its business in a bloodbath of confusion and misdirection. The Canadian division held at Ypres at a cost of 6,035 casualties but it failed, understandably, in attacks at Festubert and Givenchy. For the 2nd Division, the tragic lesson was the attempt to hold the St. Eloi craters in April, 1916, a desperate struggle made hopeless by the inept staff work of the divisional commander and a brigadier. Because they were Canadians, they stayed. It was Alderson, the Corps commander, who was fired for the disaster and for his open criticisms of the Ross rifle. Under Alderson's successor, Sir Julian Byng, the raw 3rd Division faced a harsh baptism. On June 2, the division was blasted out of its positions on Mont Sorrel and its commander perished in the bombardment. Counterattacks by the shaken soldiers failed. However, given time to plan, the veteran 1st Division, commanded by a Victoria real estate agent, Arthur Currie, recaptured the position. Of all the formations in the Corps, only the 4th Division began its service with a victory when it took Regina Trench in October, 1916, an objective which had eluded the battered 2nd Division only a month before.

Canadians became tough, effective soldiers but only at the cost of heavy casualties and setbacks. The test of battle eliminated incompetent officers and set standards which the survivors were eager to meet. In some ways, the First World War suited Canadian strengths and weaknesses. Like most wars, it was full of new lessons; those with few old lessons to unlearn could begin their study sooner. To the mingled amazement and dismay of British regulars, Canadians not only insisted on rising to the top commands in their Corps, they managed them well when they arrived. In June, 1917, when Sir Arthur Currie replaced Byng, the only British generals in the Canadian Corps were two senior staff officers and an officer who had been serving in Canada when the war broke out. The kind of static warfare that developed on the Western Front after 1914 was far more tolerant of inexperience and of slow-moving staff work than the more mobile conflict of earlier or later wars. Certainly, under Byng and Currie, the tactical style of the Canadian Corps was ponderous. Their successes owed much to masses of artillery ammunition, wire, thorough tunnelling, intelligence surveillance and rehearsals. Currie, a former gunner, encouraged aerial artillery spotting and target registration. Senior British commanders were exasperated by Byng's lengthy preparations for the capture of Vimy Ridge in April, 1917 and by Currie's management of the Hill 70 battle to grind up assaulting German divisions. They could hardly criticize the results. Canadian soldiers could be grateful—though they scarcely knew or recognized it—that their lives were more carefully guarded than their British, Australian or American counterparts. In due course, too, when the war finally entered a more mobile phase, Currie and his staff had the experience and confidence to adjust. For them, too, the experience was painfully won.

Men in the ranks were unlikely even to be aware of their staff or commanders. *Generals Die in Bed* is the title of one of the few angry memoirs from the CEF, and Will Bird, author of *Ghosts Have Warm Hands*, recalled seeing only one general in the trenches, Sir Archibald Macdonell, the redoubtable "Batty Mac." Bird and other veterans brought home few fond memories of their officers. W. D. B. Kerr recalled his distaste for General Currie when the stout corps commander insisted on opening the men's haversacks to see if they held the regulation contents: "a regular Paul Pry." Soldiers resented Currie's order of the day during the successful German offensives in 1918, commanding the Canadians to do their duty. Few soldiers really felt that they needed such a message. Inexperienced officers, owing their commissions and their comfortable privileges to political or paternal influence, won no respect from soldiers like Bird or Kerr. Oddly enough, soldiers had no more fondness for officers chosen from the ranks. Like other ugly features of a temporary existence, officers were accepted like puttees, fatigues and short-arm inspections, but most Canadian soldiers found nothing natural in the hierarchy and they protested successfully after the war when officers were initially granted higher pensions than other soldiers. They would have been unimpressed by Professor A. M. J. Hyatt's discovery that Canadian generals with the Corps suffered higher casualty rates than other soldiers, 42 per cent compared to 37.5 per cent for the entire CEF.

There was one burden of military life most junior officers shared. As platoon and company commanders, their life expectancy in action was shorter than any other rank. Officers, like men, sometimes failed in their duty and although none of them was included among the twenty-five Canadians shot by firing squad for desertion or cowardice, several were cashiered or imprisoned for such offences.

Thousands of young Canadians chose even greater risks to escape the squalid horrors of trench warfare. Among the wartime innovations, like high explosives, poison gas, flame throwers and tanks, few made more spectacular tactical or technological progress than air warfare. More than 20,000 Canadians served in the Royal Flying Corps, the Royal Naval Air Service or, after their amalgamation, in the Royal Air Force. Many came from the ranks of the Canadian Corps or from officers of the broken-up battalions. Many more were recruited and trained in Canada after the Royal Flying Corps opened its own training schools in Ontario in 1917. Canadians contributed some of the most successful fighter pilots of the war: Major W. A. Bishop, V.C., with seventy-two victories, and Major Raymond Collishaw, with sixty, ranked third and fifth among the top air aces of the war. By the end of 1918, almost a quarter of the flyers in the Royal Air Force were Canadian but it was only very late in the war that any serious effort was made to form a separate Canadian air force. Its two squadrons, organized in England, never saw active service.

Generals, pilots and privates could agree on one thing: their contempt for Canadian military administration, particularly in England. It was there that the Hughes influence was strongest, though his agent Colonel Max Aitken, later Lord Beaverbrook, regularly carried the minister's directives to France. Back in Canada, Hughes's failings gradually compelled colleagues to take over his work, with a War Purchasing Commission, a Military Hospitals Commission, Flavelle's Imperial Munitions Board and, in 1916, a parliamentary assistant to manage the departmental routine Hughes invariably ignored. Only in the training camps and overseas did the minister remain pre-eminent. To enhance his authority, Hughes promoted confusion. In early 1916 three

Canadian generals in England claimed to be in charge and all of them could produce documents from the minister to prove it. The nimblest was Major-General John Wallace Carson, a Montreal mining promoter and financier, who manipulated a vague mandate to look after the soldiers' comfort into a position of dominance, largely by exploiting his well-known friendship with Hughes. Despite his aggressive image, Hughes was indecisive. His lack of administrative skill was reflected in the Canadian organization in England. Training, reinforcements, medical care, rehabilitation of casualties, the handling of stores, transportation, personnel records, pay and finances led to a burgeoning of ill-co-ordinated offices, camps, hospitals and depots. Repeatedly Hughes was urged to create a more efficient and economic system. In the summer of 1916, an overly-patient Borden gave him a last chance. Instead, Hughes spent months in England reviewing huge parades, teaching bayonet fighting and visiting. Finally, he proclaimed an "Acting Overseas Sub-Militia Council" with Carson as chairman and his own son-in-law as secretary. An exasperated prime minister preferred his own expedient: a Ministry of the Overseas Military Forces of Canada based in London with a dependable friend, Sir George Perley, in charge. When Borden stuck by his plan, a furious Hughes resigned. The amateur era of Canada's war effort largely ended with his departure.

One of the political puzzles of the war is why Borden waited until November, 1916, to replace his Minister of Militia. From the moment the government was formed in 1911, Hughes was an embarrassment. Scandals in purchasing for the CEF shattered the party truce in 1915, and the munitions scandal in 1916, demonstrating Hughes's fidelity to a shady promoter named J. Wesley Allison, gave Liberals the hope of an early comeback. In his diary, Borden complained often about Hughes's erratic behaviour and his neglect of routine duties. Critics may agree with Hughes's own assessment of the prime minister, "as gentle hearted as a girl." They might suspect that Borden was physically or morally cowed by a big, burly colleague with a talent for verbal abuse. Yet Borden owed Hughes a lot for his loyalty in opposition. The war added its own reasons for tolerating a turbulent minister. It seemed almost disloyal to abandon a colleague under fire whether in the trenches or in Parliament. It was humiliating (and politically dangerous) to admit that critics of the Ross rifle had been right. Until recruits jeered Hughes at Camp Borden in July, 1916, it was easy for the prime minister to believe that his colleague was as popular in the army as he was with his fellow newspapermen. Most important of all, some of Hughes's apparently erratic judgements proved correct. Borden had been shocked by Hughes's violent denunciations of British generalship at Ypres; after his own visit to England in the summer of 1915, the prime minister concluded that Hughes was right. Hughes's perennial contempt for military professionals—common ground with his fellow Canadian, Max Aitken—became a justification for the chaos and influence-peddling in the militia department. Hughes's intense nationalism, symbolized in the apocryphal legend that he had dressed down Lord Kitchener for threatening to disperse the 1st Canadian Division, reflected Borden's own developing mood. Sam Hughes was close to becoming a caricature of Canadian attitudes to the war.

Hughes was fired in 1916 because both Canada and the war were changing. By the end of 1916, Canada could no longer afford the wasteful enthusiasms of voluntarism. At the new Overseas Ministry in London, Perley discovered that almost every element of Canadian administration, from the chaplains to the veterinary service, needed overhaul. His solution, in most cases, was to bring back senior officers from France. Perley knew that their prestige was built on merit, not on Hughes's favouritism. The most serious problem was the Canadian medical service, bitterly divided by a report commissioned by Hughes and prepared by Colonel Herbert A. Bruce, a Toronto surgeon and founder of the Wellesley Hospital. Bruce denounced the permanent force officers who had organized the Canadian medical system and complained that Canadian wounded had been transferred to British hospitals, delaying their return to the front. Bruce's report, with its undertone of nationalism and its implication that Canadian casualties were cosseted by British nurses, outraged most CEF doctors and led the eminent Sir William Osler to resign his position in the Canadian Army Medical Corps. Perley restored peace by disavowing Bruce (making himself a virulent enemy), summoning new leadership from France and discreetly introducing many of Bruce's suggestions. Meanwhile, with help from his new military commander, Major-General Richard Turner, V.C., who had been transferred from the command of the 2nd Division, Perley trimmed the Canadian establishments in England and coerced a small army of surplus officers either to serve at a lower rank or to go home to Canada after a short "Cook's Tour" of the front.

One reason why reform was so necessary overseas was the growing recruiting crisis in Canada. In 1916, 176,919 Canadians joined the CEF, the largest total for any year, but after mid-summer, enlistments fell sharply. The expansion of agriculture, the growth in munition production and the demands of the army placed Canada in an acute manpower squeeze. Sam Hughes had been almost oblivious of the problem. Only General Gwatkin, as Chief of the General Staff, had wondered in 1915 whether Canada had enough volunteers to maintain more than two divisions at the front. Now there were four, each requiring at least 20,000 able bodied new soldiers each year to replace the dead and the permanently disabled. In one of his final orders, Hughes had ordered formation of a 5th Division in England to provide a command for his son, Garnet, and to appease the wrath of battalions about to be broken up. He also promised that a 6th Division would follow. On Perley's insistence, the 5th Division remained in England.

In Canada, those who had led the recruiting drives were the first to warn of imminent failure and to demand the only alternative they could see, conscription. J. M. Godfrey, a Toronto lawyer and Liberal who had managed effective recruiting drives in the nearby county of Peel, turned his energy to the obvious problem of Quebec's alienation from the war effort, Godfrey's response, backed by leading Toronto businessmen, was a "Bonne Entente" movement, designed to introduce good will and mutual understanding to French-English relations. Some prominent Quebeckers responded but there was little to show for the visits, banquets and oratory. Regulation 17 remained; so did the stubborn refusal of Quebec's French-speaking majority to match the remarkable recruiting record of the province's English-speaking minority. Colonel Lorne Mulloy, blinded veteran of the South African war and inspiration of the Hamilton Recruiting League, demanded conscription. So did Chief Justice T. G. Mathers of Manitoba. Their arguments soon became familiar. Volunteering was taking the best and bravest Canadians. Bourassa himself had deplored the folly of English Canadians in leaving the country to be taken over by racially inferior immigrants. Pro-conscriptionists even argued that volunteering hurt the war effort. Men with skills vital to munitions factories were as likely to be drawn into uniform as rich men's chauffeurs or distillery workers.

As in other wartime problems, Canada could look to Britain for an example. National registration had been a first stage in rationalizing British recruiting problems; Canada must follow suit. Borden's government appointed a National Service Board under R. B. Bennett, a Calgary lawyer and Conservative MP. To allay resistance from Quebec and organized labour, Borden insisted that registration be voluntary and he journeyed to Montreal to assure Archbishop Paul Bruchési that the measure was not the first step to conscription but merely an effort to identify men who could be invited to enlist. The reassurance was promptly undermined when Borden refused to promise a trade union delegation that he would never contemplate compulsory service, but Trades and Labour Congress leaders still urged compliance. So did Bruchési and so did the entire apparatus of patriotic enthusiasm. When J. S. Woodsworth condemned registration in a letter to the *Manitoba Free Press* he was immediately dismissed from his government position and launched on the long pilgrimage that would make him a Vancouver longshoreman, an MP and a founder of the Co-operative Commonwealth Federation. Other Canadians protested more quietly. A fifth of the registration cards were never returned. Of 1.5 million replies, only 286,976 came from men apparently suitable for military service. A canvass of 2,000 of them in Winnipeg produced not a single volunteer. During December, just over 5,000 enlisted in the CEF; a year before, the total had been 22,713. By the end of 1916, Canada's casualties totalled 67,890. Only a year after his brave commitment of 500,000 soldiers, Borden must either find more men or reduce the Canadian Corps.

Almost from the outbreak of war, Sir Robert Borden chafed at the lack of information and consultation from London. British ministers and officials had their own problems. They ignored Canadian sensitivity, commandeered

Canadian coastal shipping, appointed and promoted officers in the CEF and even built submarines in a Montreal shipyard unbeknownst to the Borden government. One good reason was security: Ottawa's bureaucracy was notoriously leaky. Another less pleasing reason was that Britain's wartime leaders could find neither the will nor a way to treat the Dominions as equal partners in the war. Andrew Bonar Law, the Canadian-born colonial secretary in the coalition government, infuriated Borden with his bland treatment of the problem: "I fully recognize the right of the Canadian government to have some share in the control in a war in which Canada is playing so big a part," he admitted late in 1915, "I am, however, not able to see any way in which this could practically be done . . . if no scheme is practicable, then it is very undesirable that the question should be raised." Borden's outrage contributed to his dangerous New Year's promise of half a million men. It also inspired a bitter letter to his friend Perley in London:

> It can hardly be expected that we shall put 400,000 or 500,000 men in the field and willingly accept the position of having no more voice and receiving no more consideration than if we were toy automata. Any person cherishing such an expectation harbours an unfortunate and even a dangerous delusion. . . . It is for them to suggest the method and not for us. If there is no available method and we are expected to continue in the role of automata the whole situation must be reconsidered. . . .

In fact, it was Borden who reconsidered, withdrawing a letter written under the strain of anger and ill-health. The point was clear. When Britain experienced her own cabinet revolt at the end of 1916, with the fall of Herbert Asquith and the ascent of David Lloyd George, both the need and the means of consultation were discovered. Faced with a war effort going disastrously awry, the new British prime minister could only turn to the Dominions: "We want more men from them," he explained to his officials, "We can hardly ask them to make another great recruiting effort unless it is accompanied by an invitation to come over and discuss the situation with us." The invitation was despatched, the Canadian House of Commons dutifully adjourned and on March 2, 1917, the first meeting of an "Imperial War Cabinet" opened. Though the colonial politicians by no means shared as much influence or information as they may have imagined, they soon had more than enough facts to convince them of the dire state of the war. They learned of the imminence of Russia's collapse, of widespread mutinies in the French army, of the frightening success of Germany's submarine offensive. For Borden, the war cabinet was the institutional answer he had long sought to the problem of co-ordinating imperial policy, and he was acutely aware that the price of consultation and involvement in policy-making was an honourable commitment to provide the means. Britain not only wanted more men; she must have them if the war was not to be lost. In his spare moments, Borden visited the

Canadian Corps in France, Canadian camps in England and every military hospital he could reach. The impact was profound. Borden saw what Canadians at home would never see: wounded men who were destined to return again and again to the trenches until they were dead or so terribly mangled that not even the military surgeons would pass them for active service. At home, there were those who concluded that such men had volunteered for their fate; to Borden, sending them reinforcements was a matter of national honour and he shuddered to think what might happen if the CEF returned to a Canada that had not kept faith with it. Feelings in the Australian Imperial Force had been divided on conscription. In two plebiscites in 1916 and 1917, Australian voters rejected compulsory service and many in the AIF had claimed that their units would be disgraced by the arrival of conscripts. Some men of the CEF might have agreed. Censors also noted letters to Canada urging younger brothers to stay out of uniform so that parents would have at least someone to support them in old age. However, as Borden talked with senior officers and wounded soldiers, one message was clear. Canada's honour demanded that the Corps be kept up to strength and only conscription would do it. While he was in England, the Corps achieved its greatest single triumph. On April 9, 1917, the four Canadian divisions advanced in line through a snowstorm and drove the Germans from an apparently impregnable Vimy Ridge. By the standards of the war, the victory was a triumph of planning over the usual butchering methods but the toll was still a numbing 23,000 dead and wounded. They would have to be replaced.

When the prime minister returned to Ottawa to announce his commitment to conscription, British officials could smugly conclude that their efforts had succeeded. In fact, Borden believed that conscription was now the price Canada must pay for a new and more dignified status in the world. Not only victory but Canadian autonomy were at stake, he told Parliament on May 18. Later, politicians and even some historians would claim that Borden introduced conscription in May, 1917, to save his party's political fortunes or even to divert attention from his plans to take over the two foundering transcontinental railways. Both charges were absurd. It is true that the Conservatives were in serious trouble. Their provincial support was reduced to W. R. Hearst's bumbling Ontario government. Pro-war and anti-war forces agreed that Borden's wartime administration had been inept, uncertain and probably corrupt. Laurier's response to the conscription issue and to Borden's subsequent offers of a coalition were coloured by a wholly legitimate belief that his party would sweep the next general election. The earlier agreements to prolong the life of Parliament had lapsed. Borden himself had no confidence that conscription could ever prove politically popular. Beyond the noisy chorus of pro-conscription editors, politicians and letter-writers was a nation he knew to be deeply divided. Quebec's opposition was certain; he knew it even before his few remaining French-Canadian ministers expressed their fears. Other opponents were equally certain. Organized labour might be feeble but who could assess the loyalties it could claim from factory workers, employees in vital public utilities or the radical coal miners of Cape Breton or the West? What about the farmers of Ontario and the Prairie provinces, traditionally suspicious of the Tories and now anxious lest conscription rob them of the sons and labourers they needed to get profitable crops off the land? Such opponents might be quiet but they had votes.

In French Canada, they would not even be quiet. By mid-1916, recruiting parties risked open assault in Montreal. When P-E. Blondin, Borden's postmaster-general, and Major-General F. L. Lessard, Quebec's most distinguished soldier, set out in the spring of 1917 in a last effort to recruit a battalion, they were mobbed and threatened in small towns and returned with a total of ninety-three volunteers, most of them unfit for service. By now, Bourassa's speeches and editorials were no longer unique; others might be more discreet, less openly abusive of England, imperialism and Canada's war effort, but the message was the same. If Archbishop Bruchési in Montreal backed the government, Cardinal Bégin in Quebec was distinctly lukewarm, and parish clergy all over the province were frigidly cold. On May 24, a week after Borden's conscription announcement, riots broke out in Montreal. Bruchési wrote at once to the prime minister, recalling earlier no-conscription pledges and warning of a rising current of hatred and violence.

Like so many of the disputes between French and English in Canada, the conscription debate was a dialogue of the deaf. Borden dismissed Bourassa as a narrow-minded provincialist, fanning grievances which were petty by the scale of the world conflict. To Bourassa, Borden was an imperialist, pouring out Canadian money and lives at England's command. Both, in fact, were nationalists, pursuing utterly divergent versions of Canada's destiny that would, ironically, intersect in the postwar world. To Borden, and to western Liberals like J. W. Dafoe, the influential editor of the *Manitoba Free Press*, Canada fought Germany essentially in her own right. Britain not only had to be reminded that Canada was an ally but also, in Borden's view, she had to be urged to fight with far more earnestness and efficiency. Bourassa, like a great many Americans before the United States entered the war in the spring of 1917, was convinced that the war was hardly Canada's affair. Her security, her institutions and her economic well-being were not at stake. Canada was safe behind the Atlantic. The front line of Canada was Canada, not the trenches of France and Flanders. By all means use the war to get rich, Bourassa argued, but that meant keeping men at home to produce food and shells. To the Prime Minister, who had heard and answered such arguments in the United States during his personal efforts to bring Americans into the war, Bourassa's argument was servile and unworthy. Defying the stereotype of Canadians as a cold and materialistic people, Borden sought a higher national destiny and his reputation would perish in the attempt.

On the means, he was flexible. To the dismay of some Tory colleagues, Borden set out at once to forge a national coalition with Laurier. The Liberal

leader refused. Borden offered to delay conscription until a national government had won a general election. Again Laurier refused. The Liberal leader
was angry that Borden had announced conscription before opening coalition
negotiations. Laurier also believed that his party would stick with him, an impression confirmed in June and July when coalitionists were repudiated at
Liberal meetings in Toronto and Winnipeg. Above all, Laurier feared that if
he went with Borden he would again be humiliated in his own province by
Bourassa.

Laurier was wrong on one point: the conscription issue had shattered
Liberal unity. Party stalwarts, united by hope of victory and hatred of Tories,
could pass resolutions. Liberal editors, provincial politicians and English-
speaking MPs had to deal with the public and their perceptions of both public
opinion and the war were very different. Laurier also under-estimated
Borden, as he always had. Threading his way past the Liberal leadership, rid-
ding himself of his own blindly partisan "Minister of Elections," Bob Rogers,
Borden reached out to second-rank Liberals. Finding them still nervous and
indecisive, the prime minister turned back to Parliament and armed himself
with two weapons. The Military Voters Act extended the Soldiers' Voting Act
of 1915 which the Liberals had opposed. The franchise was extended to
every man and woman in the CEF. As part of the solution to the problem of
running an election across a U-Boat infested ocean, soldiers would vote
simply for the Government or the Opposition candidate in a constituency
which those without close home links could choose for themselves. Obviously, as the Minister of Justice sweetly confessed, both parties might avail
themselves of the chance to switch votes to where they might do the most
good. Much more important and questionable was the Wartime Elections
Act. It simultaneously extended the vote to the mothers, wives and sisters of
serving soldiers and took it away from any Canadians of enemy origin
naturalized since 1902. Women's votes, explained Arthur Meighen, would
speak for those who had given their lives; the disfranchised would also be exempt from conscription. Closure was needed to quell a furious and, for once,
united Liberal opposition.

Both measures had their effect. The enfranchised women were those
most likely to support any means of bringing help to their men. The disfranchised had become a key element of Liberal support, particularly in western
Canada. Within days, prominent Liberals began to reconsider their options.
On October 6, Parliament was dissolved. Five days later, Borden announced
his Union government. An admiring Tory colleague confessed that he would
match Borden against Job in a patience contest any day. With the union
came the promise of backing from every provincial premier but one, Lomer
Gouin of Quebec. One coalition Liberal, Major-General S. C. Mewburn,
took the militia portfolio. His Tory predecessor, Sir Edward Kemp, would go
to London. Perley, who would reluctantly manage the overseas election for
the new government, was confirmed as Canadian High Commissioner in

London. In Quebec, Laurier was secure, with a resentful Bourassa compelled to offer support; elsewhere the proud Liberal party was in ruins. Even the ambitious former Minister of Labour, W. L. Mackenzie King, had quietly offered his services to the Unionist government. Rebuffed, he salvaged his political career by running for Laurier in Ontario. There were few such prominent Laurierites except in the Maritimes, where party loyalties seemed to outweigh even war fever.

By October, the new Union government was certain of sweeping victory. As the weeks passed, its confidence faltered. The local struggles to compress Liberal and Tory ambitions into a single Union candidacy produced a host of quarrels, particularly in Ontario. In Nova Scotia and parts of the West, pledges of Liberal backing proved almost worthless. Elsewhere, Tories refused to share power. Outside the patriotic rallies, Unionist politicians found deep hostility to conscription, even among the troops. A hurried directive commanded that the next-of-kin of serving soldiers would not be conscripted. At Kitchener, anti-conscription demonstrators howled Borden off the stage for the first time in his career. General Mewburn, touring rural Ontario, felt obliged to announce that farmers' sons would not be conscripted. His order was immediately confirmed. Farm voters breathed a collective sigh of relief. Indeed, by election day, it was easy to believe that the Unionist campaign had become a crusade of English-speaking Canada against a Bourassa-run Quebec and that conscription would fall almost exclusively on "slackers" and French Canada.

The results confirmed the impression: 153 seats for the Union government, 82 for the Liberals, all but 20 of them in Quebec. It was the most one-sided election outcome Canada had ever seen. Labour, which had tried for the first time to offer itself as an alternative party for English-speaking Canada, had been humiliated. Yet the popular support for the Unionists was by no means as one-sided as the seat totals. With only the civilian vote, Borden had a lead of only a hundred thousand. The service vote, published in March, added two hundred thousand, changing the outcome in fourteen constituencies. Thanks to W. F. O'Connor, the Chief Returning Officer, most of the soldiers who had used the apparent loophole in the act to switch their ridings had their votes set aside.

The election outcome meant that conscription could begin in earnest. Contemporaries wondered why the historic compulsory features of the Militia Act were not imposed. The answer was not that militia service was only for home defence (though such a legal decision was possible) but that balloting was simply too indiscriminate. Instead, the Military Service Act created categories by age and marital status, provided grounds for exemption, examination and appeal. "Freely denounced as an engine of oppression," Sir Charles Lucas observed, it "contained so many safeguards against oppression that it had been made in no small degree inoperative." Key to its functioning were 1,253 local tribunals appointed by Boards of Selection in which the government and opposition were equally represented. Local appeals passed to 195 appeal courts and thence to a central appeal judge, Mr. Justice Lyman Duff of the Supreme Court. When the first class, unmarried men and widowers from twenty to thirty-four years, was called in October, 404,395 reported before the end of 1917; 380,510 sought exemption. Local tribunals proved unpredictable. Most Ontario Mennonites gained exemption but not even Duff accepted the arguments of Plymouth Brethren or Jehovah's Witnesses. In Quebec, French-speaking applicants were granted almost blanket exemption but, according to Duff, "they applied conscription against the English-speaking minority in Quebec with a rigor unparalleled." When the first men were called for training on January 3, 1918, only 20,000 appeared, 1,500 from Quebec. Voluntary enlistment in 1917 totalled only 63,611.

The 1917 election had revolved around a single issue, conscription. The Union government, however, embodied far more in the eyes of its members and supporters. Sir Robert Borden had long chafed at partyism. His 1907 Halifax programme had embodied a more progressive and idealistic vision of Canada than either party or, indeed, most Canadians found comfortable. The war had made idealism and sacrifice fashionable. If there was not change and reform, how could one justify the fiery furnace through which Canada had passed? Almost every progressive cause, from the single tax to a patronage-free civil service, could be revived in the atmosphere of war and given fresh justification. A nation stripped down for the struggle could not afford the evils of corruption or the self-indulgence of alcoholic drink. "To Hell with Profits," proclaimed Joseph Flavelle to shocked businessmen after he returned from visiting soldiers in France. Reports that his bacon exporting business had, in fact, been profiting enormously from its wartime trade arrived soon after Flavelle was made a baronet. The news demolished Sir Joseph's public reputation and helped justify the abolition of hereditary titles for Canadians.

By 1917, long crusades to win votes for women and to ban the sale of liquor had triumphed in the western provinces and Ontario. War provided the decisive argument. Women, who had often advocated the vote on grounds that mothers would never vote for war, were rewarded for their undoubted patriotic fervour. Just as important for women was the expansion of employment opportunities created by manpower shortages. Accompanied by cloying publicity and specially designed costumes, women worked as "conductorettes" on street cars, as "farmerettes" in harvesting crews and, by the thousands, in munitions factories. Unions demanded equal pay for women—as much to prevent the competitive advantage of cheap labour as for social justice—but they usually asked in vain. Instead, employers provided extra rest periods, lunch rooms and a few modest attempts at day care. Press censors agreed to suppress any reports of assaults on women going home from work for fear of the impact on their morale. The Union government carried out its promise to complete the shameful half-measure in the Wartime

Election Act and, early in 1918, the vote was extended to Canadian women in federal elections. The government also banned the import, sale and transportation of liquor for the duration of the war and for one year after, ostensibly as a measure to conserve scarce grain. Other ideas fermented as though their time, too, had come. W. C. Good, an Ontario farm leader, wrote a book urging the single tax. The Rev. William Irvine wrote *The Farmers in Politics.* In Winnipeg, the Rev. Salem Bland paused in his work for the Union government to produce *The New Christianity,* a tract on Christian socialism that at once attracted the suspicions of the Royal North West Mounted Police. In New York, Mackenzie King completed the turgidly idealistic *Industry and Humanity,* an amalgam of Christian uplift and industrial relations theory that would help to sell King as a man of modern ideas to the 1919 Liberal convention. Perhaps nothing illustrated the impact of war on a conservative mind better than an essay by Stephen Leacock, an economics professor at McGill University: "Put in the plainest way," he wrote in *The Unsolved Riddle of Social Justice,* "we are saying that the government of every country ought to supply work and pay for the unemployed, maintenance for the infirm and aged, and education and opportunity for the children. . . ."

Although Canada's welfare state certainly did not grow out of the First World War as it unquestionably would from the Second, some seeds were firmly planted. The Canadian Patriotic Fund, charged with maintaining soldiers' families whose breadwinners earned a meagre $1.10 a day, soon demonstrated that poverty was a function of family, not individual income. Its work provided arguments for the inter-war campaign for family allowances. As Sir Herbert Ames, its chairman, confessed, the work of the Fund forced its officials to come to terms with such unfamiliar phenomena as the "unmarried wife." Over the protests of Catholic and Protestant politicians, such women received financial support and pensions. The wartime activism of government may have been unequal to the devastating 1918 influenza epidemic but the response was permanent: a federal Department of Health. Public medical responsibilities broadened when the government cared for sick as well as wounded soldiers. Victims of tuberculosis and other medical disabilities were eligible for full treatment and pensions from Lougheed's Military Hospitals Commission and a new Board of Pension Commissioners. Out of the war came arguments for unemployment and health insurance.

Government in Canada in 1914 had done few of these things; after four years of war it could be expected to do anything. In 1915, Borden had pledged to Parliament that his policy was "not to interfere with the business activities of the country." By 1918, a fuel controller was threatening coal merchants with prison if they were found to be hoarding. A food controller, a cost of living commissioner, a chief censor and other officials, appointed because of wartime need or supply crisis, had acquired enormous powers under the War Measures Act to investigate, direct, advise, inspect and control. Voluntarism had run its limits in recruiting and much else. The Military Hospitals Commission, the Natural Resources Commission, the Canadian Wool Commission and, most controversial of all, the Canadian National Railway Company, managed for the government what had once been sacred to free enterprise. The new managers, it is true, were themselves the pre-war heroes of free enterprise like Flavelle, Sir Henry Drayton and other bankers and businessmen. No one else would have been acceptable to a nation reluctant to believe that public ownership did not also mean political patronage or that the new CNR would not be the corrupt and meandering Intercolonial Railway writ large. Wartime, with its demand for personal sacrifice, provided arguments unheard in peacetime. As Food Controller, for example, W. J. Hanna of Imperial Oil rejected rationing on principle and ignored the public expectation that his proper role was to curb soaring food prices. Instead, Hanna preferred public preaching of conservation, advertising campaigns and ingenious schemes to alter food consumption. His food board sponsored a "Keep a Pig" campaign, issued a thousand Ford tractors to farmers at cost, delivered fish display cabinets to butchers at half-price and publicized a "Sea Food Special," an express train that raced freshly-caught fish to Quebec and Ontario. It was the Food Board that proposed the regulation that most delighted Borden: an "anti-loafing law" that offered punishment for any man or boy not suitably employed. The Fuel Controller had an even grimmer task. American entry into the war threatened Canada's chief energy source, the Pennsylvania coal fields. Labour trouble remained endemic in the mines of Cape Breton and Alberta. A Director of Coal Operations was granted extensive powers to keep Canada's mines operating while the Fuel Controller, working through provincial and municipal authorities, managed allocation, ordered "Fuel-less Days" and negotiated earnestly with his American counterpart.

Wartime pressures even broke Sir Thomas White's determination not to introduce direct taxation. In 1916, political demands drove him to insert a small Business Profits Tax in his budget. In April, 1917, White again rejected income tax. By July 25, bowing to demands that the government conscript wealth as well as manpower, the tax was adopted. Advertisements piously insisted that the Dominion War Income Tax would be levied only in wartime. Initially, the tax hit incomes of over $1,500 for single people, $3,000 for families. In 1918, only 31,130 Canadians had to pay taxes when they completed their new T-1 forms. As cynics predicted, the rates rose, the bite dug deeper and a federal income tax became one of the hardier survivors of the First World War.

Government intervention in the economy seemed necessary. By the last year of the war, food and fuel were in desperately short supply. Fearful that it could not feed its own people, Ontario in 1917 ordered farmers to plant more crops, but not even armies of students, school children and soldiers could harvest the crop efficiently. The war grew as grim as the economy. At Halifax, on December 6, a French munitions ship exploded after a collision, levelling much of the city and neighbouring Dartmouth, killing 1,630 and leaving many more blind and mutilated. The tragedy brought some cruel wartime reality to Canada. There was worse news to come. On March 21, 1918, with reinforcements from the Eastern Front, German storm troopers smashed into the British Fifth Army. The entire Allied line reeled back for miles. In a war in which the defence had almost always succeeded, the disaster was inexplicable and its dimensions could not be concealed. A horrified Borden summoned Parliament into secret session and announced the cancellation of all exemptions. Every draftee under the Military Service Act would be ordered to report for duty.

Outrage was inevitable. Farmers, on the eve of the planting season, watched sons depart. Quebec, so far buffered from conscription by mass exemptions, responded in fury. Throughout the Easter weekend, crowds roamed the streets of Quebec City, attacking soldiers, military police and the draft registration offices. The government sent General Lessard and its only available troops, CEF drafts from Toronto. In a violent clash, shots were fired by both sides. Five civilians lay dead; many more on both sides were wounded. A shocked clergy ordered peace and submission. The city, French Canada and most of Canada obeyed. In British Columbia, a prominent radical labour leader, Albert Goodwin, was shot by military police when he fled arrest. Later that spring, farmers from Quebec and Ontario brought their grievances to Ottawa. Borden heard their complaints but refused to reinstate exemptions. An election promise could not outweigh a war crisis. The farmers left in a seething rage, infuriated as much by sneering editorial comment as by duplicitous politicians.

In 1918, most of the enthusiasm and voluntarism of the Canadian war effort were gone. War was a grim struggle. For the first time, at the insistence of C. H. Cahan, a Montreal lawyer and prominent Tory, the government authorized secret agents to hunt for sedition. They discovered very little, but over the objections of the RNWMP, Cahan won approval to suppress the Industrial Workers of the World, branches of the Social Democratic Party and other organizations he deemed "seditious." Publications in the "enemy" languages were banned in 1918 unless they secured a licence and translated every word into English. A wartime labour code approved the principle of organization, collective bargaining and equal wages for men and women but banned strikes and denied workers any effective means of forcing employers to meet their demands. Despite the ban, strikes occurred and the government abandoned the order as unenforceable.

Overseas, the mood was just as grim. The belligerents, as Ivan Bloch had predicted, were exhausted. After the 1917 mutinies, the French army could make no serious exertion. If the Fifth Army collapsed before the German offensive, it was because its battalions had been bled white in the terrible Flanders offensive of the previous autumn. The Canadian Corps had been there too, holding back at Currie's angry insistence, until its guns were ready and then going forward to capture Passchendaele, the final objective. As Currie had predicted, the Corps lost almost sixteen thousand men to take a meaningless ridge in the Flanders mud.

Ironically, the Canadians escaped the brunt of successive German offensives in 1918. Currie had refused to weaken his divisions to match the new British organization of nine battalions to a division though it would have meant an Army command for himself and two smaller Canadian army corps. Instead, to the fury of surplus officers yearning for staff positions, Currie kept his four-division corps and insisted on the breakup of Garnet Hughes's 5th Division. While Borden imperilled his government by cancelling the Military Service Act exemptions, drafts from the 5th Division filled the ranks of the Corps and kept them full until the Canadians and Australians smashed through the German line at Amiens on August 8, 1918, to begin the final stage of fighting. Conscripts only began reaching the Corps during the hard, casualty-filled days of the advance to Mons. If the war had lasted until 1919, the MSA men would have been needed. Most experts believed that the war could even last until 1920.

At Amiens, on August 8, the Canadian Corps was probably at its finest pitch. It had fully justified its reputation as the most effective fighting organization on the Western Front if only, unlike the Americans, because it had a wealth of fighting experience and, unlike the Australians, it could count on reinforcements. As a result, its men were far more physically fit than their British counterparts. By 1918, the British accents of the Old Originals of 1914 had largely vanished. The Canadian-born were now sergeants as well as privates and their leadership style was often different from those who had modelled themselves on the rigidity and verbal abuse of British regulars. The Corps had its own organization, its own procedures, a special expertise in counter-bombardment thanks to Brigadier-General A. G. L. McNaughton, a former McGill University chemistry professor, and its own motorized machine guns. In London, the Overseas Ministry was different too. Its headquarters, Argyll House, was as detested as ever but the new Overseas Minister had imposed his style on the place. Perley had let the generals run their own organization; Kemp insisted on creating an Overseas Military Council on the Ottawa model, so that civil authority could be clearly established. Next, over the resistance of the War Office and the British general headquarters in France, Kemp had established a direct liaison with the commander-in-chief, Sir Douglas Haig. The new Canadian Section was also a direct link between Kemp and the Canadian commander in the field, Sir Arthur Currie. It was the kind of arrangement that anyone should have expected from a junior but sovereign ally.

That status was reaffirmed when Sir Robert Borden returned to England in the spring of 1918. He had reason to be angry. For all the previous year's air of openness and consultation, no one had discussed the planned drive through the Flanders mud to Passchendaele. When Borden summoned Currie to advise him on the failed offensive, and on reasons for the disastrous defeats in March, the Canadian prime minister had further reasons to be indignant. Undoubtedly happy to score on some former British superiors, including the hapless Sir Hubert Gough of the Fifth Army, Currie delivered a long, merciless indictment of sloth, bad intelligence, stunting of talent and lack of foresight in which the Canadians, naturally, stood as brilliant exceptions. Borden was outraged. "Mr. Prime Minister," he told Lloyd George, "I want to tell you that if there is a repetition of the battle of Passchendaele, not a Canadian soldier will leave the shores of Canada so long as the Canadian people entrust the government of their country to my hands." The British prime minister, delighted that someone else would indict his generals for a change, was not at all displeased. Instead, he proposed a committee of Prime Ministers which set out in the course of the summer of 1918 to review not only the past and future conduct of the war but a good many other matters as well. Admittedly, the significance of the committee could easily be exaggerated. Its draft report remained unsigned when Borden returned to Canada on August 16 and its recommendations, based on husbanding the British army through 1919 for a decisive blow in 1920, were soon rendered obsolete.

Dealing with London remained for Borden and many Canadians a recurrent frustration. In 1914, like many others, the prime minister had been a theoretical imperial federationist, hopeful that Canada would find its destiny as a major influence in the greatest empire the world had ever seen, and confident that someone would come up with efficient means. Four years of war had come close to confirming Bonar Law's gloomy judgement of 1915. Only when Borden was in London could he influence imperial policy; even there it was a desultory, unsatisfying performance. Banquet speeches and public acclaim did not conceal the fact that key decisions were made elsewhere. A prime minister like Lloyd George might feel more kinship with colonial politicians than with his aristocratic colleagues but power was not governed by social intercourse. If anything, Borden found it easier to deal with Canada's oldest enemy, the United States. Washington might be confused about Canada's status, and the British embassy in Washington would be the last place to concede that Canada had a voice of her own. However, when diplomats could be sidestepped, Americans would talk business and make decisions. Flavelle had profited from that fact during the British financial crisis in 1917. His agent, Lloyd Harris, became the logical person to head a Canadian mission to the United States, by-passing the British embassy officials. When the Admiralty warned that U-Boats might become active in the western Atlantic in 1918, it was the United States that sent naval escort vessels and seaplanes from its naval air service, supplementing a hurriedly assembled collection of ill-armed trawlers organized by the Canadian naval service. When the British opened their network of flying schools in Canada in 1917, short-cutting the older methods of pilot training, Texas became the alternate location in the winter. Borden's government might consider itself proudly British in allegiance but it was almost dangerously easier to negotiate with the Americans.

Canadians could not forget, of course, that they had borne the war for three years longer than their powerful neighbour. When the Armistice came on November 11, 1918, with unexpected suddenness, the Canadian losses, 60,661 dead, were still far greater than the American toll. In the postwar years, resentful about American claims to have won the war and a little nervous about the steady Americanization of their own country, Canadians would take pride in the magnitude of their own war effort and perhaps engage in a little boasting of their own. In the immediate aftermath, there was very little evidence of such national pride. Canadians celebrated the Armistice—a little cautiously, perhaps, because they had already celebrated a false report of peace on November 7. Mainly, they set out to liquidate the war as ruthlessly as Sir Joseph Flavelle dismantled the munitions industry and disposed of the national factories. Helped by a Senate amendment that gave Canadians a year to reconsider and stock up, most of Canada experimented with provincially-controlled prohibition and cheerfully abandoned it within a few years. Women retained the vote but they used it not for moral uplift or social reform, as the suffragists had promised, but like anyone else.

The war effort had endeavoured to unite Canadians. Instead, it divided them: French and English, farmers, labour and business; Union Liberals, Laurier Liberals and those who ducked the crossfire; patriotic Canadians and "slackers," British Canadians and "enemy aliens." Then there was the deepest division of all: those who had spent the war years in Canada and those who would now return from months and years overseas.

The Long Truce

4

Few if any Canadians realized that the armistice of November 11, 1918 was no more than the start of a long truce. People had christened the conflict the Great War. Whether or not Canadians believed that they had waged "the war to end war," they could never return to the naive illusions of 1914. The rewards of war had proved few; the costs were frightfully high.

Australians would find a nation-building pride in the exploits of the AN-ZACs; Canadians knew only that war had divided their country, and even their own proud achievements were drowned out by American self-congratulation about the Argonne or St. Mihiel. Very few Canadians could appreciate the international status Canada had achieved by its war effort. Even Sir Robert Borden's cabinet colleagues could not understand why he insisted on spending the postwar months in London and Paris, robbing the Union government of badly needed leadership. It was hard for ailing, exhausted ministers to summon much interest in how or where Canada's name was placed on the final draft of the Treaty of Versailles.

Financially, Canada emerged from the war surprisingly unscathed. The national debt had soared from half a billion to two billion dollars during the war years but much of that was due to the generous treatment of investors in the bankrupt Canadian Northern and Grand Trunk railways. The cost of Canada's soldiers overseas, based largely on a five shillings a day per capita and a surcharge for artillery ammunition, was $252 million. What was owed to Britain was massively offset by Britain's debt for Canadian munitions. The real loss was human. More than a quarter of Canada's young men of military age, 230,000 of them, had been killed or wounded in the war. The loss of 60,661 dead, just under one per cent of the entire population, could never be measured. The cost of pensions for the bereaved and disabled, for medical and hospital care, training and re-employment seemed staggering for a country which, in the past, had been able to reward war veterans with a few more acres of its inexhaustible supply.

Not even with time would Canadians romanticize the First World War. At most, they would hunt for the rewards which must surely follow such an ordeal. In the 1920s most of them would seek in vain. Disillusionment bred one conclusion: Canadians would go crusading no more. Henri Bourassa had been reviled when he preached isolationism and self-interest as a basis for Canadian nationalism; in the postwar years, he was the prophet of Canada's attitude to war and the world. In 1922, Arthur Meighen responded to the Chanak crisis and the risk of an Anglo-Turkish war with Laurier's words of 1914, "Ready, aye, ready!" He was utterly disavowed. Safe behind its Atlantic moat, protected as much by the new United States Navy as by the British fleet, Canadians wanted no commitments and few responsibilities.

The immediate impact of the end of hostilities could not be easily or swiftly escaped. In late 1918, a quarter of a million Canadian soldiers were scattered from Le Havre to Vladivostok, from Archangel to Baku. As many more, employed in the IMB factories and other war-related industries, faced immediate layoff. Food, clothing, fuel, consumer goods of every description were in short supply. Prices, instead of dropping as the experts had predicted, soared to new heights. Young women began wearing tiny potatoes as earrings to celebrate unprecedented grocery bills. Canadians demanded a release from wartime controls and, simultaneously, decisive government action to bring down the cost of living. Clinging to its wartime style, the cabinet appointed a Cost of Living Commissioner with impressive powers. Then it replaced him with a Board of Commerce, ordered to restore a free market by means of strict regulation. The Unionists broke the Tory promise to scrap the income tax, increased it to new heights and rolled out the old slogans to sponsor a final Victory Bond drive.

A government dominated by businessmen and financiers felt a pressure to get back to normal. Bankers insisted that rapid deflation was the answer to rising prices. Helpless before arguments he would have used himself, Sir Thomas White consented. The result was a brutal, if short-lived depression in 1919-20, aggravating every problem of reconstruction. Farmers, who had been mollified by the $3.15 a bushel the new Wheat Board got them in 1919, saw prices cut in half when marketing returned to private hands. The Board of Commerce, rendered impotent by internal conflict, was judged unconstitutional six months after birth in a ruling that claimed that Ottawa's wartime emergency power had lapsed. Prohibition, frustrated by the Senate for a year, left a patchwork of provincial bans on liquor which gradually discredited temperance reformers and annoyed the returned soldiers.

Yet when liquor returned to most provinces within five years, it was invariably as a government monopoly. The businessmen and bankers did their best to rebuild the free enterprise, *laisser faire* economy they remembered from pre-war years but they could not entirely succeed. The war left the federal and provincial governments with a host of responsibilities they had never really exercised before. The Patriotic Fund had been financed as a private charity but the huge task of administering welfare for soldiers' families had been managed by the government in Ottawa. The disastrous influenza epidemic of 1918 gave birth to a national Department of Health. The Union government continued a wartime habit of leadership by providing grants to provinces to promote highway construction, vocational and technical training, venereal disease control and the development of a national employment service to meet the needs of munition workers and discharged soldiers. To Borden's immense pride, forty thousand public employees were rescued from the vagaries of political patronage by transfer to the aegis of the Civil Service Commission. A "veterans preference" rule gave politicians a back door for their more military friends.

The biggest and most unfamiliar task for the government was coping with the returned soldiers. In 1917, to soldiers about to attack Vimy Ridge, an emotion-filled Borden had sworn: ". . . no man, whether he goes back or whether he remains in Flanders, will have just cause to reproach the Government for having broken faith with the men who won and the men who died." It was a bold promise for a government that had no experience of veterans' needs or expectations. A few thousand dollars a year, managed by the Militia department, had provided meagre pensions for survivors of the Fenian Raids or the 1885 campaign. Now, 640,000 Canadians had served in uniform; 400,000 had gone overseas. In 1915, a Military Hospitals Commission under Senator Sir James Lougheed of Alberta had relieved the Department of Militia of responsibility for coping with returning sick and wounded soldiers. Working in a morass of medical jealousies, political patronage and jurisdictional battles with provincial authorities and voluntary organizations, Lougheed's commission could report 11,700 beds in service by the end of 1917 as well as an array of rehabilitative facilities. In 1916, the government appointed a Board of Pension Commissioners, relieving the Patriotic Fund of responsibility for war widows and the disabled. Building on the 1907 pension regulations for the permanent force, which allowed a totally disabled private the princely sum of $150 a year, the Board steadily improved the rates, initially to $480 a year for a totally disabled CEF private, $264 for a permanent force private's widow. By September, 1919, a widow with three children could claim up to $81 a month. Complaints from veterans' organizations steadily eliminated the gap between officers and other ranks: by 1920 a disabled private or lieutenant each got $900 a year if single, $1,200 if married.

Unlike the Americans, whose Congress refused to permit postwar planning, Borden's government began considering the problems as early as 1916. In February, 1918, Senator Lougheed entered the cabinet as minister for a new Department of Soldiers' Civil Re-Establishment. A Repatriation Committee of the cabinet under J. A. Calder prepared plans and legislation for a host of postwar problems. Nothing illustrated better the influence of wartime in expanding government power and initiative. An elaborate demobilization scheme, patterned on the British model, arranged to release CEF members on the basis of the priorities of restoring a peacetime economy, with coal miners and skilled mechanics given preference. After debating the merits of training the disabled for highly-skilled trades, Lougheed's department opted for a cheaper alternative of adapting wounded soldiers to light work in their old jobs. The government was determined that its main concern would be the mentally and physically disabled. A modest gratuity and loans to establish qualified would-be farmers on the land would be the major concessions to the able-bodied.

For re-establishment planners, the war ended at a very inconvenient time. Munition workers were laid off at the start of the slack winter season. By the time soldiers could come home from Europe, the only ice-free ports were Halifax and Saint John. Canadian officials insisted that war-worn railway lines to the Maritimes could carry no more than 20,000 soldiers a month. Indignation at conditions on one of the early troopships, the *Northland,* forced Canadian officials to insist on even higher quality ships than the Americans demanded at a time of grave shipping shortage. Despite the backing of employers, labour unions and veterans' organizations, the government's go-slow demobilization plan collapsed before the rebellious impatience of soldiers anxious to come home. Urged on by Sir Edward Kemp and Sir Arthur Currie, Borden persuaded his cabinet colleagues that troops had better come back to Canada as fast as possible. His argument was underlined by riots and disorders in Canadian camps in England. At Kinmel in north Wales, several thousand Canadians rioted on March 4 and 5, 1919 to protest the lack of spending money and cancellation of sailings. The toll was five dead and twenty-five injured. More ships were found. In May, after British dock strikes caused more shipping problems, Canadians rioted at Witley, Seaford and Ripon. Friction with their British hosts led to street fights in Guildford. A savage fight in Epsom left a British police sergeant dead. Within weeks, the Overseas Ministry could report that all but a remnant of Canadians had gone home, well ahead of schedule.

Canadians met the returned soldiers with speeches, bands, bunting and hidden fears. How far had war and military service transformed sons and husbands? Would the returned men appreciate that those at home had also endured shortages of sugar and butter and put up with meatless Fridays and fuel-less Mondays? Had years of army life crushed initiative or embedded the evil habits of swearing, drunkenness and gambling? The long wait in England had allowed the completion of army documentation and soldiers returned to civilian life with surprising speed. Typical of many CEF units, the 20th Battalion arrived at Toronto's Union Station on May 24, 1919. The unit formed up, marched along Yonge Street through cheering crowds and dispersed, never to parade again. Men who needed a bed spent the night at the Canadian National Exhibition grounds. Next morning, men lined up for back pay and, if they needed them, tickets to their final destination. They were through with the army. There was no postponing the process. Troops of the 27th Battalion were asked whether they would mind remaining in uniform to provide the government with a reserve in Winnipeg during the 1919 General Strike. The men would mind very much. Though the regimental baggage was used to transfer Lewis guns and ammunition to the troubled western city, the battalion broke up as rapidly as the others.

The wounded and sick returned less glamourously. Sufferers from venereal disease remained in almost penal segregation in England while a transatlantic controversy raged about whether they should be allowed to carry their contagion across Canada or whether there would be a national scandal if they were kept in a single hospital in Toronto. Public opinion had to be shielded from the less than virginal qualities of Canada's soldiers. By the time reluctant consent was obtained for dispersal, the problem had solved itself. The sufferers had been discharged as cured. There was no such happy outcome for others. Despite horrible wounds inflicted by high explosives and the almost invariable infection from the polluted soil of Flanders, medicine and surgery made dramatic progress during the war. Advances in antisepsis, bacteriology, radiology, blood transfusion and irrigation of wounds meant that more blinded, maimed and limbless soldiers survived. The war saw strides in plastic surgery, physio-therapy and prosthetics, particularly in France.

After previous wars, the wounded survivors had usually been abandoned to join the ranks of beggars and indigents, sometimes with a meagre pension. It took years after the Civil War before veterans' organizations persuaded the American government to assume full medical responsibility for the human wreckage of the conflict. From the time the first sick and wounded began trickling home in 1915, Canadian public opinion made it clear that it expected care and rehabilitation for returned soldiers. Such responsibilities were as new to Canada as war itself. Medical services were a provincial or municipal concern, limited largely to charity care for the indigent. Lougheed's department had to establish hospitals, clinics and a small industry to serve the needs of rehabilitation. In its 1921 report, his staff reported the issue of 32,000 pairs of orthopedic boots, 25,000 artificial arms and 9,000 legs. Its boards had approved 60,000 disability pensions and identified 196 sightless veterans. The year found 6,520 in-patients in the department's hospitals, 1,634 out-patients and 8,993 dependent on clinical care. Lougheed's highest priority was vocational training for the disabled. By June of 1924, when the postwar rush was over, the department reported that 55,771 ex-soldiers had been found eligible for training, 52,284 had begun training and 42,993 had finished. However, only 63 per cent found jobs in fields for which they had been trained. Some found employment only in sheltered workshops run by the Red Cross or by Vetcraft, a veteran-sponsored organization that produced poppies for a newly approved occasion, Remembrance Day.

The government cheerfully congratulated itself on its achievements. Canada's vocational training programme led the world, and its pensions, in many cases, were more generous than those of the prosperous United States. A totally disabled American veteran could receive no more than $1,200 a year; a Canadian in a similar state, with a wife and three children, could claim $1,644. In 1921, Canadian taxpayers learned that they had paid out $36,671,000 in pensions to widows, orphans, parents and the disabled.

Medical treatment cost them another $13,562,012. Much of the money had probably been spent on soldiers whose medical problems long pre-dated their enlistment and officials of the Pension Commission tried remorselessly and with the usual bureaucratic callousness to separate civil from military disabilities. Their efforts brought an explosion of protest from veterans' organizations.

Returned soldiers nourished a more immediate grievance in the immediate postwar years: the government's neglect of the able-bodied. Canadians could feel relieved. The returning veterans proved to be generally cheerful, law-abiding and glad to be home, though newspapers tended to underline every crime in which an ex-soldier might be involved. In 1918, when the 17,000 member Great War Veterans' Association met in Toronto, some Greek restaurants were ransacked and scuffles with the police sent a few from both sides to hospital. Veterans attacked radical union officials in Vancouver in 1918. In February, 1919, ex-soldiers in Winnipeg broke up radical meetings, demolished the offices of the local Socialist party and threatened to drive out "enemy aliens" working for Canada Packers and the CPR. As a rule, the returned men were more restless than troublesome. Even those who returned to their old jobs often abandoned them. More than 80,000 applied for land under the Soldiers' Settlement Act but only 30,000 took up grants. Many gave up, partly because most of the available land was marginal, partly because of a collapse in farm prices but also partly because of a kind of emotional turbulence. The government's discharge gratuity, ranging from $210 to $420 for men with at least three years' service, was soon spent. The hero's welcome soon wore off. During the two-month general strike in Winnipeg in the spring of 1919, it was largely the returned soldiers who provided the action, meeting, marching and demonstrating for the strikers on one side, and volunteering as guards and special constables on the other.

The most obvious outlet for their energies was organization, and the target was a government which obviously should have been doing more. After 1916, the Great War Veterans' Association had emerged as the largest organization for returned men. Its inspiration was W. D. Lighthall, a Montreal lawyer and municipal reformer, but the leadership soon passed to men wounded at Ypres. The GWVA demanded conscription, denounced half-heartedness and threw itself behind the Unionist campaign in 1917. That won it official recognition. Membership grew from 18,000 at the end of the war to an inflated claim of 250,000 by mid-1919. The Association's egalitarianism—addressing all members as "comrade" and demanding equal pensions for privates and generals—worried politicians but they took heart when the GWVA denounced Bolshevism and the radical One Big Union. The GWVA, in fact, tried hard to walk on both sides of the street. According to its national secretary, Grant MacNeil, its members in Winnipeg split about evenly on the general strike. Jack Moore, a future president of the Canadian Legion, led an attack on the headquarters of the anti-strike Citizens' Committee. The

GWVA official statement after the strike was evidence of many painful compromises:

> this Association is fully in sympathy with that portion of organized labour which is striving to better the conditions of the working men through lawful and constitutional means and which is in no sympathy whatever with factions controlled by extremists who strive by all means to overthrow British institutions and incessantly breed discord and advocate riot or revolutions and that we are unalterably opposed to all capitalistic combines which seek by economic or financial pressure, to control, to an unwarranted degree, the governing bodies of this fair Dominion to the detriment of the majority of the people of Canada.

Despite the anti-officer bias of the GWVA, it and most Canadian veterans' organizations were usually ready to choose officers for their leaders. On one issue, however, rank and file members took the bit in their teeth. The notion that veterans were entitled to a handsome lump sum payment for their services was of uncertain origin though it may have come from the United States. In both countries, a bonus seemed like overdue justice when they discovered how well their fellow-citizens had fared during the war and how little was left for soldiers who had served for $1.20 a day. In a resolution drafted by the Calgary branch of the GWVA in February, 1919, the veterans demanded $2,000 for any man who had served in France, $1,500 for any who had gone to England and $1,000 for those who had served in Canada. On the strength of the demand, thousands of veterans joined the association. For all the protests and machinations of the GWVA's officials, the Calgary resolution became policy. In August of 1919, before it chose William Lyon Mackenzie King as its new leader, the Liberal convention solemnly endorsed the gratuity proposal. The Union government was less crass. At the amounts proposed, the GWVA demand would add the then-stupendous amount of a billion dollars to the national debt. Borden and his colleagues said no.

Frankly, the GWVA leadership would cheerfully have forgotten the idea had it not been for J. Harry Flynn. An American-born teacher of commercial subjects, Flynn set out to build a postwar career on the gratuity issue. He launched his own United Veterans' organization, promised to push the issue into politics and took over branch after branch of the GWVA. A worried government created a parliamentary committee, summoned Flynn to testify and did its best to impugn his war record. For stay-at-home politicians to question anyone's heroism was not the way to the veterans' hearts. Instead, time and the GWVA's responsible leadership beat back the demand. By the summer of 1920, most returned men had found jobs and remembered that they were taxpayers too. Their main organization reflected the new maturity. "I do not want men voting in convention any longer because they are afraid of the crowd back home," MacNeil told delegates to the GWVA's 1921 convention, "I know that there are men in this convention who do not believe that it is possible to get a cash bonus and they tell me this on every hand. They vote this, that and the other way at the meeting and they come around to me and say: 'we know all that stuff, MacNeil, but you know we cannot get it, it is impossible."

Despite expectations, the veterans made surprisingly little political impact. Fewer veterans were elected to the House of Commons in 1921 than in 1917. The returned men spoke with many voices. The GWVA battled Brigadier-General W. A. Griesbach's Army and Navy Veterans, Flynn's organization and an array of smaller competitors, not to mention battalion and corps associations, a secret society called Fourandex and a religious association, Toc-H. Unity was delayed when the GWVA's MacNeil denounced the Pension Commission for a "contemptible and cold-blooded conspiracy" to deprive ex-servicemen and their families of their rights. Griesbach, a senator, felt personally affronted by MacNeil and responded with charges that the GWVA had mismanaged the Poppy Fund and the Vetcraft enterprise. A Royal Commission headed by Lieutenant-Colonel J. L. Ralston, a distinguished CEF battalion commander and Liberal MP, disposed of most of MacNeil's charges; a parliamentary inquiry did as much to Griesbach's claims. In the aftermath, unity finally seemed possible.

Propelled by the hope of sharing in wartime canteen profits, shoved from behind by their wartime commander-in-chief, Earl Haig, Canadian veterans' organizations finally came together at Winnipeg in November, 1925. Though the Tuberculous Veterans, the Amputees and Griesbach's organization found reasons to stay out, most remained to form a Canadian Legion, part of Haig's British Empire Service League. Despite the anti-officer bias of the earlier veterans' organizations, the new Legion was headed by Sir Richard Turner, Sir Percy Lake and an array of colonels and generals. MacNeil quietly departed; his style had little value in the new mood of discretion, moderation and persistence. Official veteran influence in Canada would be carefully conservative.

No one asked whether that suited the mass of ordinary CEF veterans because their impact on Canadian society as a whole remains one of the unposed questions of Canadian history. More than half a million men, a tenth of the adult population, had shared the experience of military service, many of them for several years. They had experienced discipline and regimentation, had worn uniforms and shared army food. They had been separated from normal relations with women and families. We are still left to conjecture about the impact of that experience on Canadian society as a whole.

Most of the returned men, like those of the 27th Battalion, appeared determined to put military service behind them forever. Others, in time, would turn back from the disappointments of civilian life to seek the comradeship and security they had known in uniform. That could not happen soon enough for a frightened Union government. In Winnipeg, where affluent citizens interpreted the general strike as a Bolshevik revolution,

Brigadier-General H. D. B. Ketchen had to fill the militia ranks with elderly, overweight businessmen. Sir Thomas White wired Borden in Paris to arrange for a British cruiser to anchor at Victoria or Vancouver to overawe local radicals. Instead, Borden ordered a squadron of the RNWMP serving with the CEF to return to Canada. General Mewburn announced that the maximum strength of the permanent force would be raised from 5,000 to 10,000. Postwar reorganization of the Canadian defence forces began in an atmosphere of confusion and panic.

Sam Hughes's mobilization in 1914 had produced two Canadian military organizations, the old volunteer militia and the new CEF. The task of combining them was given to a committee headed by the venerable "father of the force," Major-General Sir William Otter. The result was rather more political than military. Both Otter and the new inspector-general, Sir Arthur Currie, agreed that it was far more important to maintain military interest across Canada than to design a balanced militia army. They might quietly sympathize with enthusiasts like Major H. M. Mowat who campaigned in Parliament for universal military training; they knew perfectly well that peacetime Canada would still depend on voluntary enthusiasm to keep up a military organization. If a good CEF battalion like the 3rd Toronto refused to mix with the two historic regiments which had created it in 1914, let the unit survive on its own. The result of Otter's Committee was a huge paper organization of eleven infantry and four cavalry divisions, with a company or even a regiment for any community that might be even remotely interested. To ease the transition, new regimental titles replaced the old numbers. At the suggestion of Brigadier-General A. G. L. McNaughton, Otter proposed that the CEF's only French-speaking battalion join the permanent force as the Royal 22nd Regiment. The West also got its own regular regiment, the Princess Patricia's Canadian Light Infantry.

Soldiers had traditions to help them win post-war re-establishment; other services were less fortunate. The belated attempt to create a Canadian air force in England and another effort at Halifax to build a Canadian naval air service both faded in the postwar months. Few Canadians even realized the extent of the Royal Canadian Navy's patrolling operations off the Atlantic coast during the later war years and it was not a task that inspired legends. The navy had almost died in 1913; it almost did so again. Lord Jellicoe, the former British First Sea Lord, recommended a variety of postwar naval organizations ranging in cost from $4 to $20 million a year. Borden's navy minister, C. C. Ballantyne, settled for a modest plan costing $2.5 million. When cabinet colleagues denounced even that meagre proposal, Ballantyne marched out and furiously despatched telegrams disbanding the entire service. "The Navy League spent half its revenue on messages," Sir George Foster recalled, "Halifax and Esquimalt were up in arms and the rest of the Ministers were asking 'who did it?' " Ballantyne's navy—a light cruiser, two destroyers, a couple of submarines and the Royal Canadian Naval College—was saved for the moment.

An air force was more popular. Thousands of former service flyers flocked back to Canada, their exploits already renowned among old and young. It was easy to argue, in a country always preoccupied with transportation, that flying would become as vital as canoes or trains had been. Barnstorming pilots excited crowds with aerobatics and short flights before the postwar economic depression put most of them out of business. In June of 1919, a seven-member Air Board was appointed to regulate Canadian civil aviation. Even the GWVA demanded a Canadian air force, with "the workers sharing in the management." The Air Board devised a cautious compromise: a militia air force would give former pilots and mechanics a month's service every two years while a permanent cadre, serving from year to year, would provide the staff, the instructors and the government's own air service. This was possible only because Britain contributed $5 million worth of aircraft, spare parts and equipment from its war surplus while the Americans donated twelve seaplanes brought to Halifax in 1918. By the summer of 1920, government pilots were busy proving that aviators could spot forest fires, observe smugglers, deliver treaty money to remote Indian bands and even report on geological formations. In April of 1920, the Air Board announced its three branches: Air Operations, Civil Aviation and a Canadian Air Force headed by a newly fledged Air Vice Marshal Sir Willoughby Gwatkin.

By 1921, the Union government had exhausted itself and the country. "I think any person who holds office . . . at any time during the next five years is entitled to a measure of sympathy," J. W. Dafoe of the *Free Press* had written at the end of the war. "It is going to be demanded of him that he do things which cannot be done; things which are mutually contradictory and destructive, and whatever he does will have more critics than friends." Tired ministers had done what they thought best for the country, often in the face of public opinion. On December 6, 1921, public opinion had its revenge. The new fourteenth Parliament was unlike any that Canadians had seen before. The Liberals, under King, emerged as winners with 117 seats. The government (once more Conservative) salvaged a meagre fifty. For the first time a third party had emerged to challenge tradition. The balance of power would be held by a coalition of sixty-four western and Ontario farmer-MPs with three Labour members and an independent.

It was a Parliament that could agree on very little save the folly of defence spending. "The people of this country do not propose to submit to the god of militarism," the *Farmers' Sun* had warned, "We have just fought a five years war in order to make wars to cease." J. S. Woodsworth, who gravitated to the leadership of the labour group, was a devout pacifist. So was Canada's first woman MP, Agnes Macphail. From the first, she seized attention with speeches against war and militarism. She made hazing at the Royal

Military College a national issue and informed parents (with no evidence) that boys in cadet corps were marched to abattoirs to inure them to the sight of blood. Macphail and Woodsworth went farther than most Canadians but applause came easily in the 1920s to anyone who denounced general staffs, "Merchants of Death" and doctrines of military preparedness. The Liberal government could only slowly win over Progressives to its policy on tariffs or freight rates but on defence, agreement was easy. Quebec Liberals had a special score to settle with the military. In the 1922 session, C. G. Power, a cocky Quebec backbencher and CEF veteran, demanded a cut of $300,000 in militia training estimates. In the party caucus, other members demanded and won a cut of $400,000 in training and a $300,000 reduction in other defence spending.

The new prime minister was not displeased. As James Eayrs has noted, Mackenzie King had "a marked aversion to the military life and the military mind, whose workings he failed to understand and whose virtues he ignored." In opposition, he had attacked every Union defence proposal. He had tried to remove the $800,000 budgeted for the new Canadian Air Force while his lieutenant, Ernest Lapointe, raised the familiar argument that the new service would commit Canada to imperial defence. What enemy, King demanded, had the government decided to arm itself against? The answer, all too plainly, was the people themselves. The sight of militia patrols in Winnipeg and Vancouver in 1919 left bitter memories. King himself was embarrassed when local magistrates requisitioned most of Canada's permanent force to protect the Cape Breton coal mines during the strikes of 1922 and 1923. The Militia Act was changed at last to place both the responsibility and the cost for aid to the civil power directly on provincial governments.

In addition to slashing militia spending, the new government cut the Air Board estimates by 43 per cent, ending the CAF as a reserve force and condemning government pilots to another year of flying in worn-out World War aircraft. Next, when the great powers met in Washington to haggle over naval disarmament, the Liberals proudly announced a sudden 40 per cent cut in Canada's own naval budget. The cruiser, the submarines and the naval college were immediately eliminated. In exchange, companies of a thousand-member Royal Canadian Naval Volunteer Reserve began to sprout across Canada. For a service whose chief weakness was national indifference, the navy's reserve was probably the shrewdest investment it could make for peace or war.

The fate of the Canadian air force remained in question while the Liberals pressed forward with their only positive defence policy, a unified defence department. The idea had emerged from the reforming minds of generals like Currie and Major-General James MacBrien, the new Chief of the General Staff. A single authority, MacBrien argued, could prevent competition for personnel and resources and it would underline the interdependence of the three services. Sir Eugene Fiset, retiring as deputy minister of the Militia Department, claimed that amalgamating all three services and the RNWMP could save millions of dollars as well as providing a complete force for aid to the civil power. Though the mounted police was to have a separate destiny as the Royal Canadian Mounted Police, King had been impressed by the arguments. His new Minister of Militia, George Graham, announced his National Defence bill in April, 1922. "What I want to accomplish, if I possibly can," he explained, "is to have a well-organized, snappy defence force that will be a credit to Canada without being too expensive." Parliament offered no resistance. Graham's entire 1922–23 defence budget, $12,242,930, cost the average Canadian only $1.46, a fifth of the burden on the average American.

For Canada's military, Liberal defence policy was more cheap than snappy. Probably their pre-war predecessors, inured to political pressure, meaningless training and social satisfactions, would have been more content. The war had raised expectations and given Canada what she had never had and could not now use: military expertise. Sir James MacBrien, Captain Walter Hose of the navy, and Brigadier-General A. G. L. McNaughton led an impressive array of intelligent, ambitious and professionally competent officers in all three services. Slowly they were forced to realize that their career horizons would be limited to the pair of tiny destroyers, aging equipment brought home by the Canadian Corps and the obsolete, reconditioned aircraft for which the Royal Air Force had no further use. Sir Arthur Currie left early for the principalship of McGill University; MacBrien went in 1927 after a long, humiliating correspondence in which he had pleaded for at least as much pay as a British major-general.

In some ways, unifying the new Department of National Defence made matters worse. Far from ending or resolving inter-service competition, the struggle intensified in the new Defence Council, where the three service chiefs brought unequal resources to the struggle for defence dollars. MacBrien, as Chief of Staff, was supposed to be more than the voice of the army but he was still a soldier and his voice was reinforced by the presence of the Adjutant-General and the Quartermaster-General. Hose, as Director of the Naval Service, raged at his subordination to an army general and he found an ally in the Deputy Minister, Georges Desbarats, civil head of the naval service since 1910. Humblest of all was the director of the Canadian Air Force, a mere associate member.

For two years, the air force stayed in limbo while the new ministers discovered for themselves how useful aviation had become for federal and provincial government operations. Gwatkin and allies on the Air Board rejected the claim that the British gift had been restricted to a military air force. General MacBrien even conceded, by December, 1922, that the Canadian air force would be separate from the militia and navy and, on Gwatkin's assurance that the new service was now securely established, it was granted the title of "Royal" on February 15, 1923. A year later, on April 1, 1924, the Canadian government formally recognized the new Royal Canadian Air Force. Most of the officers and men of the old force transferred to the new organization and adopted the uniforms, badges and youthful traditions of the British model.

The British connection suggested a potential conflict of roles for a service whose civil flying duties far overshadowed military training. It was J. A. Wilson of the Air Board who had insisted that any Canadian venture into air power "must be based on a sound economic development for Peace uses. On any other basis, its maintenance in Canada must be artificial and burdensome in time of Peace." The RCAF earnestly made itself useful. Aerial survey and mapping, ferrying government officials and policemen, and mercy flights and rescue missions in remote areas gave the new service an importance its rivals could not match. Not until 1928, when Colonel Ralston had become Minister of National Defence, did the RCAF receive its first real fighters, a handful of elderly Siskin and Atlas biplanes.

The RAF connection was a constant reminder that the Canadian force was more than an organization of bush pilots. Canadian officers turned to the RAF for their advanced professional training. An occasional year in Britain helped to imbue them with Lord Trenchard's doctrines of independent air power and the potential of aerial bombardment. Then they returned to the dreary flying routines of Jericho Beach or Rockcliffe. The British connection was just as important for the militia and the navy. Nowhere had national pride and self-confidence burned higher than in the Canadian Corps, but peacetime officers could look only to Britain for contact with modern tactics and mechanized equipment. At Camberley and at the new Imperial Defence College, senior Canadian officers unwittingly made contact with their future wartime commanders and colleagues. Denied its own training college, the RCN depended entirely on British resources to train officers and skilled ratings. If they returned with the Royal Navy's attitudes and accents as well as its expertise, the responsibility lay with the Canadian government as much as with themselves.

As frustrated professionals, Canada's peacetime officers sought outlets for their ideas and their talents. MacBrien launched the *Canadian Defence Quarterly* in 1923 and it circulated quietly for years as a vehicle for reprinted articles from the British service press and for the writing of Canada's own small officer corps. Until it was discovered by the anti-military Canadian Institute of International Affairs, the *Quarterly* escaped comment. Thereafter it was an easy target for anyone eager to be shocked that service officers would write about war. They would have been even more horrified to discover Defence Plan No. 1, devised in 1921 by Colonel J. Sutherland Brown, the Director of Military Operations and Plans, as a mobilization scheme for war with the United States. Brown's plan might, of course, have seemed less absurd had anyone realized that American officers had developed their own "Red Plan" for the invasion of Canada. Both sets of plans were really little more than staff exercises and a framework for war games and militia exercises. It was Canada's other defence plans which should have created political turmoil. No. 2 envisaged war with Japan, with Canada either involved or neutral; No. 3 spelled out mobilization plans for a new CEF in a European war; No. 4, in memory of 1899, considered how a brigade of volunteers could help in an imperial war—perhaps a black uprising in South Africa or trouble on the northwest frontier of India.

If Mackenzie King had ever discovered plans like these, his life-long suspicion of generals would certainly have been confirmed. They represented precisely the ideas he wanted to purge. Canadians had died so that their country could have a voice in the world; King found that there was very little that he wished to say. The League of Nations would only rarely be subjected to his lectures on morality and conciliation; imperial conferences would learn that there would be no unit rule in imperial foreign policy. King had learned from Borden's experience that there could be no words without commitment. Canadians had gone to Siberia and Archangel in 1918 because their prime minister had insisted on re-opening the Russian front. King would never be so beguiled. Article X of the League covenant, with its commitment to mutual security even to the extent of armed force, poisoned King's attitude to that otherwise harmless organization. Even when Article X had been thoroughly trampled, King's suspicions remained. The Liberal leader never denied that Canada would be obliged to support Britain in a major war; equally, he did his utmost to avoid any risk of that commitment being called. To assume any added obligation which might draw Canada into war on grounds of mutual security was, in his eyes, as immoral as it was unnecessary. "It is for Parliament to decide whether or not we should participate in wars in different parts of the world," King explained in 1923, "and it is neither right nor proper for any individual nor for any group of individuals to take any step which in any way might limit the rights of Parliament in a matter which is of such great concern to all the people of our country." This, of course, was sanctimonious cant. Parliament would almost certainly approve whatever the government dictated, but a country in the process of gaining its own right to declare war was understandably jealous about handing on that right to the League of Nations.

King has been much criticized for his unenterprising role in the world of the twenties and thirties. It seemed ignominious that Canada should win her international status by signing a Halibut Fisheries Treaty in 1923 or by hesitantly opening a legation in Washington in 1927. In a low, dark, selfish era in human affairs, surely Canada could offer the world more than Senator Raoul Dandurand's smug little boast that Canadians lived "in a fire-proof house, far from inflammable materials." Yet the statement was correct. Canada faced no threat greater than Colonel Brown could conjure up. There was no logical criterion by which soldiers, politicians or philosophers could claim that Canada was unprepared for a palpable threat. There was only the moral certainty that someday, somehow, Canada's armed forces would be needed in circumstances no one could predict. Canadians ignored such a grim but fuzzy forecast. It was a prospect that could only be brought closer by preparing for it.

Denied public support or a clear military purpose, the Canadian forces slid back to their old stultification. Militia officers still handed over their pay to the regimental fund, revived old techniques for attracting and holding recruits and grumbled that military rank no longer commanded the old social status. The country, after all, had been flooded with generals and colonels. Instructors who had survived Vimy and Amiens swung gas rattles and pretended that they were machine guns. Battery commanders reminisced about wartime barrages and husbanded the ten rounds a year they were allotted for peacetime practice. Permanent force sergeants became expert at detecting "snowbirds," men who would join in the fall and desert in the spring when the drill season began. Canada's soldiers could see tanks, anti-tank guns, armoured cars and machine gun carriers—but only in the newsreels. Canada had none. Slowly, during the 1920s, a little of Canada's prosperity trickled into the defence estimates. By 1929, the total had climbed to $21,070,015. As minister, Ralston commanded more respect than his predecessors though his painstaking insistence on reviewing every single decision drove subordinates like General McNaughton to the verge of resignation. More serious was Ralston's refusal to authorize new military equipment or to permit the development of a government arsenal where it might be built. Canadians, under a Liberal government, would not become Merchants of Death, even in their own interests.

McNaughton would certainly have resigned as Chief of the General Staff had Canadian voters left the Liberals in office in 1930 to face the full rigours of the depression. Instead, they turned to the Conservatives. Richard Bedford Bennett won office with a stridently military pledge to blast Canada's way into the markets of the world. His defence minister was D. M. Sutherland, a former CEF major and medical doctor, who promptly authorized McNaughton to buy six Carden-Loyd machine gun carriers with a promise of more to come. Depression constraints intervened. Canada's mechanized army would remain a family joke.

Militia and naval officers had envied the RCAF's civil flying responsibilities as a source of favourable publicity and a handy lever for public funds. As a military counterpart, MacBrien had promoted the Northwest Territories and Yukon Radio System, a network of stations manned by the Royal Canadian Corps of Signals that began at Mayo and Dawson in 1923 and soon spread across the southern Arctic. McNaughton, the former chemistry professor, encouraged military collaboration with the National Research Council in fields ranging from photogrammetry and ballistics to his own work on a cathode ray direction finder. The RCN, divided between two coasts and kept short of fuel, could do little beyond "showing the flag" in Canadian and Caribbean ports. By instinct, the new Conservative government would probably have preferred to be more sympathetic to the defence department than its Liberal predecessor. It was trapped. Every sector of the Canadian economy was vulnerable to the world slump. Raw material and wheat prices collapsed. In the West, the recurrent drought cycle, rust and grasshoppers coincided with the economic disaster. Tax revenues tumbled. Bennett's own plans to restore prosperity proved to be blustering failures. As prices fell, wages followed and hundreds of thousands of Canadians faced unemployment and ruin. Prominent among them were war veterans, fleeing the marginal farms of the Soldier Settlement plan or laid off from jobs created only by prosperity. By the summer of 1932, a quarter of Canada's work force was hunting for jobs. Federal, provincial and municipal governments scrambled to organize relief for the destitute and to find the funds to pay for it. In seven years, Canadian governments poured a billion dollars into help for Depression victims. To recipients, it seemed painfully meagre.

In Ottawa, politicians and officials ransacked budgets for economies. Defence was an obvious place to look. Warned of widespread Communist organizing among the unemployed, the cabinet decided not to cut deeply into the militia or the permanent force. The other services were more vulnerable. The prime minister concluded that civil air operations had become a luxury a depression-wracked country could not afford. His defence minister did not need to be persuaded. In opposition, Sutherland had regularly protested that the RCAF was degraded by such duties. Far from finding safety in its civil role, the air force faced orders to fire 78 of its 177 officers and 100 of its 729 airmen. The "Big Cut" crumpled the morale of the RCAF and left a deep bitterness at other services that suffered less drastic reductions. In 1933, presented with orders to trim a further $3,673,023 from the defence budget, General McNaughton decided arbitrarily to scrap the RCN by cutting $2 million from its $2.4 million allocation. Coast defence, he reasoned, could be handled by aircraft. Commodore Hose, the Director of the Naval Service, turned and waged a brilliant rear-guard action for his beloved navy. The Treasury Board relented.

McNaughton's active mind also contributed to the Bennett government's most ill-starred attempt to cope with the Depression. The economic disaster left thousands of young men drifting hopelessly in search of work, pushed on by municipal officials who wanted no more mouths to feed. To McNaughton, these were the men who would be Canada's soldiers in any future war. Now they wandered across the country, demoralized, dirty, a prey to disease, injury and, he suspected, to Communist agitators. The army could act. Staff officers worked out the details. For a dollar a day, men could be housed, fed, clothed and put to work—with twenty cents a day left over as spending money. There was plenty to be done. Building the St. Lawrence Seaway, an early suggestion, was rejected because it would need heavy engineering equipment and might enrage the construction unions. With simple tools and their own strength, the single unemployed men could rebuild crumbling fortresses like Fort Henry at Kingston or the Citadel at Halifax. They could erect barracks and, above all, clear landing fields for the Trans-Canada Airway that McNaughton had dreamed of building. Bennett, approached through his brother-in-law, W. D. Herridge, was intrigued. In October, 1932, the plan was approved. By the summer of 1933, McNaughton could report that 8,000 men were at work. During four years of operation, more than 170,000 single unemployed passed through the army-managed relief camps.

Relief camps should have been a success. In the United States, Franklin Delano Roosevelt's Civilian Conservation Corps was one of the acknowledged triumphs of the New Deal. Like the Canadian camps, the CCC was administered by the army and its members did rough bush work for a small wage. One difference was that the CCC wore uniforms and shared an *esprit de corps*. In Canada, McNaughton had been the first to insist that the camps must be as civilian as possible. Engineer officers wore civilian clothing. Workers were issued overalls and bulky sweaters. A military atmosphere spilled out in other ways—ex-CEF sergeants hired as foremen, camp regulations framed like military orders, a firm ban on collective grievances or union organization. Effective as a stopgap, the relief camps turned sour when the depression dragged on for months and years. The relief camp workers felt forgotten, condemned and derided by their tiny wage. They called themselves the Royal Twenty Centers. Far from being immunized from radical agitators, they were the best recruiting ground for the Communists in the thirties. From McNaughton's camps in British Columbia came the young men who filled the streets of Vancouver in 1934 and 1935, "tin-canning" for their own support. Relief camp workers formed the On-to-Ottawa trek that ended in tragedy in Regina on Dominion Day, 1935. When Canadian voters went to the polls that September, the relief camps had become a national symbol of R. B. Bennett's failure to deal with the Depression.

In the 1935 election, Canadians chose King, not Chaos, but the Liberal slogan fitted the world as well as a depression-ridden Canada. In 1931, Japan had found a pretext to invade Manchuria and the world found excuses not to intervene. China, after all, was a remote, misgoverned country; Japan had grievances; the horrors of war could no longer be lightly risked. The same arguments would be adapted and used again. In Germany, Hitler came to power in 1933 and brusquely withdrew from the Geneva disarmament talks when other nations refused to concede his new Reich the status of a great power. In March of 1936, Germany scorned the Versailles settlement by resuming compulsory military service; months later, Britain accepted Germany's naval rearmament. Then it was Italy's turn, defying the League of Nations to fulfil an old colonial ambition, the conquest of Ethiopia. League members debated sanctions. Caught without instructions amidst the 1935 change of government in Ottawa, Canada's permanent delegate, W. A. Riddell, took the podium to move that the only products Italy really needed, oil, iron and steel, be added to the embargo. In Ottawa, King was furious.

Without authority, Riddell had risked war with an Italian dictator who had too many admirers among Quebec Catholics and nationalists. Worse, the chancelleries and editorial offices of the world buzzed with the significance of what they called "the Canadian initiative." At King's command, it vanished from the League agenda. So, too, did Riddell. An accident had allowed Canada to play its own brief, ignoble part in the collapse of collective security.

It should have surprised no one. King had acted with complete consistency. Among Canadians, only Dafoe of the *Free Press* showed the least dismay. He would soon have much more to deplore. When Hitler invaded the Rhineland in 1936, King's response was as clear as he could make it: "I believe that Canada's first duty to the League and to the British Empire, with respect to all the great issues that come to us, is, if possible, to keep this country united." Not just Quebec but much of Canada showed no will to fight for the Treaty of Versailles. They would not fight the *Anschluss* of 1937 either and they would cheer a Munich agreement in 1938 that gave much and then all of Czechoslovakia to the Nazis in return for Neville Chamberlain's hope of "Peace in our time." Canada would not even help more than a tiny handful of the horde of Jewish and political refugees fleeing from Nazi horrors the world could not yet conceive. Jewish immigration would, after all, offend influential ministers like Ernest Lapointe and Fernand Rinfret, to say nothing of anti-Semites across Canada.

Not all Canadians turned inwards. For some, the fight against Fascism could be waged in Spain. A merciless civil war between the Soviet-backed Republicans and a military junta dependent on Italian arms and Nazi air power became, for a time, the idealists' perfect crusade. When the Communist International funnelled thousands of volunteers into Spain to form the international brigades, at least 1,200 came from Canada, proportionately more than from any country except France. According to Victor Howard, surviving records suggest that the Canadians were older, on average, than the 3,300 American volunteers with whom they were mixed and that very few were teachers or students. Instead, most had emerged from the relief camps where General McNaughton had hoped to save the military manhood of Canada. In the Republican cause, they found the purpose that the Depression had denied them. As many as a third of them never returned. Despite the auspices, the Canadians in Spain were more like Canadian soldiers in France or South Africa than most of them realized. After serving in the Lincoln and Washington battalions, they pleaded successfully for their own unit and, in July, 1937, the Mackenzie-Papineau Battalion was formed. From the first futile assault at Fuentes de Ebro on October 12 to the final retreat to the Ebro on September 23, the Mac-Paps served as what they themselves would ironically describe as "premature anti-Fascists."

In Canada, their services were hardly appreciated. Maxime Raymond was one Quebec nationalist who did not deplore their departure: "it will rid us of these undesirable people, provided they do not return here." Ernest Lapointe, as Minister of Justice, pushed through a Foreign Enlistment Act threatening two years of prison for any Canadian who served against a friendly power. He then applied the law to both sides in the Spanish civil war. When the international brigades were finally repatriated late in 1938, Canadian officials carefully ensured that private sponsors guaranteed to pay the costs of transportation and medical rehabilitation. The Mac-Paps would not be numbered among Canada's veterans. O. D. Skelton, Under-Secretary of State for External Affairs and guardian of Canada's isolation, had the grace to acknowledge that some people had stood up to the European dictators: ". . . there is a lot to be said for the conclusion that if the people of Canada really wanted to get into somebody's war, they might choose Negrin's instead of Neville's." Still, it was Britain's Neville Chamberlain who had set the pattern of appeasing the dictators and it was a policy which King and his colleagues showed no sign of criticizing.

Perhaps they were realists. The newsreels had their impact. Gradually Canadians realized that they were no longer far from inflammable materials and they had never been fireproof. In the United States, long-range bombers had been developed by 1936 which, with only one refuelling stop, could reach Europe across the Arctic Circle. By extension, a European power could hit back with similar aircraft by seizing a base in Canada's Arctic. Canada would be helpless to interfere. The Bennett years had endowed the armed forces with splendid new barracks at Barriefield, Trenton and Bennett's own constituency of Calgary but that was all. In 1932, the Tory government had authorized an RCAF reserve, but its five squadrons each mustered four DeHavilland Moths. In his final appeal before becoming chairman of the National Research Council, McNaughton warned that Canada had not a single anti-aircraft gun. The fortress armament at Halifax and Esquimalt was obsolete and defective. Canada had only twenty-five service aircraft, all of them obsolete, and not a single bomb. Never had Canada been so defenceless.

McNaughton's memorandum greeted the returning Liberals. Mackenzie King had no more taste for military spending than he ever had and his choice for Minister of National Defence, Ian Mackenzie, was a hard-drinking CEF veteran from British Columbia, unlikely to stir the cabinet. The Depression had not made Canadians warlike. Maurice Hankey, secretary of the British Committee of Imperial Defence, concluded that French Canadians had been joined in their hostility to the defence alliance by "great blocks of unabsorbed aliens" and by the "highbrows" of the Canadian Institute of International Affairs who "talk a lot of dreadful 'slop'." For the first time, Hankey's superiors began seriously to wonder whether they really could count on Canada in a future war. The government sent senior Canadian officers to Washington to make contacts Mackenzie King now discouraged with the War Office in London. Americans must be reassured that Canada would defend her share of the hemisphere. The commitment was stated publicly when President Roosevelt came north in 1938 to receive an honorary degree from Queen's

University. The people of the United States, declared the American president, "would not stand idly by if domination of Canadian soil is threatened by any other empire." "We too have obligations as a good, friendly neighbour," King replied, "and one of these is to see that, at our own instance, our country is made as immune from attack or possible invasion as we can reasonably be expected to make it. . . ."

Continental defence created entirely new and unfamiliar military priorities for a country whose strategic thinking had rested somewhere between "Buster" Brown's Defence Plan No. 1 and the despatch of the CEF. Now it was the turn of the neglected RCAF to grow and even for the humiliated RCN to expand while the militia, useful mainly for expeditionary forces, was relegated to third place. Indeed, in a drastic exercise urged by the staff since 1931, its paper strength of fifteen divisions was cut in half. Understrength militia units were disbanded, forced into amalgamation or converted to artillery, tanks or armoured cars (without, of course, buying the necessary equipment). Even with new funds and modest encouragement, only 46,251 militia trained in 1938-39 compared to 55,000 on the eve of war in 1913. There would not have been arms or equipment for more.

By previous humble standards, there was no such restraint for the navy. Between 1936 and 1939, permanent force strength doubled to 191 officers and 1,799 ratings. Two more destroyers were purchased each year and Canadian shipyards delivered four new minesweepers. Air force expansion was far more dramatic. Even the Bennett government had ordered a few fighting aircraft before it fell but the RCAF's budget soared from $3,130,000 in 1935-36 to more than $30 million by 1939-40. Late in 1936, the air force finally lost the civil aviation tasks that had carried it through its early years. New squadrons were authorized and in 1938 the RCAF finally emerged from subordination to the Chief of the General Staff and his local military district commanders. A Chief of the Air Staff, Air Vice Marshal G. M. Croil, controlled the expanding RCAF through Eastern and Western Air Commands and an Air Training Command. For the militia, King's government offered only modernized coast defences, guns that would never fire in anger.

In her belated drive for rearmament, Canada found herself in a new arms race with most of the western world. Britain's armaments industry, to which Canadian officers instinctively turned, found itself hopelessly backlogged as the British themselves struggled to re-equip their forces. Thanks to Ralston's refusal in 1929 to develop a Canadian arms industry, the Canadian forces could only wait while manufacturers cautiously pondered the arguments for entering a risky and innovative field. Industrialists were hardly encouraged by the experience of Toronto's John Inglis Company. A Department of National Defence contract to manufacture 7,000 Bren light machine guns was diligently transformed into a major scandal by Colonel George Drew, an Ontario Conservative. The charge that the Liberals had handed the Bren contract to a washing machine factory was false but it sounded delightfully plausible to citizens indoctrinated to associate arms production with original sin.

Britain, struggling to overcome its own desperate unreadiness, also turned to Canada to place a few orders for airframes. It also wanted men. Since 1919, a steady trickle of Canadians had crossed the Atlantic to join the RAF, maintaining some of the wartime link. In 1938, the British turned to Canada with an invitation to sponsor a modest aircrew training programme for the RAF. They were firmly rebuffed. The reason was simple. If Canada were to go to war, there was one aspect of preparedness that would be infinitely more important than trained pilots or modern equipment. The country must be united. To bring British training to Canada in peacetime would arouse a violent chorus of opposition from Quebec and beyond. It could not be risked.

In 1938, it seemed inconceivable that Canadians would agree to involvement in a war to save Europeans from themselves once again. Only the Communists and their friends preached incessantly for war against Hitler. Their limited credibility as upholders of democracy crumbled with news of Stalin's show trials and purges. In French Canada, clerical and nationalist opinion favoured Mussolini and Portugal's Dr. Salazar if not necessarily Hitler. Quebec's seemingly eternal allegiance to the Liberals had been badly shaken in 1936 by the election of Maurice Duplessis at the head of a coalition of conservatives, nationalists and isolationists. King and his colleagues had to be cautious. Quebec was not alone. Twenty years was not long enough to forget the horror of the earlier war. The illustrated magazines and the newsreels told Canadians that any new war would expand those horrors out of recognition. The bomber, a British prime minister had warned in 1935, would always get through. Frank Underhill, a sergeant in the CEF, a professor of history at the University of Toronto and editor of the *Canadian Forum,* caught a mood when he wrote: "Elderly sadists of the last war are emerging from their obscurity to join the war-dance again, their eyes glistening and their mouths watering as they think of the young men whom they will send to slaughter." Canadians, he warned, should stuff their ears with the tax bills of the last war and ignore the European war cries.

In all of Mackenzie King's long political career, nothing was more astonishing than his achievement in bringing Canada united into war on September 10, 1939. There had never been any doubt in his own mind that Canada would be at Britain's side. "If a great and clear call of duty comes," he had declared in 1923, "Canada will respond, whether or not the United States responds, as she did in 1914. . . ." King could feel a bitter resentment at the forces which dragged Canada back to the maelstrom. "The idea that every twenty years this country should automatically and as a matter of course take part in a war overseas for democracy or self-determination of other small nations, that a country that has all it can do to run itself should feel called upon to save, periodically, a continent that cannot run itself . . . seems to many a nightmare and sheer madness." Yet it was a nightmare and a madness that King sadly prepared himself to face.

Throughout the winter of 1939, King spared no pains to warn that if Britain faced the threat of air bombardment, Canada would be in the war. Even clearer was another message: if Canada went to war, there would be no conscription. It was a pledge promptly echoed by King's new Conservative opponent, R. J. Manion. A wartime medical officer and Bennett's Minister of Health, Manion sought to appeal to Quebec voters with a French Canadian wife and the one promise that might reconcile Quebeckers to the Conservatives. King's own sentimental allegiance to England, if not to its political leadership, led him to the master stroke of his pre-war preparations, the Royal Visit of 1939. The tour of the soft-spoken, diffident king and his gracious, out-going consort accomplished what not even monarchists could have imagined as possible. For a few weeks, Canadians were lifted out of themselves. Communities vied with each other to achieve pageantry and colour. The emotions would sometimes be short-lived. Montreal's Mayor Camillien Houde would be interned little more than a year after the warmth of his welcome to the royal couple had astonished Canadians.

What mattered was that Canadian isolationism had been mildly anaesthetized. It still slept on September 1, 1939, when Hitler's tanks plunged across the Polish border.

Total
War
at Home

5

Even before war broke out in September, 1939, the meagre Canadian defence forces had taken every possible precaution. Four destroyers left Esquimalt on August 31, bound for Halifax via the Panama Canal. The torpedoing of the *Athenia* on September 3 was warning enough that the U-Boat war would resume where it had ended some twenty years earlier. The RCAF sent its aged aircraft to war stations on the coasts. Some of them, forced down in Maine by bad weather, narrowly escaped internment. A few American-built aircraft, purchased before the war, were flown to border locations and painfully winched across. American neutrality laws were bent but not broken since Canada was not at war.

Mackenzie King had promised that Parliament would decide and it did. Not until September 10 had Canada formally declared war on Germany and a mixture of accident and inexperience delayed the actual royal signature of the declaration until November. The charade saved face for Quebec Liberals like Ernest Lapointe. After all, Canada was in the war for much the same reason as in 1914, not for an overdue reckoning with Nazism but because of a continuing sentimental link with Britain—shared as fully by Mackenzie King as by any of his countrymen. That link divided Canada as much as ever. In Quebec, nationalist organizations met to denounce any involvement in the war. French Canadians were not alone. In Parliament, J. S. Woodsworth of the CCF spoke out for the pacifist wing of his party when he joined two Quebec members in lonely opposition to the declaration of war. Outside Parliament, the Communist crusade against Fascism had ended abruptly with the Molotov-Ribbentrop pact of August 27, 1939. Fresh orders from Moscow sent the disciplined Communist cadres out to disrupt the war effort, particularly by influencing key labour unions.

At first, there did not seem to be much of a Canadian war effort to impede. For all his emotional commitment to Britain and the Crown, King looked on the war with a sense of profound despair. If Hitler did not win, Stalin would. Was any effort worth it? Canada's three chiefs of staff had put together a mobilization plan estimated to cost $500 million. The cabinet promptly chopped it in half. Instead of three infantry divisions, the army must be content with two and only one of them would be sent overseas "for the time being." Naval expansion was similarly trimmed and only the RCAF plans to expand aircrew training passed virtually unscathed. An enlarged air force could be justified for home defence; it did not threaten conscription and, above all, the money would stay in Canada.

Few Canadians faced the war with enthusiasm. Some English-language newspapers, led by Dafoe's *Winnipeg Free Press* and George McCullagh's newly merged *Globe and Mail* opened a patriotic chorus but their main effect was to alarm Quebec. The national mood owed something to memories of an earlier war and even more to the morale-sapping Great Depression. Most of the men who crowded recruiting depots were looking for a job, not a crusade. French-speaking units (this time carefully included in the mobilization plan) were among the first to meet their quota of recruits. Later, soldiers would jokingly refer to the men of the 1st Canadian Division as the "Breadliners." Guided by their fathers' memories, recruits showed a marked preference for the artillery or even the medical corps.

King and his colleagues had only one guiding light as they set out to lead Canada through the war: they would avoid any policy which had brought division to Canada and disaster to the Conservative party in the earlier war. The menace of conscription was obvious. So was the politically corrosive effect of inflation, profiteering and hoarding. One of the first applications of a newly revived War Measures Act was a Wartime Prices and Trade Board. At first modest in its powers and their exercise, the WPTB and a flock of related agencies would expand to affect the existence of every Canadian. The earlier war had been financed by debt and inflation: under two austere Nova Scotians, J. L. Ralston and his successor, J. L. Ilsley, the new war would be conducted, so far as possible, on a pay-as-you-go basis. To King, Sir Robert Borden's fundamental error had been in sacrificing his party, his country and himself for an allied victory. In the Second World War, sacrifice would certainly be demanded of individuals and almost 45,000 Canadians would give their lives. For Canada as a whole, however, there would be no talk of the last man or the last dollar. The Second World War was and would remain, except perhaps for the desperate summer of 1940, a war of limited liability.

Just how limited became apparent when the British government revived its 1938 request for Canadian participation in a major aircrew training programme. To train the 50,000 pilots and navigators the Royal Air Force estimated as its wartime requirement, Canada's huge spaces and safe skies seemed ideal. In the earlier war, pilot training in Canada was a major explanation of the fact that a third of RAF pilots in 1918 had been Canadian. When Mackenzie King was approached on September 26, 1939, his reaction mingled delight and dismay. If only Chamberlain had approached him ten days earlier, the government might not have felt obliged to offer even a single infantry division as an overseas expeditionary force. Aircrew training would mean that wartime spending would remain mostly within Canada. No matter how many young Canadians might be sent overseas as pilots or observers it was inconceivable that their numbers would ever have to be reinforced by conscription.

King's satisfaction was muted when serious negotiations for the British Commonwealth Air Training Plan began. Like some other Canadians, King's attachment to England did not always extend to Englishmen. Lord Riverdale, a blustering Sheffield businessman, was ideally suited to arouse Canadian prejudices. Both Britain and Canada wanted a bargain but both sides needed a settlement. The RAF needed aircrew; King wanted a wartime activity that would forestall any risk of conscription. The rancorous negotiations concluded on December 17, the prime minister's birthday and always a propitious moment for the superstitious King. He had won most of his points. Canada would administer the plan; Britain would find Canadian dollars to pay for Australian and New Zealand cadets. The official statement dutifully proclaimed that the BCATP was Canada's "most effective contribution to the war effort." King and his colleagues seemed untroubled by the fact that most Canadian graduates of the plan would be absorbed in the RAF or that new RCAF squadrons to be formed in Britain would be manned by British ground crew and paid for by British taxpayers. Principles which Canadian soldiers had respected since 1899 were overlooked for Canada's youngest service.

During the BCATP negotiations, an angry King had blurted the comment, "This is not our war." The phrase might have caused some domestic outrage had it been widely publicized but it certainly reflected a lot of Canadian feeling in 1939. King's caution and shrewd political timing allowed him to administer a lesson to both the pro-war and anti-war flanks of public opinion. Quebec's Maurice Duplessis, whose Union Nationale had held power since 1936, judged that the war offered him a chance to restore his fragmented, fumbling regime to power. Surely Quebec voters would respond to a furious assault on conscription and Ottawa's centralizing ambitions. King and Ernest Lapointe met the challenge. Liberal cabinet ministers barnstormed Quebec constituencies pledging to resign their portfolios if Duplessis won the election and swearing undying opposition to conscription. Duplessis's bombast and his record of broken promises assured his own defeat on October 25; federal intervention guaranteed it.

In neighbouring Ontario the government was Liberal but the premier, Mitchell Hepburn, was about as fond of King as was Duplessis. The basis of the quarrel was old, personal and political but the war opened up a new front. Hepburn toured the makeshift barracks and drafty exhibition halls where Canada's new army mustered, denounced the all-too-evident lack of uniforms and equipment, and forced a stinging vote of censure on the federal government through the Ontario Legislature. When Parliament reassembled early in 1940, members dutifully listened to the speech from the throne, adjourned and returned to discover that King had dissolved the House of Commons in their absence. Not Parliament but the people would decide. Opposition members raged but to no effect. In Canada's second wartime election, the national war effort was again an issue. "Fighting Bob" Manion, chosen as

Tory leader because his charm and his French-Canadian wife would placate Quebec, opted instead for a National government and a whole-hearted commitment to the war. His proposal chilled Quebec and aroused little warmth elsewhere. On March 26, 1940, Canadian voters delivered the most massive electoral landslide in their history: 184 Liberals to only 39 Conservatives, 10 Social Credit, 8 CCFers and 6 assorted independents. The aged pacifist, J. S. Woodsworth, barely held his Winnipeg seat; Manion was personally defeated. If King's war effort was as phony as the war along the distant Maginot line, it was entirely to Canadian taste.

Barely two weeks after Canadians had endorsed the government's half-hearted mobilization, the storm broke. On April 9, Hitler's troops struck at Norway. A month later, as the British and French struggled to help the Norwegians, the German blitzkrieg smashed into the Netherlands and Belgium. Within eleven days, the German columns had reached the English Channel. The threatened catastrophe of 1914 and 1918 had occurred with terrifying speed. On June 4, German soldiers entered Dunkirk, ending the desperate, harrowing struggle to rescue the British Expeditionary Force. Eight days later, General Maxime Weygand advised the French government to seek an armistice.

In the crisis, Canada had done her pathetic best. The 1st Division, short of every kind of equipment, had reached England in the winter of 1939. King had reluctantly approved the appointment of Major-General A. G. L. McNaughton as its commander. The old general might be a Tory but he was eager to use science and technology to save lives. In the circumstances, King might forgive his advice to Bennett and his troublesome urging of pre-war preparedness. During the 1940 crisis, McNaughton's division had been considered first for the Norwegian campaign and then as part of a desperate bid to retain a foothold in the Brittany peninsula. A complete Canadian brigade was landed at Brest and then even more hurriedly evacuated, minus most of its painfully acquired guns and vehicles. Meanwhile, Canada's four available destroyers were despatched to Britain and her single modern squadron joined a Canadian-manned RAF squadron already in England as a tiny but useful contribution to the Battle of Britain.

The magnitude of the 1940 disaster dawned only slowly. Within a month Britain's major allies had been knocked out of the war. By joining Hitler, Mussolini's Italy carried the war to the Mediterranean and Africa. As the largest Dominion, Canada was suddenly Britain's biggest partner. As the British struggled to arm and equip the soldiers rescued from France, McNaughton's raw division found itself almost alone in the front line of Britain's defences. In such a crisis, there could be no haggling about prices and contracts. Everything Canada could conceivably produce would be needed somewhere. The most urgent need was aircraft for the BCATP. Britain could no longer be the source. Canada must seek equipment wherever it could be found, in the neutral United States or from its own ill-developed aircraft industry. There was hardly a protest when Parliament passed the National Resources Mobilization Act, giving the government sweeping powers to control manpower—though for home defence only. When Montreal's popular mayor, Camillien Houde, protested at national registration, he was immediately swept into an internment camp. So were hundreds of pro-Nazis, pro-Fascists and Communist labour leaders, all of them suddenly intolerable with the advent of "total war."

In the crisis, the phony-war constraints on the three armed forces were forgotten. The RCN's ship-building programme was expanded to meet a German U-Boat threat which could soon be launched from virtually the entire coastline of Europe. The army was the service most affected. The new Chief of the General Staff, Major-General H. D. G. Crerar finally cut a historic knot in the summer of 1940 by proclaiming that the militia would henceforth be known as the "Canadian Army." A second and a third division were authorized for overseas as soon as they could be organized. A proposed armoured brigade would expand into a 4th and then a 5th Armoured Division. Meanwhile, it would train with First World War Renault tanks, dug out of the Texas sand by Major-General F. F. Worthington and purchased as scrap. At the outset of war, King switched the defence portfolio from the genial but often inebriated Ian Mackenzie to his own protege, Norman Rogers. On June 10, 1940, when Rogers died in an aircraft crash, J. L. Ralston returned to the Department of National Defence. His integrity as shining as his high domed forehead, his appetite for painstaking detail undiminished, Ralston could hardly have been a greater contrast from the previous war's Sam Hughes. As Associate Minister for Air, Ralston inherited a colleague who was both bibulous and shrewd: C. G. "Chubby" Power. He soon acquired, as Associate Minister of National Defence for the Navy, Angus L. Macdonald, summoned from the premiership of Nova Scotia. It was an impressive team for a task of superhuman magnitude.

Between the wars, it had been fashionable for Canada's representatives to boast that they were producers, not consumers, of security. Their fireproof house would never be threatened; even their meagre defence effort was maintained for the benefit of others. In 1940, the truth was very different. A disarmed and helpless Canada depended on the battered remnants of Britain's defenders to keep the war from her own shores. Suddenly, Canada was also dependent on the United States. Before the war, President Roosevelt had used two occasions to remind Canadians that they shared the protection of the Monroe Doctrine; with the collapse of Britain seemingly imminent, Canada might now need that protection. The Americans, launched on their own rearmament drive, had no illusions about Canada's defenceless state. After thinking about the problem, Roosevelt lifted his telephone early on the afternoon of Friday, August 16, 1940, summoned the

Canadian prime minister and arranged to meet him next day at Ogdensburg opposite the little St. Lawrence town of Prescott.

King was ecstatic. Only American intervention could save the allied cause. At Ogdensburg, as Britain's senior allied leader, he would become that misnamed "linchpin" between the old world and the new. A politician who shied away from even the faintest hint of commitment to any British military scheme now enthusiastically welcomed Roosevelt's suggestion of a joint commission on common defence problems, particularly on Canada's Atlantic coast. King wanted it called a "board," Roosevelt added the word "permanent" and, in a splendid example of diplomacy by press release, the Permanent Joint Board on Defence was announced. Parliament was given nothing to decide. In return for consultation, Canada opened her territory for American defence installations. A delighted King envisioned himself as the architect of a new Anglo-American alliance. In London, Winston Churchill, successor to the feeble Neville Chamberlain, grumbled that there might be "two opinions" about that.

Indeed, to his quiet indignation, the Canadian prime minister was largely ignored in his chosen role as intermediary. When Churchill and Roosevelt met off Argentia, Newfoundland, in 1941 to issue their resounding Atlantic Charter, King was not invited. The much more important destroyers-for-bases deal of October, 1940 ignored Canada's obvious concern about permanent American bases in Newfoundland. Britain's urgent need for escort ships, however obsolete, and American concern with hemispheric defence paid no heed to Canadian sensibilities. Canada had to be content with six of the aged American destroyers. In Newfoundland, she outbid American ranks and numbers with her own military and air garrison.

The key sector for Canadian-American joint defence was not the Atlantic but the Pacific. The dawn raid on Pearl Harbor on December 7, 1941 not only opened the Pacific War but culminated generations of atavistic concern for the "Yellow Peril." After 1938 Ottawa had taken Pacific defences less seriously although Ian Mackenzie's political interests had ensured that, by 1939, Esquimalt was better armed than Halifax. Ignorance of Pacific realities also helps to explain why the government, on General Crerar's advice, blithely permitted two ill-trained Canadian battalions to be despatched to Hong Kong in November, 1941. A month later, they were fighting for their lives. Of the 1,975 Canadians who left Vancouver, 557 perished in battle or in Japanese prison camps. The survivors were permanently marked by their savage ordeal.

In Canada itself the Pacific War had relatively very little direct impact. On June 20, 1942, a Japanese submarine lobbed a few shells in the general direction of the Estevan Point lighthouse. It submerged hurriedly with the record of having launched the first enemy attack on Canada since 1814. The indirect consequences of the war were more serious. For many British Col-

umbians, the war was an opportunity for a final solution of part of their perennial grievance against oriental immigration. A 1940 investigation had confirmed that neither the army nor the RCMP believed that Japanese Canadians presented any significant security risk. That made no difference at all in
a province where Liberal politicians like Ian Mackenzie had exploited anti-
Oriental prejudice to get elected. On the shabby pretext that Japanese Canadians needed protection from angry whites, 1,700 male Japanese nationals
and then all 19,000 Japanese Canadians in British Columbia were interned.
In a clumsy and sometimes callous programme, the internees were relocated
in makeshift camps and ghost towns in the province's interior. At Slocan, they
spent the winter in tents and a leaky hockey rink. Meanwhile, their market
gardens and fishing boats were sold to white neighbours at absurdly low
prices. Entire families, from grandparents to small infants, crowded into
internment camps. The men were segregated and moved to the Prairies and
Ontario for agricultural or forestry labour. Treatment of the Japanese Canadians contrasted with the treatment of German and Italian internees and of
Nazi and Fascist sympathizers. King's government and white British Colum-
bians shared the responsibility for a national shame but few Canadians outside the Protestant churches and the CCF bothered to protest the treatment of
their fellow citizens.

The Japanese-Canadian internment of 1942 diverted resources needed
elsewhere. So did the panic-stricken demand for troops to defend the British
Columbia coast. In March of 1942, Ottawa approved creation of a 6th and
part of an 8th Division for a new Pacific Command and, for no very good
reason, a 7th Divison for the Atlantic coast. Most of the men were found
through the National Resources Mobilization Act. Instead of the original
thirty-day training period, men were drafted for longer periods of service and
eventually for the duration of the war. Conscription for home defence was no
breach of the government pledge, even in Quebec opinion. By the summer of
1942, 34,000 Canadian soldiers were located in British Columbia. The
Americans faced a more immediate threat to their territory. The Japanese
had occupied the rocky, fog-bound outer islands of the Aleutian chain. It was
easy to believe, as Japanese power spread irresistibly across Southeast Asia,
the Philippines and Indonesia in the winter and spring of 1942, that it could
also reach out easily to seize a foothold in North America. If the threat was
far-fetched militarily, it was politically all too real.

The result was an extraordinary drive of American military and then
civilian manpower to ram through the Alaska Highway and to bring fuel from
the Imperial Oil field at Norman Wells along the Canol pipeline. For the most
part, Canadians were utterly unaware that the United States Army had simply
made itself at home in the Northwest, treating native claims, environmental
concerns and Canadian sovereignty with affable indifference. At the height of
construction, 33,000 Americans were working in the Canadian North.
Ottawa offered no protest and not until the British High Commissioner,

Malcolm MacDonald, reported on his visit to the region was Mackenzie King much concerned. The government response was to appoint a former Canadian Legion official, Major-General W. W. Foster, as "Special Commissioner for Defence Projects" and to send him west in an RCAF aircraft to show the flag.

The Americans made some amends. Having lost heavily in a bloody battle to recapture Attu in the Aleutians, an American general invited Major-General George Pearkes of Pacific Command to contribute some of his men to an expedition to take the neighbouring island of Kiska. The friendly offer triggered a flurry of diplomatic exchanges as Americans discovered that, in Canada, politicians and not soldiers approved the disposition of soldiers. The result was an anti-climax. The 13th Canadian Infantry Brigade, largely composed of NRMA men, trained vigorously, adapted to American methods and finally joined in the landing on August 15, 1943 only to discover that the Japanese had unobtrusively departed. For six months, the Canadians remained on the barren island while their officers engaged the Department of National Revenue in a fascinating dispute. The Canadian camp was a few miles west of the International Date Line and technically outside the Western Hemisphere and hence exempt from income tax. Since NRMA conscripts could not legally serve outside the hemisphere and Ottawa wanted the taxes, the claim was ignored. Ottawa wanted taxes because Canada's war effort, at least at home, was no longer limited.

There was one activity of the earlier war which had not really resumed in 1939: munitions production. The 1938 Bren gun scandal had only deepened King's antipathy to peacetime arms production. It alarmed Canadian industrialists, too. When war came, the British had their own high unemployment to overcome with defence contracts and very little business—twenty-five pounder field guns in Sorel, airframes in Fort William—was available for Canada. Manufacturers refused to tool up for a Canadian military market which would be small and possibly unprofitable.

That changed in April, 1940. Clarence Decatur Howe was an American-born engineer with an impressive reputation as a designer and builder of Canadian grain elevators. With little business in the thirties and much to criticize, Howe had gravitated to the Liberal party and to Parliament in 1935. King made him Minister of Transport and watched nervously as his devoutly free enterprise colleague created the publicly-owned Trans-Canada Airlines. On April 9, 1940, Howe became Minister of Munitions and Supply. Almost overnight, he became Canada's most dynamic war leader. Short in stature, terse in manner, Howe wore a perpetually rumpled look. Part of his brilliance was in finding able subordinates, judging their limitations and putting them to work. "Howe's Boys," most of them leading businessmen, brought a badly needed and infectious dynamism to Ottawa's corroded decision-making. Howe's second strength was a constructive vision, backed by the courage to see ideas through. The spring of 1940 was his challenge and his opporunity.

"We have no idea of the cost," he admitted to aides, clamouring to know what to produce, "but before the war is over everything will be needed so let's go ahead anyway."

To beat the competition, he approved dummy corporations to purchase machine tools, silk and rubber. Between the War Measures Act and the emergency legislation creating his new department, there was virtually no economic power Howe could not claim. Even the provinces could be compelled, under emergency powers, to hand over their natural resources. Controllers were appointed to allocate scarce stocks of steel, timber, oil, machine tools, metals and power. With aircraft for the BCATP as his highest priority, Howe created Federal Aircraft, one of the first of twenty-eight Crown corporations he would devise, and ordered aircraft engines in the United States. Determined to penetrate the confusion over Britain's own war needs, Howe set off for England late in 1940. He survived the torpedoing of his ship and returned a popular war hero, with a lengthy shopping list.

Like Flavelle in the earlier war, Howe was surrounded by critics, and his brush with death probably saved his career. Furious quarrels disrupted aircraft production. H. R. Macmillan, the Timber Controller, plotted Howe's downfall. J. L. Ilsley and the Finance Department were horrified by Howe's freewheeling policies. Mackenzie King, on the advice of his secretaries, prepared to split the department. Yet Howe's power survived intact. His dynamism was vital to a government suspected of being half-hearted. King had hoped that Canada's main war effort would be in industrial production and Howe was making that hope come true. Within the cabinet, his demand for more and more workers made him a competitor for the manpower demanded by the three service ministers. Meanwhile, the half-million unemployed of 1939 had dwindled to only 200,000 in 1941 and to virtually zero in 1942.

In two years, Canada's gross national product grew by 47 per cent. The automotive industry, most easily adapted to war needs, tripled its deliveries while iron and steel production doubled. Howe boasted that Canadians could produce anything and he proudly presented Canadian-made binoculars to anyone who might be impressed. In fact, Canadian factories could not produce aircraft engines, operational tanks or warships larger than a frigate. The Ram and Grizzly tanks, designed in Canada by General Worthington, were assembled largely from American components and never saw action except as gun mounts and armoured personnel carriers. Most of what was produced came from British or American designs and Canadian factories were sometimes slow in adapting their products to the latest technical improvements. Yet Howe had good reason to boast. Canada delivered most of the vehicles that carried the British Eighth Army across North Africa. Workers in plants that had not even been a dream in 1940 put together Mosquito and Lancaster bombers, artillery guns, wireless sets, radar equipment and some of the apparatus from which the first atomic bomb would be developed.

Ilsley's concern about Howe's carefree spending was well-founded. As in the First World War, Canada's war production depended on a three-sided trading and financial relationship with Britain and the United States. Canada could buy vital components (as well as more routine civilian needs) from the Americans only as long as Britain could pay for her purchases in dollars. By early 1941, the system was about to collapse. The huge reserves and investments that had carried Britain most of the way through the 1914-18 war had never been rebuilt. The British were bankrupt and Canada's own trading deficit with the United States was out of control. Britain's crisis was solved, at least for the war years, when the United States Congress approved lend-lease. However, the terms of lend-lease required British orders to be placed in the American market. Canada might eventually qualify for her own lend-lease arrangement but only after all her assets in the United States had been sold. Postwar trade with the United States would become virtually impossible.

While Ottawa feverishly bought time by guaranteeing payment for British purchases, King, Howe and Clifford Clark, the Deputy Minister of Finance, sought a way out. The answer came, as in 1918, from the United States' own rearmament programme. As before, Canada needed American credit and Americans needed arms and military supplies. The result, with rather more fanfare than Sir Robert Borden's earlier arrangement, was the Hyde Park agreement, personally negotiated between King and Roosevelt at the President's Hudson River estate on Sunday, April 20, 1941. Americans would buy in Canada through Howe's Department of Munitions and Supply. Britain's debt to Canada could pile up in London as an unconvertible sterling balance. In E. P. Taylor, an agile and quick-minded entrepreneur, Howe found the ideal Canadian agent to cruise the American market for defence orders.

Hyde Park solved one problem. There were many more. Answers often inspired new Crown corporations like Research Enterprises, developing radar and optical equipment, or Polymer Ltd., created in 1942 to manufacture artificial rubber from a German patent when natural stocks had been cut off by the victorious Japanese. At Malton, National Steel Car's big aircraft plant was plagued with trouble. When the company ignored Howe's final ultimatum, he seized the factory in October, 1942, reorganized it as Victory Aircraft, and made it a success. Organized labour was harder to manage. Like Flavelle at the Imperial Munitions Board, Howe was caught between anti-union employers and a determination by union organizers to make gains in a period of full employment. The worst crisis came in July, 1942, when workers at the giant aluminum smelter at Arvida, Quebec, went on strike. Company officials insisted that the strike had been fomented by an enemy agent and warned that the giant smelter pots would "freeze" if they were not started within twenty-four hours. Alarmed at the threat to aircraft production, Howe believed them. Troops must be sent. No one had told him about the law. Troops could not move without a requisition from Quebec's attorney-general. He was not available. The acting Minister of Justice was ill. General Crerar, as chief of staff, would obey only the law. The pots froze. A furious Howe resigned and returned only when granted full power to call out the army in cases of sabotage. An investigation revealed no saboteurs at Arvida. The culprits were excessive heat and a language barrier between company officials and their French-speaking employees.

Howe and his dollar-a-year men found themselves more at home with corporate managers. Like most Canadians, Howe expected that postwar Canada would slump back into depression conditions. Manufacturers were converted to defence production not by the official coercion applied to humbler citizens but by the ingenious device of accelerated depreciation. Between 1940 and 1945, depreciation privileges cost the remaining tax-payers $514 million, most of it for machinery and equipment. Howe could argue that the country's capital stock was improved and Canadian workers had acquired new skills in mass production that might be applied to jobs undreamed of in the Canada of the thirties. Businessmen, accustomed to dealing with provincial governments, found a tough but like-minded authority in Ottawa and they gradually learned to appreciate the experience. Ottawa's capacity to manage the postwar economy had its roots in Howe's wartime department.

Canadian self-congratulation and Howe's infectious dynamism established an impression of legendary wartime productive achievements. A moribund industrial base was revived, retooled and set to tasks that would have seemed unimaginable in 1939. Industrial backwardness could even be an asset. It would have been wasteful to convert American factories to produce British-pattern equipment. Canada was a more logical source since its production would be a net addition, not a diversion. There was a price in starting from scratch. Inland shipyards, accustomed to building cheap, uncomplicated vessels for the Great Lakes, adjusted painfully to the complexities of warship construction. Aircraft production, a brilliant success story in the building of an industry, was much less impressive in meeting its production targets. In 1943, when Canadian war production reached its peak, 1,239,327 Canadian men and women delivered $8,725,350,000 worth of industrial production. Wartime cost accounting tended to hide the inefficiency of workers and managers learning their jobs. The wartime pay-off in ships, planes and military vehicles was respectable but the real benefit of the industrial effort was to give Canada a chance to be competitive in the postwar world. That was C. D. Howe's greatest vision.

Not all of Howe's colleagues appreciated his dominance. Canada's own military needs often held third place in Howe's priorities behind the United

States and Britain. Canadian generals, admirals and air marshals were as unwelcome in munitions policy-making as they were in most other branches of the Liberal government. When Ralston sought Canadian repesentation on the allied Munitions Assignment Board, Howe instead manoeuvred Canada onto two smaller committees dealing with raw materials and with production. In Howe's eyes, these were more central to his concerns and they included no military representation. In fact, the chief issue between Howe and Ralston was the competing demands of industry and the fighting forces. In his usual blunt fashion, Howe shared his frustrations with the House of Commons in June, 1942: "our whole war effort," he claimed, "is being distorted at the present time by the undue emphasis now being placed on men for the army overseas."

Howe's public complaint went to the heart of one issue neither he nor his colleagues could resolve: eleven million Canadians, fewer than eight million of them over eighteen years of age, were not enough to meet civilian and military needs. A country which had too many people in the 1930s now had too few. Even in June of 1940, the problem had loomed. A National Labour Supply Council had wrestled with the problem. So had an Inter-Departmental Committee on Labour Co-ordination, three months later. With mixed feelings, all three armed services had established women's branches in July, 1941. The Labour Supply Council claimed that 2,124,000 of 7,863,000 adult Canadians might potentially be available for war needs but confessed that only 609,000 were actually free to serve and then only "if the most drastic measures were adopted." Companies must stop competing for manpower. More women must be employed in key industries. If workers would not move to jobs, the jobs must move to the workers.

Exhortation had severe limits. By October, 1941, the establishment of National Selective Service gave the government the means to act. A succession of regulations issued during 1942 gradually brought most working Canadians under the control of the NSS. In March, all farmers were frozen in agricultural occupations. In May, any unemployed man was compelled to register with NSS and, by June, no man or woman could take a new job without an NSS certificate. In September, women between twenty and twenty-four were ordered to register. No fit man, seventeen to forty-five could work as a stenographer, a taxi-driver, in advertising, real estate or in the manufacture of beer, bread, sporting goods, toys or a variety of "non-essential" occupations. It was, Mackenzie King boasted, "the negative compulsion of restrictions," not "the positive compulsion of allocation." From September 1, 1942, Selective Service demanded seven days' notice before an employer could fire or an employee could quit. Jobs could be advertised only through the NSS and its officials could compel an unemployed or an underemployed person to accept a designated job.

Yet, despite sweeping government powers, critical manpower shortages remained. All three armed services faced some difficulties but only in the army were they acute. The reasons were not surprising. Unlike 1914-18, young Canadians could choose among three services although high language barriers channelled most French-speaking recruits to the army. The RCAF was flooded with applicants for aircrew training. Romance, glamour, an officer's commission and a chance to learn a new skill were attractions to set against the exacting educational and physical standards. The navy, for many of its would-be seamen, operated in a remote and even exotic environment. Anyone with a father or an uncle in the World War knew what to expect from the army and what to avoid. Talk of a new, mechanized army fooled no one. One change in army recruiting policy aggravated its problems. A lesson of the previous war was that infantry needed high physical and mental standards to endure the strain of battle. Much of the cost of postwar rehabilitation could have been saved if the CEF had imposed higher medical standards. Politicians were indignant to discover that the army was rejecting men who would probably have been acceptable cannon fodder in the First World War. To Mackenzie King, it was only one more confirmation that the generals had deliberately set out to sabotage his no-conscription pledge.

Undoubtedly there were officers who, like other Canadians, believed in conscription. There were others who wanted an all-volunteer army. The truth was that they had very little to do with manpower policy. It was the politicians, not the soldiers, who insisted on holding large army garrisons and substantial air strength on each coast. The army had little enthusiasm for training NRMA men on thirty-day courses though they soon learned to use every kind of strategem, benevolent and malevolent, to persuade home defence conscripts to volunteer for general service. Their efforts, partially successful, left behind a bitter residue of men whose pride compelled them to take all the pressure and abuse the army could hand out. Such men would even glory in the contemptuous title of "Zombie." Fit and fully trained for a war that would virtually certainly never come to Canada, the NRMA men remained in uniform because coastal communities clamoured for their presence (and their business) and because Colonel Ralston knew that they were the only pool of trained reinforcements at his disposal.

Public pressure for conscription certainly existed. To many Canadians, it was the only logical response to the catastrophe of 1940. "Germany must be defeated," argued *Saturday Night*, "even if we all have to live like the Germans." The *Canadian Forum*, Underhill's magazine, wondered whether proconscriptionists were as keen on conscripting wealth as they were about getting men for the army but the message of total war was spreading. When Hitler attacked the Soviet Union in the summer of 1941, the message reached Canada's Communists. No longer was the war the dying gasp of capitalism but a patriotic struggle for democracy. The message did not reach French Canada. Ernest Lapointe's death in November, 1941 robbed Quebec of a powerful voice in Ottawa. His heir, P. J. A. Cardin, was no successor. Shock at the fall of France in 1940 had been followed by widespread Catholic and *nationaliste* approval of the Vichy regime of Marshal Philippe Petain, with its slogan of "Work, Family, Fatherland" and its hostility to Jews, Communists and Freemasons. General Charles de Gaulle's Free French found no such sympathy in Quebec.

Late in 1941, a leaderless Conservative party turned to its venerable stalwart of the 1920s, Arthur Meighen. Meighen was never quite the ogre Liberal propaganda had depicted to Quebec. He had struggled to understand French Canada. By proposing, long before, that a referendum precede any declaration of war, he had infuriated loyal Tories without reassuring Quebec. Indeed, Meighen believed that such a vote would give Ottawa the most powerful imaginable mandate for waging a serious war. As the new Conservative leader, he believed that he could rally his party and country behind an appeal for total war and conscription. The supporting evidence was easily mustered. The Canadian Legion, tired of merely organizing welfare and education programmes for soldiers overseas, had thrown its heart and soul into a "Call for Total War," rallying 500 national organizations in its support. Across English-speaking Canada, it was easy to make a fat collection of pro-conscription editorials and service club resolutions. Mingled in the strident appeals to imitate the Soviet and British examples of sacrifice were heavy traces of the old atavism. "There is among English-speaking Canadians," warned *Saturday Night,* "a wide-spread feeling that the real motive of the French-Canadian attitude toward conscription is the desire to improve the numerical strength of that element in the Canadian population, by avoiding its full proportional share of the casualties."

Ironically, the total war movement was fed by the government's own propaganda appeals for greater sacrifices and by its own decisions. A summer recruiting programme in 1941, backed by the government's full prestige, was a success. In its wake, General Crerar and Ralston persuaded a reluctant prime minister to endorse their overseas programme of five full divisions and their dream of a two-corps Canadian Army in the field. It might seem little enough for a country that had kept four rather larger divisions in the field during the earlier war, but armies had grown huge tails of service, maintenance and administrative personnel. Moreover, there had been no RCAF and little RCN competition for manpower.

The growing conscription crusade made King acutely nervous. A November, 1941 Gallup Poll showed 61 per cent of Canadians satisfied with the war effort but 60 per cent wanted conscription. Then came Pearl Harbor. In the United States, a peacetime draft for military training had been in effect since 1940; now it extended in earnest. In January, 1942, New Brunswick's Liberal premier, J. B. McNair, publicly called for conscription. A Toronto "Committee of 200," reminiscent of Godfrey's "Win-the-War League" in 1916, published advertisements for conscription. They might as well have campaigned openly for Arthur Meighen, seeking a parliamentary seat in a by-election in the Toronto riding of York South. King's old enemy, Mitch Hepburn, made no secret of his support for Meighen. The resourceful prime minister decided to kill the issue: he would announce a plebiscite to allow Canadians to decide whether or not to release him from his no-conscription pledge. It would satisfy a divided cabinet, reassure a dubious Pierre Cardin and undermine Meighen. Georges Pelletier, editor of *Le Devoir*, received solemn assurances that a plebiscite would divert the pro-conscription movement.

In the short term it proved a brilliant stroke. Robbed of his main issue, Meighen was cornered by his CCF opponent, Joe Noseworthy, for his antediluvian social and economic views. To national amazement York South voted CCF on February 9, 1942. A party bound for oblivion by its pacifist reputation and its support for Japanese Canadians suddenly found an astonishing surge of popular support. Yet the plebiscite had to be faced. All across Canada there were opponents of conscription, yet most people understood that King's promise had been offered specifically to Quebec, a fact underlined by the federal Liberal role in Quebec's 1939 election. Opposition to conscription, ranging from the St-Jean Baptiste Society to the Montreal Catholic Labour Council, rallied behind *la Ligue pour la défense du Canada*, led by Georges Pelletier, Maxime Raymond, the Liberal MP, Jean Drapeau, a future mayor of Montreal, and André Laurendeau, the future editor of *Le Devoir*. Quebec Liberals insisted that King had no intention of introducing conscription; the *Ligue* answered that no one asks to be released from a promise unless one intends to break it. Elsewhere in the country, the plebiscite vote seemed little more than a register of patriotism. Only in non-Anglo-Saxon constituencies was there much "No" support. The result of the April vote seemed predictable: 2,945,514 voted to relieve King of his pledge, 1,643,006 voted against. Support ranged from 82.4 per cent in Prince Edward Island and 82.3 per cent in Ontario to 69.1 per cent in New Brunswick. Military voters were 84 per cent in favour at bases in Canada but only 72 per cent in favour overseas. In Quebec, the outcome was almost precisely reversed: 72.9 per cent would not release King from his pledge. It was a proportion generally reflected in French-speaking constituencies outside Quebec.

The debate switched to Parliament. Pro-conscriptionists now had a mandate for action. King's answer gave Canadians a memorable quotation: "conscription if necessary," he promised, "but not necessarily conscription." By Bill 80, the National Resources Mobilization Act was amended to allow conscripts to be sent anywhere beyond the Western Hemisphere but only after Parliament had again been consulted. It was a compromise that seemed to enrage everyone. Cardin, embarrassed by his promises in the 1939 provincial election, quit. Furious that conscription would again be delayed, Ralston submitted his resignation. The Tories split on whether or not to vote for Bill 80. The CCF wandered between motions to conscript wealth and the tempting opportunity to appeal to Quebec's anti-conscription mood. Liberal MPs weighed the significance of a 61-7 vote in the Quebec legislature favouring voluntary recruiting. Months passed and slowly King's compromise prevailed. On July 7, when Bill 80 came to a vote, the outcome was 158-54, with 48 Quebec Liberals and 6 CCFers opposed. Ralston, tired and ailing, consented to forget his resignation. The prime minister, carefully filing the letter, did not.

The prime minister could reasonably assume, by the summer of 1942, that conscription might not, indeed, be necessary. For all the terrible setbacks of the year, the sinking of the *Renown* and the *Prince of Wales*, the unexpected fall of Singapore and Tobruk, 1942 was the turning point of the war. The huge resources of the United States had at last been committed to the allied cause. Soviet troops blunted the blitzkrieg at Stalingrad. At the end of the year, British soldiers finally defeated General Erwin Rommel's Afrika Korps at El Alamein. Canada had her own small share of disasters—Hong Kong at Christmas, 1941 and Dieppe in August, 1942. The total losses in dead and prisoners were less than five thousand, modest by the standard of even the Americans. Indeed, mingled with Ottawa's anxiety about conscription was a rival concern that Canada might not be seen to have done quite enough in the war. It never ceased to annoy King that most Canadians drew their inspiration from war leaders like Winston Churchill or Roosevelt and rarely from their own fussy, verbose prime minister. Politically, that might also damage the Liberal party.

In the earlier war, Sir Robert Borden had built Canada's overseas effort on his demand to be consulted, at least within the imperial family. For King, that family was symbolic at most, an encumbrance more often. In Canada's brief period as senior ally, he had sought no voice in grand strategy and Churchill would have been among the last British politicians to have conceded it. Once the Soviet Union and the United States were in the war, Canada was again a very junior partner, treated sometimes with scant ceremony. King rarely complained. As in peacetime, consultation always brought the risk of commitment. Twice the British and American war leaders met at the Chateau Frontenac hotel in Quebec City; both times the Canadian prime minister was invited to join Churchill and Roosevelt only for the photographs. Though both conferences settled matters that would affect Canadian forces, King cheerfully accepted his modest role in return for a little flattering publicity and some kind words.

King and most Canadians had chosen independence instead of the Empire but there was a price. The prime minister, claims Charles Stacey, was prepared to believe the worst of the British and the best of the Americans although, according to the record, Canadians seem to have been better treated by the Whitehall than by Washington. King counted heavily on his personal relationship with Roosevelt; to the American president and his advisers, Canada's claims to consideration only provided a dangerous precedent for Brazil, Costa Rica or other humble and opportunistic allies to demand equal time. According to Lester Pearson, who spent much of the war in the Canadian embassy in Washington, Mackenzie King "normally accepted the situation with a mild complaint or none at all." His friendship with the imperious Roosevelt was both too delicate and too politically valuable to be jeopardized by any disagreement.

Even in their own territory, Canadians might have found much to complain about. Militarily, both the Alaska Highway and the Canol pipeline turned out to be costly white elephants. So was the Crimson Route, a line of airfields across the northeastern Arctic, which the PJBD's Fiorello LaGuardia had insisted on constructing. Such undertakings kept up to 33,000 Americans busy in the Canadian North and presented Canadians with a postwar bill for permanent facilities. Ottawa paid it, as the price of continued Arctic sovereignty. In contrast, the British found Ottawa far less tolerant. To be fair, King found Churchill to be no more confiding an ally than Roosevelt. Britain wasted none of her influence in trying to squeeze her Commonwealth partners into any of the boards or committees through which the allied powers co-ordinated their efforts. The "functional principal," devised by Norman Robertson of the Department of External Affairs to justify Canadian inclusion in discussions of food, resources and munitions where she was a major contributor, proved more acceptable to Washington than to Whitehall. Canada's continued diplomatic link with the Vichy Republic after the fall of France exasperated the British, particularly when Canada denied Britain access to $400 million in French gold shipped to Ottawa early in the war to aid in American purchases. Quebec sentiment was the simple explanation. British interests had better luck in Toronto. In January, 1944, Lord Halifax, the British ambassador in Washington, delighted a business audience with arguments for a joint imperial foreign policy for the postwar world. Mackenzie King was furious when he learned of the speech: "Hitler could not have improved on the proposals as a way to break up the Empire," he fumed to an unsuspecting governor-general.

Official British influences on Canada started small and dwindled steadily during the war. In contrast, unofficial influence and example were pervasive. Whether it was the management of a wartime economy or the shaping of postwar policies which would make the struggle worthwhile, Britain was the source for a remarkable range of ideas. One of the more dramatic examples in the immediate pre-war years was the conversion of key civil servants in Ottawa and even some of King's more openminded cabinet colleagues to the doctrines of John Maynard Keynes. Counter-cyclical economics, as propounded by the brilliant Cambridge don, offered remedies for both a depressed and an inflated economy. Time and timidity prevented Canadians from discovering whether a country could really spend its way out of a depression but the war offered plenty of incentives for trying to save one's way out of an inflation. The rapid imposition of sweeping economic powers at home—in some contrast to the timid war effort overseas—gave civil servants and newly recruited officials like Donald Gordon of the Wartime Prices and

Trade Board the means. Keynes gave them the direction. Inflation, pushing prices up 15 per cent in the first two years of the war, gave the stimulus. With full employment, rocketing public expenditures (Ottawa spending rose from $553 million in 1939 to $5,322 million in 1944) and shrinking civilian production, desperate remedies were needed.

While Selective Service controlled where and how Canadians would work, Gordon's WPTB rapidly expanded its mandate to control wages and prices. From December 1, 1941, price ceilings were set at levels reached between September 15 and October 11 of that year. With each contortion of the economy, more regulations followed. Wages, tied to 1926-29 levels, could be notched up only with the rising cost of living. By war's end, the Board could boast that the Canadian consumer price index had climbed from 101.5 in 1939 to only 120.4 by 1945 and that most of the increases had come before the imposition of effective controls. Rationing was introduced soon after Pearl Harbor, as Japanese advances and German submarines in the Caribbean cut off sources of sugar and rubber. Gasoline, meat, butter and, in most provinces, liquor were also rationed. Canadians got by on half a pound of sugar a week. Gasoline rationing and a tire scarcity persuaded car owners to put their vehicles on blocks. By 1944, anyone moving to an area of housing shortage like Ottawa or Vancouver needed WPTB approval.

Wartime controls caused no real suffering. By British or European standards, Canadians were unbelievably well off. Clothing and most food were not rationed although some items, like nylon stockings, virtually vanished. Most Canadians soon discovered what officials already knew: voluminous and complex regulations can only be enforced by consent. Patriotic appeals to sacrifice, busy-work in collecting empty bottles and newspapers for scrap and other efforts to mobilize Canadians on the "Home Front" had diminishing impact. Grocers usually managed to keep a little extra butter or meat under the counter for faithful or well-heeled customers. The knowledgeable soon learned where a little gasoline could be purchased without coupons and certainly without questions. A favoured few obviously had no difficulty in acquiring silk stockings, a set of tires or vintage Scotch. In cities like Montreal, the WPTB writ did not run very far, and Montreal's example grew contagious with war-weariness.

To J. L. Ilsley, at least the puritanical side of the Keynesian doctrine was attractive. Provincial governments were warned that Ottawa would raid their taxing domain as if constitutional barriers did not exist. Dutifully, all nine provinces rented their income and corporate tax fields to Ottawa in return for a guaranteed payment of the 1938-39 revenue. By 1941, Ottawa's income tax revenue had reached $296 million, six times the pre-war level. Wartime also justified a measure passionately debated during most of the previous decade, unemployment insurance. Duplessis's 1939 defeat broke a constitutional roadblock to federal legislation in 1940 but it was the need to drain away purchasing power from workers' incomes that led to establishment of the Unemployment Insurance Commission in 1942. Ironically, the programme was established at the precise moment when no Canadian needed it.

Almost as important as Keynes's economic notions were the social reforms urged by another influential Englishman, William Beveridge. War-weary Britons were deliberately encouraged in their sacrifices by the promise of cradle-to-grave security when victory was won. In Canada, developments were remarkably similar. Ian Mackenzie, moved from National Defence to the Department of Pensions and Health, emerged as the minister most concerned with postwar reconstruction. A committee under his wing, headed by Principal F. Cyril James of McGill University, was gradually overwhelmed in a bureaucratic battle with a rival Economic Advisory Committee headed by W. A. McIntosh of Queen's University. Its major achievement outlasted both committees. Aided by a few like-minded colleagues, James's research director, Leonard Marsh, emerged from the Chateau Laurier hotel in Ottawa in mid-January, 1943, with a blueprint for social reform in some ways even more comprehensive than the Beveridge report, if only because Canada had so much farther to go. Marsh argued for drastic measures to fend off a postwar depression. Canada, he insisted, must be committed to full employment and to full-scale social insurance plans to meet the universal risks of sickness, old age and poverty. Since the number of children was a basic factor in pulling many Canadian families below the subsistence line, Marsh offered a fervent case for family allowances as a basic income supplement regardless of means.

Wealthy and influential Canadians gave the Marsh proposals a savage reception. Walter Gordon, a rising official in the WPTB, flippantly noted that Marsh and his friends had taken thirty hours to decide how to spend a billion dollars and wondered how much they would have spent if they had worked for a week. Mackenzie King, torn between his innate conservatism and his desire to be considered progressive, decided that his government's first concern should be the soldiers, not the poor. In truth, he was more than a little piqued that a young Englishman like Marsh should outflank his own reforming instincts. Yet Marsh was closer to the public mood than King realized. As in 1914-18, the war had opened minds to new ideas. The Soviet Union had been transformed from a fearful socialist bogey into a rapturously admired ally. Even the Conservatives had shifted. Arthur Meighen had contributed unwittingly to the process when he persuaded John Bracken, head of Manitoba's Progressive government, to become the Tories' new national leader. Part of Bracken's price was the linking of Progressive and Conservative in his party's title. Reform-minded Tories met at Port Hope in the summer of 1942 and their ideas, mixing conscription and free enterprise with a modest commitment to low-cost housing, full employment and free collective bargaining for labour, became part of the Bracken programme.

Most disturbing to King was the steady rise of the CCF during 1943. In July, Ontario's Liberal government went down to ignominious defeat. What was amazing to almost everyone was that the CCF came from nowhere to win thirty-four seats, only a handful short of power. Moreover, the Conservative winner, George Drew, had edged out the CCF with a surprisingly radical political programme. In August, four by-elections all went against King's Liberals, three of them to the CCF. A September Gallup Poll found CCF support at 29 per cent with the Liberals and Conservatives tied at 28 per cent each. The Marsh Report, commented the *Canadian Forum*, might be "the price that Liberalism is willing to pay in order to prevent socialism."

Closely tied to the popular surge in the CCF's strength was the alarming militancy of organized labour. Canada's unions had emerged from the Depression more divided and weaker than ever. The dynamic Congress of Industrial Organizations had swept into Canada in 1937 but its victory at General Motors in Oshawa was a lonely triumph. Without legislative protection, unions remained vulnerable to any powerful and determined employer. The war changed everything. Full employment by the end of 1941 removed the fear of lockout or dismissal. Inflation between 1939 and 1941, with accompanying allegations of profiteering and speculation, justified wage demands. King, supremely proud of his standing as a labour expert and still proud of his masterpiece, the Industrial Disputes Investigation Act of 1907, thought he knew how to keep the unions on his side. If Sir Robert Borden had ignored labour, King consulted regularly with men like Tom Moore, president of the conservative, craft-oriented Trades and Labour Congress. In 1942, King brought in a ponderous veteran of independent labour politics, Humphrey Mitchell, as his Minister of Labour. The appointment solved nothing. It was not Moore's organization but the newer, radical industrial unions which invaded war industries and the mines and smelters vital to the defence economy. The IDI Act, extended to all war industries, continued to be more effective in preventing or defeating strikes than in helping workers. Kirkland Lake's 2,800 gold miners followed its procedures to the letter but employers easily crushed their 1941 strike. Old-fashioned unionists like Humphrey Mitchell or Moore or his successor in 1943, Percy Bengough, were little better than King himself at reading the minds of frustrated war plant workers. Wage controls, administered by the War Labour Boards, developed infuriating anomalies for workers and they turned to both TLC and CIO unions in their thousands. In 1940, Ottawa had urged employers in war industries to pay fair wages, to allow unions and to bargain fairly but the directive had no penalties and C. D. Howe's dollar-a-year men were unlikely to impose them.

In 1943, Canada experienced its worst year of strikes since 1919. In Windsor, the Ford plant was closed for a month. Steelworkers shut down the huge mills at Sydney and Sault-Ste-Marie. In Montreal, 21,000 aircraft workers staged the biggest strike since the Winnipeg general strike of 1919. Through the year, civic workers, streetcar drivers and even the city police tied up Montreal. The militancy caught even union leaders by surprise. The political significance was highlighted when the three-year-old Canadian Congress of Labour, formed largely of the militant new industrial unions, voted formally to endorse the CCF. For advice in its labour crisis, the government turned to the National War Labour Board. Its chairman, Judge C. P. McTague, was a Tory but his experience in trying to settle the 1941 Kirkland Lake strike had given him a clear insight into the key problem of 1943: union recognition. Unless a satisfactory procedure established the rights of both unions and employers, the trouble would continue. A solution was also available: the National Labour Relations Act or Wagner Act in the United States, a key New Deal reform of 1935. McTague's report, delivered in the autumn of 1943, virtually imported the Wagner Act to Canada. Transformed into an order-in-council as P.C. 1003, McTague's recommendations became the most significant labour legislation in Canadian history. For the first time, without condescension or false neutrality, a Canadian government endorsed labour's right to organize and set up machinery to make the right effective. The National War Labour Order allowed bargaining units to be defined, unions to be certified and unfair practices by both labour and management to be rectified. The government's reward was extraordinary labour peace for the balance of the war.

That was not all. Labour militancy and CCF growth accomplished what Marsh's passionate arguments had failed to do. So did the shrewdly devised questionnaires of the government's War Information Board. The final development from a succession of attempts to handle wartime propaganda, ranging from genial news management by Charles Vining to the earnest educational uplift of the National Film Board's John Grierson, the WIB emerged as a sophisticated instrument for public opinion research. Surveys, censorship reports and regular communication with 140 different communities across Canada allowed the WIB chairman, Davidson Dunton, to warn the government that Canadians by 1944 were fed up with rationing and price controls and that postwar rehabilitation measures for veterans were widely misunderstood.

Dunton himself worried about whether such information, officially collected, might give the party in power an unfair advantage. He was right. However, Mackenzie King's political intuition and experience needed no surveys to convince the old prime minister that his government had to change or face a postwar defeat. Still, reform went against the grain. Surely, he argued, family allowances would demoralize Canadians and sap their sense of responsibility. His secretary, Jack Pickersgill, had a strangely effective answer. His own mother, a widow from the earlier war, had raised her Winnipeg family on a slim government pension and certainly her boys had not been lacking in initiative. King was convinced. His paranoia began to add new and more absurd arguments. Surely it was significant that the strongest cabinet opponents of social reform, Ilsley, Ralston and even Howe, had all become outspoken proponents of conscription. Clearly they were at odds with that true spirit of Liberalism which King felt himself to embody. If pro-conscriptionists opposed reform, it must be right.

Out of such reasoning, wartime Canada could be made the foundation for a postwar welfare state. The speech from the throne on January 24, 1944 had little to say about the war and Canada's role in it. Instead, it promised a Canada in which social security and human welfare would be the primary goals of government and in which family allowances, as a first instalment, would help to transform the poor from a majority to a minority in Canadian society.

Once again, war had brought social revolution to Canada.

Limited
War
Overseas

6

By 1942, most Canadians could believe that their country really was engaged in what the propagandists called "total war." To a degree unimagined in the earlier war, men and women were regulated, directed, rationed and exhorted. The voluntarism of CEF recruiting and the Patriotic Fund was channelled into Victory Bond campaigns with their opportunities for fervid patriotic speeches. School children handed in their sticky quarters for war savings stamps. Community organizations collected books, knitted socks and rolled bandages. Family life was disrupted and rebuilt around mothers doing shift work and children in factory nurseries. Radio, unknown in 1914-18, added immediacy to war news and a special authenticity to wartime propaganda. Older media did their best to compete. Advertisers built their messages into a warlike setting. Comic book publishers were allocated paper only for patriotic themes. Dutifully they informed their young and not-so-young readers that Germans and Japanese were brutal, merciless and thank goodness, dumb. Adult fiction purveyed the same message with only a little more sophistication.

Yet, in reality, Canada's war effort was not total. Politicians and civil servants carefully measured the sacrifices demanded of their fellow citizens. When Elliott Little, director of Selective Service, proposed to take 27 per cent of the male labour force from non-essential industries to meet a military call for 400,000 more men, the cabinet bowed to warnings from the WPTB that this would lead to widespread rationing, spartan living and an end to exports of furs and rye whiskey. Little was ordered to find the men elsewhere. Instead, he soon resigned. Other Canadians were also puzzled by the gap between the propaganda of total war and the reality of limited exertion. Much steam behind the conscription crusade of 1941-42 was generated by the ambiguity. The NRMA removed the title of "slacker" from the wartime vocabulary but its replacement, "Zombie," was no improvement. Yet what else could the government expect when it appealed to Canadians for total commitment, yet refused to send fit, trained soldiers where they were obviously needed?

Mackenzie King did his best to preserve his objectivity about the war. In the earlier war, Sir Robert Borden had spent every possible moment visiting Canadian wounded. From their sacrifice, he had found the courage to impose conscription in 1917. King did not submit to such temptations. Warned, during a 1941 visit to England, that he would be expected to address the troops, he confessed: "I felt what was like a dart pass through my bowels. It made me quite sick and faint . . . I cannot talk their jargon of war." Forced to wait for their national leader in the driving rain, the soldiers showed their own feelings by booing King. Politically, the prime minister understood that he should be photographed and identified with war heroes like the moody Montreal-born air ace, George "Buzz" Beurling. Privately, King experienced his own wartime tragedy when his nephew, a surgeon-lieutenant in the RCN, failed to survive the sinking of the *St. Croix* in 1943. Yet the Liberal leader remained surprisingly immune from the emotions of war.

As a war leader, King has had persuasive admirers, from R. MacGregor Dawson to J. L. Granatstein. He took the country into war in 1939 and out again in 1945 in a far more united state than anyone had a right to expect. His reward was the long postwar hegemony of his Liberal party. Yet King failed the admittedly difficult task of making Canadians understand their role in the war or the limitations which their fragile national unity imposed on them. He may have been the leader Canada needed and deserved but few Canadians would ever understand why.

Of course, few Canadians understood very much about war. The peacetime squeezing of defence budgets and the constant sniping at "warmongers" and "militarists" had more enduring consequences than the desperate shortage of trained men or modern equipment in 1939. Canadian political leaders had no idea of the cost or complexity of the world-wide struggle that had burst on them, and their few professional advisers were ill-equipped to give them much advice. Canadian naval and air force officers had been able to escape the monotony and penny-pinching of their own tiny services only by serving with the Royal Navy or much less frequently, the RAF. Almost inevitably the Canadians absorbed the strategic ideas and the values as well as sometimes the accent of the British services. The army, slightly larger and more self-confident because of its First World War experience, might be more independent in outlook, but deadening peacetime routine produced competent staff officers, not battlefield commanders. With the exception of General McNaughton, no senior officer of any service became a household word to Canadians during the war years, and McNaughton's military career ended in 1943, a year before his vision of a Canadian Army in the field was realized. Without personification, it was hard for Canadians to understand the role of their fighting services or to appreciate their problems and achievements.

The war certainly revived some old myths. Canadians found fresh arguments for their old faith in military amateurism. Tiny corvettes, crewed by seasick prairie youngsters, had tracked down Hitler's U-Boats. Ontario high-school graduates had out-flown Luftwaffe aces and flattened Ruhr factories. Given half a chance by blundering generals, raw Canadian soldiers had battered Wehrmacht veterans into submission. Such claims were very partial truths. Since the war ended in victory, they would not be seriously challenged. They automatically acquitted voters and politicians of any responsibility for pre-war unpreparedness. They ignored the fact that other allies had borne the brunt of the struggle, absorbed the costly lessons and given Canada time to prepare. Above all, the myth of military amateurism ignored the price Canadians themselves paid for inadequate equipment, inexperienced leaders and political confusion over how, where and why Canadian forces would make their contribution to the war.

In the First World War, Canada's role had at least been unambiguous. Her soldiers, from the outset, were swept up in a strategy which insisted that victory could only be achieved on the Western Front. It was a strategy on which no Canadian and, indeed, very few British politicians were ever consulted, but which Canada's prime minister, at least until the summer of 1918, totally accepted. Mackenzie King had no more influence on strategy in the Second World War than the huge Communist-inspired rallies in Toronto and Montreal that shouted for a Second Front. With a certain amount of grumbling and demands for consultation, Canadian forces were used where they were needed. They grew into roles like convoy escort or the British bomber offensive against Germany which were presumed—not always correctly—to be for the common good. In return, Ottawa assumed few commitments. The only operational theatre assigned to Canada was negotiated by admirals, not politicians, and then only because the assignment recognized a fact. Elsewhere, even the doctrine that Canadians would always fight together under their own commanders was overlooked by a government with more mundane political or financial priorities.

In the First World War, Borden had insisted that Canada's front line was in France and Flanders. In the 1939-45 war, the front line lapped against Canada's Atlantic shoreline and even reached into the St. Lawrence when two U-boats wreaked havoc in the river in the summer of 1942. In the crisis of 1940, the few RCN destroyers had crossed the Atlantic to aid a hard-pressed Royal Navy, first off the coast of France and then in a struggle to control what German submarine skippers later called their "Happy Time." The RCN's mobilization plans had called for the same kind of small-ship escort and anti-submarine role that the Halifax Patrol had played in the earlier war. While yachts and small vessels were purchased or commandeered, Canadian shipyards wrestled with the task of building sixty-four corvettes, small warships based on a whaling ship design and capable of carrying at least rudimentary gear for detecting and destroying submarines. Meanwhile the reserve divisions the navy had grudgingly supported during the peacetime years gathered the thousands of recruits who swelled the 1939 strength of 3,600 into the 93,000 men and women of 1945. Canada's merchant marine produced scores of officers whose seamanship and navigating experience became scarce and vital commodities for an expanding fleet of small ships.

Anti-submarine warfare was a mystery to the RCN in 1939. Few officers had even seen ASDIC, the Royal Navy's underwater sound ranging device. Even the British lacked experience in using the equipment to detect U-Boat propeller and engine noise. Using ASDIC and experience (if they had it) destroyer, frigate and corvette commanders did their best to keep the enemy submerged and away from convoys by constant patrolling. More than two years passed before such tactics managed to sink a U-Boat. German submarine skippers were first-class professionals, aggressive, innovative and experienced. They perfected "wolf pack tactics," co-ordinated assaults on convoys. When the United States scorned convoys for its coastal shipping, U-Boats picked off hundreds of ships. Slowly, the British gained the upper hand. Submarines were limited weapons. Without air support or a surface fleet, German U-Boats lost the initiative. Radar, primitive and scarce at the beginning of the war, gradually improved. Mounted on surface escort vessels, it forced the U-Boats to stay under water. Shore-based radio direction finders located submarines when they transmitted messages. High frequency direction finders (HF-DF) on destroyers allowed escorts to pinpoint enemy submarines. Because the British had broken the German naval code, convoys could be steered away from major U-Boat concentrations. After 1943, when the Germans failed to break the Allied convoy code, their U-Boats suffered an enormous disadvantage.

Whatever else it might be, submarine warfare was not a business for amateurs. For Canadians, it was the first and probably the most dangerous struggle of the war. Once the Luftwaffe had withdrawn from the Battle of Britain, the Atlantic became the one theatre where Hitler could win the war. If the Germans could gain the upper hand and decimate the big, lumbering Atlantic convoys, lend-lease and even United States entry into the war could not save Britain. By early 1941, Canada's role in the convoy battle was set. British escort groups took convoys to Iceland and then to St. John's, Newfoundland. Canadian escort groups took increasing responsibility for the third leg to Halifax or the American seaboard. On May 31, 1941, Commodore L. W. Murray established his headquarters at St. John's. A few days later, the first three Canadian corvettes joined his command. By July, Murray's force was escorting convoys as far as thirty-five degrees west.

Hardly was the Canadian role established than it was supplanted. By sinking American vessels in 1940, the U-boats had given President Roosevelt the pretext he wanted to jerk an isolationist United States further into the war. If the United States Navy wanted to join the war, few Canadians in the summer of 1941 were likely to object. Canadians were hopelessly ill-equipped for the struggle. They were short of long-range aircraft, the latest radar and ASDIC. If they had illusions of proficiency, they were shattered by the fate of Convoy SC 42. Between September 9 and 16, fifteen of the sixty-four ships went down before a German wolfpack until RAF aircraft and a force of British destroyers arrived. The Canadian escort group, mostly corvettes, had been hopelessly outnumbered and outclassed. Given time, amateur crews became proficient but a naval staff struggling to improvise ships and crews had neither time nor the expertise to insist on new tactics, effective training or a full share of new equipment. The Admiralty, desperate to satisfy its own experienced commanders, had no reason to offer radar or ASDIC gear to Canada if they were not sought. The Americans, far behind the British in anti-submarine warfare, could offer little help. After Pearl Harbor on December 7, 1941, they could not even provide escort vessels. U-boat captains moved west into the Gulf of St. Lawrence and south as far as the Caribbean, devastating Canadian and American coastal traffic while the American admirals concentrated on avenging their humiliation in the Pacific.

The winter of 1942-43 was the most desperate of the Atlantic war. Free to operate from bases in the Bay of Biscay, German submarine strength grew from ninety-one to 212. Experience and teamwork helped Canadian ships to register four victories in the summer of 1942 but nothing that winter could curb the staggering loss of convoyed tonnage. In November, 119 ships were lost, 729,160 tons. Foul mid-winter weather reduced losses in December and January but the toll resumed—63 ships in February, 108 in March. To the Canadians there was much that was wrong. Experience and contact with the Royal Navy had taught them how primitive and inadequate their ships and equipment really were. They had also learned the value of aircraft as submarine hunters and killers but the RCAF squadrons in Eastern Air Command had no really long-range aircraft and no means of getting any. The result was a wide gap in mid-Atlantic where U-Boats reveled in their relative immunity. Above all, the command arrangements for the Atlantic war now seemed absurd. Since August, 1941, an American vice-admiral commanded the entire convoy and escort operation in the Northwest Atlantic but the American contribution of navy and army air corps squadrons and two lonely coast guard cutters was far outmatched by the RCN and RCAF contribution.

Canadian naval officers at Halifax, St. John's and Ottawa found a channel for their discontent in Rear-Admiral Victor Brodeur. A classmate of Murray in the original Royal Canadian Naval College class, Brodeur had remained resolutely French-speaking, Catholic and Liberal through all his years with the Canadian and British navies. He was, after all, the son of Laurier's first naval minister. King had chosen him and Major-General Maurice Pope as senior Canadian service representatives in Washington. The dissatisfaction of Canadian admirals coincided with deep British and American concern over the grim state of the Atlantic convoy war and the impact of U-boat sinkings on Allied plans for a European invasion. The upshot, in March, 1943, was an Atlantic Convoy Conference in Washington with British, American and Canadian naval participation. For once, discussion was crisp and to the point. Sub-committees settled vital issues of equipment, tactics and organization. In the end, Brodeur could claim a modest national victory. With American consent, Britain and Canada would share responsibility for the North Atlantic. At Halifax, Admiral Murray took direct command of an expanse of gloomy Atlantic from forty-seven degrees west and south to twenty-nine degrees north. In a world divided into operational sectors, Murray became the sole Canadian to bear such responsibilities.

By happy coincidence, the change occurred just as the tide in the convoy war began to turn. In May, thanks to the British, the RCAF finally began to acquire some of the long-range Liberator bombers it needed to cover the mid-ocean gap. The stream of new escort vessels from Canadian drydocks allowed the formation of powerful support groups able, with the help of electronic intelligence, to reinforce embattled convoys. Hurricane fighters and aged Swordfish bombers, mounted on merchant ships, gave convoys direct air support. Vice-Admiral Percy Nelles, blamed for the Canadian navy's technical deficiencies, was replaced as Chief of Naval Staff and transferred to Britain as Senior Canadian Flag Officer (Overseas). One result was modernization at last. Training, air cover and better equipment turned the tide. In May, 1943, after losing six U-boats in a convoy battle that saw eleven merchant ships sunk, the Germans pulled their submarines off the North Atlantic route. In September, they were back with a new secret weapon, the acoustic torpedo. These had some success. They sank HMCS *St. Croix* and other vessels with terrible losses but they were soon beaten by various ingenious devices, especially the so-called CAT (Canadian anti-torpedo) gear. Canadians needed to be up-to-date.

The Atlantic battle continued until the end of the war. At times, notably in the fall of 1944, it turned dangerous again. U-Boats with *schnorkels* and the promise of hydrogen-peroxide as a fuel swung the balance back to the submarines, countering the lead achieved by hunter-killer groups of aircraft carriers and destroyers. By March of 1945, the German navy had 463 boats on patrol, compared to 27 in 1939. The last Canadian warship lost in the war, the *Esquimalt*, was torpedoed off Halifax on April 16, 1945. Yet, between them, the RCAF and the RCN had turned the tide in their sector of the Atlantic. More and more Canadian seamen and ships had crossed the Atlantic to carry the battle closer to the enemy. As Douglas and Greenhous have argued, both the Canadian services showed the benefits of training and hard experience as they returned to British waters. Twenty of the RCN's twenty-seven U-Boat sinkings occurred east of the 35th meridian and seventeen took place after November 20, 1944.

To most Canadians, the RCN was identified with the bitter submarine war in the North Atlantic. At its height, by the autumn of 1943, 229 ships, 21,000 seamen, eleven RCAF maritime patrol squadrons and supporting facilities were committed to the struggle against the U-Boat. Yet the RCN was eager to do more. Having twice watched their service teeter to the edge of extinction, senior naval officers knew that the war was their best chance to prove the benefit of a balanced fleet and to ensure a stable future. Canadian officers admired the Royal Navy; from the outset of war, they had forcefully asserted Canadian autonomy against British admirals who could be condescending as well as knowledgeable. Escort groups transferred to European waters remained RCN organizations. Two motor torpedo boat flotillas were formed largely from Canadians serving in the British coastal forces. Canadian seamen were drafted into British cruisers and aircraft carriers to gain experience in working major warships. During 1944, the RCN acquired two escort carriers, *Puncher* and *Nabob,* and added two cruisers in early 1945 as part of preparations to join the war against Japan. The major fleet units of the Canadian service were still destroyers, many of them serving in Canadian flotillas with the British Home Fleet at Scapa Flow. Two of them, *Haida* and *Athabaskan,* gave the Canadian admirals the kind of tradition they wanted. On April 25, 1944, the two destroyers chased three German destroyers through a minefield and sank one of them. Three days later, in another battle, *Athabaskan* was sunk by a torpedo but *Haida* drove one of the German attackers ashore, returned to hunt for survivors and left its own cutter to make its way back to England loaded with men from the sunken Canadian ship. Three days after D-Day, *Haida* and *Huron* avenged their sister-ship with yet another German destroyer.

The fact remained that the RCN's main contribution to the allied victory was the grim anti-submarine battle in the North Atlantic. The cost of inexperience, out-of-date equipment and inadequate ships was high. In the grim winter days of 1943, the British director of anti-submarine warfare noted that 80 per cent of the merchant ships torpedoed in the previous two months had been under Canadian escort. There were justifications but most of them added up to the price of trying to create a fighting navy in only three years. Yet both the RCN and the RCAF perfected their skills, produced effective sub-killers like Commander J. S. D Prentice, responsible for three of Canada's twenty-seven sinkings, and Canadians also devised new tactics for frustrating the German wolfpacks.

Like the RCN, but perhaps less comfortably, the RCAF also resumed air roles Canada had performed in the earlier war. In 1917, Canada had also played host to a British-sponsored air training programme. She had sent a steady flow of young Canadians to British squadrons and she had struggled to organize her own coastal air patrols. The difference was that a Canadian air force, little more than a dream in 1918, had become a sturdy reality, and in the government's plans, the main component of Canada's contribution to victory.

Despite immense obstacles, including the cut-off of British training aircraft in 1940, the BCATP was an eventual success. Using private flying schools for initial training, the RCAF boasted that the Air Training Plan's facilities were virtually in place by October, 1941. By the end of 1943, the Plan's forty-seven schools were graduating 3,000 students a month. In fact, more aircrew were trained than anyone needed and the flow was cut in 1944 and stopped in March, 1945. The BCATP generated 131,533 graduates, including more than 50,000 pilots. Almost all its aircraft, from Fleet Finches and Avro Ansons to the ubiquitous Harvards, were built in Canada.

Most of the BCATP graduates were Canadian. While early graduates were needed as instructors and to man the ill-equipped squadrons of the RCAF's Eastern and Western Air Commands, the great majority flowed overseas, as their fathers had, into the ranks of the RAF. To the British, devoted to the notion of a single imperial air force, this seemed appropriate and the Riverdale mission in 1939 had not quarrelled with the niggardly Canadian refusal to pay its men in the RAF more than the difference between British and Canadian rates. Moreover, the RAF had become a multinational force. Airmen from the Commonwealth rubbed shoulders with Poles, Czechs, Norwegians, Dutch, Free French and other escapees from a conquered Europe, and with young Americans, prematurely engaged in the war with Hitler. The friction which so often had marked Anglo-Canadian relations seemed agreeably scarce in the wartime RAF.

Article 15 of the BCATP agreement had guaranteed that RCAF squadrons would be established overseas and that aircrew would be identified with Canada "to the highest extent possible." By the end of 1940, when the first graduates of the BCATP began trickling overseas, there were only three RCAF squadrons in action, all of them transferred from Canada. In May, 1941, Colonel J. L. Ralston and the British air minister, Sir Archibald Sinclair, agreed that the British would create twenty-five squadrons for the RCAF—but with British ground crew and at British expense. By the end of 1941, only 500 of the 8,595 Canadian graduates of the plan were flying with RCAF units. Ten more squadrons were formed in 1942, four in 1943 and three in 1944, while six squadrons transferred from Canada. By war's end, the RCAF overseas had forty-eight squadrons while forty had been organized for service in Canada.

Canadianization of the RCAF was a political more than a tactical issue. Few Canadians clamoured to join RCAF squadrons and some objected to being transferred. The RAF was willing to make allowances for colonial wildness; RCAF senior officers distinctly were not. The problem for Ottawa was that Canada was making a substantial contribution to the allied air effort but that effort could never be recognized so long as its airmen were part of the Royal Air Force. Sending more public relations officers overseas made no difference. Of greater concern to the RCAF's own senior officers was the stunting of their opportunity to gain command and staff experience. Youthful pilots and navigators might be obscenely contemptuous of such concerns; career officers in the RCAF knew that their service might be permanently blighted if they could not establish a separate command structure in England. Their minister, C. G. Power, did not need much instruction. As a Quebec politician and a First World War veteran, he understood both nationalism and officers.

Not even Power could overcome the root of the Canadianization problem, money. In the earlier war, Canadian authority over its Corps was built on the irrefutable fact that Canada was paying the bills. Canada could well have afforded to pay for her own overseas air force. In the immediate postwar period, she would cheerfully cancel Britain's BCATP indebtedness. Yet it was not until the spring of 1943 that King and his colleagues reluctantly accepted the financial burden of the RCAF squadrons overseas. By then, it was too late to create a force which in any sense matched Canada's manpower contribution. In the summer of 1944, 60 per cent of RCAF aircrew served in RAF squadrons. In early 1945, a quarter of the flying personnel of the RAF Bomber Command was Canadian.

Canadian flyers took part in every kind of air operation, from artillery spotting to ground strafing over France. Six squadrons served with Coastal Command, including one which gave the first warning of the Japanese attack on Ceylon and another which provided the RCAF's first Victoria Cross winner. Fourteen RCAF squadrons flew day fighters; three provided fighter reconnaisance and four manned Beaufighters and Mosquito bombers as night fighters. Two of Canada's three overseas transport squadrons furnished air lift in the Burma campaign. Ottawa suspected that they might be entangled in British imperialism; in fact they were badly needed for the Fourteenth Army's logistical lifeline across the jungle.

By the time Canadians wanted a say in how their air force was deployed, it was really too late. Air Vice Marshal Harold Edwards, the senior Canadian air officer overseas, only learned after the event that eight RCAF squadrons had helped provide air cover for the Dieppe landings in August, 1942. Even when fighter squadrons were grouped in Canadian wings, they fitted into the RAF's dispositions. In D-Day preparations, 83 Group was built up with a heavy complement of RCAF squadrons to provide post-invasion cover for the First Canadian Army. When the Second British Army was designated to manage the actual landing, Air Marshal Sir Trafford Leigh-Mallory switched 83 Group to its support. A less experienced (and all-RAF) 84 Group was assigned to the Canadians. The decision may have made good operational sense but it gave no comfort to Canadian sensibilities.

The biggest and costliest Canadian air commitment was in Bomber Command. The original case for an independent Royal Air Force had been built on the visionary claim that air power could be a war-winning weapon. Between the wars, enthusiasts like Lord Trenchard, Billy Mitchell of the United States and Giulio Douhet of Italy had passionately insisted that aerial bombardment would devastate cities and shatter civilian morale. British voters had certainly been chilled in the thirties by the slogan that "the bomber will always get through." Guernica, Warsaw and Rotterdam all seemed to prove the air power arguments. The Battle of Britain should have raised questions. It did not. With its back to the wall, with no hope of matching German military strength, Britain had few other ways of hitting back. If Air Chief Marshal Sir Arthur Harris could win the war with bombers, Winston Churchill was delighted to let him try. The 13,000 British dead from the Blitz calmed any scruples.

In some respects, Harris's strategy was about as futile as the "offensives" of the First World War. Britain's bombers were underpowered, underarmed and an easy prey for Luftwaffe fighters and anti-aircraft artillery. Daylight raids led to intolerable losses. Night bombing was hopelessly inaccurate. Propaganda insisted that raids were tightly targeted on military and industrial objectives; in fact, incendiaries and blockbuster bombs were aimed at civilian populations in exactly the same kind of terror raiding the Luftwaffe had carried out. Germany lost 560,000 killed and 675,000 injured from the Allied bomber offensive, most of them women and children, but German war production until the final months was cut as little as 1.2 per cent. As in 1914-18, Canadians had no chance to debate the strategy or its morality. If they had, the senior RCAF officers who had learned their air power doctrines at the RAF staff college would probably have raised as few questions as their British or American counterparts. Instead, officers of all three countries found themselves preoccupied with the tactical and technological problems of trying to reduce disastrous aircraft losses. Four-engined bombers, electronic navigation aids, special Pathfinder aircraft to spot targets, all helped a little, but not even the well-armed American B-17s could fend off German fighters. In 1942, when Canadians became significantly involved in the bomber offensive, only one in three crews survived to complete a thirty-mission tour. In one BCATP's navigators' course, only fifteen out of fifty survived the war, ten of them as prisoners. Young Canadians who had joined the RCAF to escape their fathers' memories of trench warfare found themselves in no less bloody and hopeless a struggle, in which their own survival became improbable and their most likely victims were women and children.

Because so much of the wartime news centred on the bomber offensive, Canadianization became a particularly acute issue. By October, 1942, four complete RCAF squadrons served in Bomber Command. A fifth, 425 (Alouette) Squadron, was formed as a symbolic gesture to French Canada although its ground crews remained British and its working language was English. At the outset of 1943, eleven Canadian bomber squadrons were assembled as 6 Group, RCAF, under Air Vice Marshal G. E. Brookes. It was overdue, essential if the RCAF was to train its own senior officers, and it was unpopular. As if the problems of the bomber offensive were not bad enough already, 6 Group seemed to make them worse. Canadians were torn from their familiar RAF crews and squadrons to join strangers who had nothing more in common than an RCAF enlistment. Canadian squadrons found themselves last in line for new aircraft and improved technology. Beginning with the obsolete Wellingtons and inadequate Halifaxes, not until August of 1943 did the first Lancaster bombers appear. The 6 Group's stations in the Vale of York were farther from their targets than any in Bomber Command

and rather more likely to be fogged in when aircraft returned from a night raid.

One result was a grim casualty rate. Between March 5 and June 24, 1943, the group lost 100 aircraft, 7 per cent of its strength. A five per cent loss was considered crippling. Morale sagged. Its symptoms were failures to take off, early returns and a soaring total of aircraft found unexpectedly to be unserviceable just before takeoff. On January 20, 1944, 147 of 6 Group's bombers were ordered out on a Berlin raid: 3 failed to take off, 17 came back early, 9 were lost. On January 21, 125 aircraft were ordered out: 11 never took off, 12 returned early and 24 were reported missing. Bomber Command was understandably worried.

Changes began with a new commander on February 29, 1944. Air Vice Marshal C. M. McEwen brought a brilliant First World War flying record, professional experience and an unwelcome commitment to traditional military discipline. Canadian pilots were forced to abandon their casual "fifty mission" look. More practically, McEwen insisted on navigational training, faster conversion to the more powerful, better armed Lancaster and improved ground crew and administrative efficiency. Best of all, Harris's bomber offensive against Germany was interrupted by preparations for D-Day. Blasting railways and German defences in France cost fewer casualties. So did the fact that most targets were close enough to permit fighter escorts. By the time 6 Group switched back to raids on Germany in October, most of McEwen's crews had been together long enough to acquire experience, technical skill and a few tactical tricks. Moreover, the new Mustang fighters had long enough range to escort bombers all the way to their targets and to tackle the Luftwaffe fighters on their own air space. At the end of 1944, McEwen could boast the lowest casualties of any group in Bomber Command and the highest accuracy. He had reason to be pleased. Thanks partly to leadership but chiefly to better equipment and a critical reprieve, 6 Group had turned around its reputation for failure.

The value of the bomber offensive against Germany remains bitterly controversial. Canadians who are willing to pronounce the Dieppe raid a needless blunder, are understandably hesitant to condemn an operation which went on relentlessly throughout most of the war. It is too painful to admit that 9,980 young Canadians, to say nothing of many thousands of airmen of every Allied nationality, died to very little purpose. Yet the Canadian death toll in Bomber Command was no smaller than the total loss of soldiers as the Canadian army fought its way from Normandy to the Hochwald forest. Because Bomber Command had priority, Coastal Command was denied the long-range aircraft needed to combat German submarines in the Atlantic. Even when the huge strategic bomber force was grudgingly transferred to support the Normandy invasion, its inexperience and unsuitable equipment sometimes made the bombers seem as destructive of the Allied forces as of their enemies. Victory denies the victorious the necessity of reflection. Faith in victory through air power survived the Second World War. Until the final stages of the conflict, so did German industrial power, allowing Hitler's armies to retain a technological lead in the quality of their tanks, guns, rockets and fighter aircraft.

By comparison with the navy and the air force, Canada's army was the Cinderella service. Canadians found airmen attractive and sailors exotic; the First World War had taught them that soldiering was a filthy business controlled by brainless generals and demanding enormous casualties. In a modern, mechanized war, soldiers were still necessary but Ottawa obviously hoped that someone else would provide them. Even the Defence Council's initial proposal to offer two infantry divisions had reduced Loring Christie, a senior official in External Affairs, to fury. Canadian generals, he charged, wanted to save British manpower. Ralston and his cabinet allies, Ilsley, Power and Macdonald, insisted that Canadian manpower had still not been tapped. Generals promised that each increase would not bring conscription. Slowly, the strength of the overseas army grew to three infantry divisions, two armoured divisions and two tank brigades, as well as a host of miscellaneous units from tunnellers to the Canadian Forestry Corps. Instead of the single corps headquarters of the earlier war, Canadians mustered the staff and ancillary units for two corps headquarters, an army headquarters and a Canadian Military Headquarters in London which would manage alone if the Canadian forces ever took the field. The number of actual fighting soldiers was very much smaller than in Currie's Canadian Corps but in 730,625 men and women eventually saw service in the Canadian Army in Canada and overseas.

Experience had taught the army some painful lessons. This time, existing militia units were mobilized instead of the *ad hoc* battalions of the CEF. Though the army was far from bilingual, it was a deliberate contrast to the resolutely unilingual RCN and RCAF. The order of battle included French-speaking infantry, artillery and armoured regiments. It was not much easier to find French Canadian volunteers than it had been in the earlier war but, in its fumbling way, the army tried to avoid being part of the problem. Whatever the prejudices of officers and men farther down the line, senior officers like McNaughton, Pope and Lieutenant-General Kenneth Stuart, a native of Trois-Rivières, were more sensitive than their First War predecessors. Recruiting remained a problem. Pope's memoirs show that more sensitive methods in Quebec brought few volunteers. The fact remained that the Canadian Army took men who could not get into the other services and who failed to find a place in industry. The NRMA call-ups persuaded some men to volunteer before they were conscripted. Others converted during their training period. They left behind the large, resentful core of conscripts who swore that they would only fight when the government forced them to do so. Officers, obliged to serve in Canada when pride or professional ambition made them yearn for active service, found commanding such soldiers a doubly demoralizing experience.

In England, Canadian soldiers might be relatively immune to debates about conscription and "Zombies" but they faced other frustrations. As the Canadian force grew from a single division in the winter of 1940 to four divisions, 125,000 men, by the autumn of 1941, General McNaughton had nourished his private dream. When the Allies finally returned to Europe in a Second Front, the Canadians would be there not merely as an army corps of a few divisions but as an entire Army, a balanced national force. Pleading with a sceptical Grant Dexter of the *Winnipeg Free Press*, General Stuart evoked national pride as an argument for the army's five-division programme: "This is the kind of army a soldier dreams of commanding, hard-hitting, beautifully balanced, incredibly powerful." The most consciously Canadian of the three armed services, the army was also acutely conscious of how difficult it would be to retain an identity and autonomy among more powerful allies. Its senior officers remembered how important it had been to assert their tactical independence from British commanders in 1917 and 1918. McNaughton's fascination with scientific and technological innovations, which had led him to the pre-war chairmanship of the National Research Council, was now directed to finding equipment and techniques to make his army more effective and its battles less bloody.

Other armies had also learned lessons from the earlier war and they went on learning them while the Canadians waited and trained in England. In 1941, the war had moved dramatically south and east. Hitler's invasion of the Soviet Union initially seemed as easy a triumph as his conquest of France. Gradually, the enormous distances, the incredible recuperation of the Red Army, and winter slowed and stopped the Wehrmacht. The Eastern Front became a gigantic meatgrinder, devouring the strength and skill of the German panzer armies. Meanwhile, in North Africa, Britain's Eighth Army struggled with its inferior equipment to match General Erwin Rommel's Afrika Korps. To all of this, the Canadians remained spectators. They were not irrelevant: Britain needed a garrison. When the Second Front came, Canada would be there. Proposals that a Canadian division or even a brigade join the other Commonwealth units in the Eighth Army were rejected. McNaughton wanted his formations kept intact. Mackenzie King was horrified at the thought: it was the business of generals and ministers to conserve lives, not to invent spectacular roles. Yet the refusal to send Canadians to Africa had made Ottawa much more vulnerable to the British request to send two battalions to Hong Kong. Service with the Eighth Army might have been a costly but beneficial learning experience for an army of raw soldiers and paper-bound staff officers; Hong Kong was a wholly predictable disaster. The same pressure to do something made it equally difficult for Canadian officers to ask searching questions when they were invited to contribute two brigades for a raid on the French coastal resort of Dieppe. It did not require hindsight to see the problem. Under Byng and Currie, Canadian staff officers had made a military trademark out of painstaking planning rehearsal and massive bombardment. None of this seemed possible for Dieppe. Amphibious exercises before the landing were marred by chaos and confusion. Serious bombardment was ruled out when Sir Dudley Pound, sensibly enough, refused to risk his capital ships in the narrow seas under an untamed Luftwaffe. Air bombardment might have helped but Bomber Command had larger targets and some experts insisted that tanks, to be used for the first time in a raid, would be impeded by wreckage.

In the event, few tanks got anywhere near the town. The landing, on August 19, was a procession of accidents, bad luck, miscalculation and tragedy. At Puys, the Royal Regiment of Canada lost 209 dead in a few minutes, the worst daily toll for any Canadian battalion in the war. Other units fared little better. Of 4,963 who had set out for Dieppe, 907 lay dead and 1,946 remained as prisoners. The best known battle of the Canadian Army in the Second World War would be remembered only as a catastrophe.

Like the bomber offensive, Dieppe remains the prisoner of widely shared popular conceptions. Canadian soldiers had not been slaughtered merely because of the chronic stupidity of British commanders like the debonair Lord Louis Mountbatten or the publicity conscious Lieutenant-General Bernard Montgomery. Other nations, with more extensive experience in the war, would have granted Dieppe a more generous perspective. Amphibious operations had always been notoriously risky. For all their prior training, the Canadians at Dieppe utterly lacked battle experience. Even a few veteran officers and sergeants might have kicked the huddled, bewildered soldiers into action. The losses were horrifying but they were lighter than many Canadian battalions had suffered on the Somme or at Vimy Ridge. Moreover, the losses were not in vain. Common sense might have argued the need for special assault tanks, vastly improved communications on the beach and a tightly organized fire support plan. Yet only sacrifice and failure could convince generals and politicians to divert scarce, costly resources to meet such needs. Failure is a better teacher than success.

After Dieppe, Canadians returned to their training with some added sense of purpose. The battered 2nd Division was rebuilt and its commander, Major-General J. H. Roberts, was not, in fact, sacrificed as a scapegoat. There were, however, doubts about most Canadian generals. Lacking the test of battle, senior officers could be tested only in complex tactical exercises. Montgomery's suspicion that any officers from the earlier war (except himself) were too old and slow soon extended to Canadian ranks. Some officers who had proudly worn the medals of 1914-18 discreetly removed them; others were themselves removed. McNaughton, at fifty-six, fell under the shadow.

In Canada, the fervid patriotism which had generated the 1942 conscription crisis did not evaporate with passage of Bill 80. In the previous war,

Canadians had boasted that their soldiers had been in action long before the Americans had even begun to fight. Except for Hong Kong and Dieppe, Canada's army seemed to have done nothing in the war while Americans had fought major battles in North Africa and the Far East in 1942. R. B. Bennett, retired to England, commented scornfully to the press that Canadians would spend their fourth Christmas in England without firing a shot. The *Winnipeg Free Press*, the Liberals' favourite newspaper in the West, demanded that the government send a division somewhere, anywhere. The *Montreal Gazette* reported that the overseas army was suffering mental illness because of inaction. In fact, most Canadian soldiers seem to have adjusted to their lot with admirable resignation and relations with their British hosts remained surprisingly friendly. Yet generals and politicians now felt the urge to act. When, after polite preliminaries, the British asked for a Canadian infantry division and tank brigade for the forthcoming invasion of Sicily, only McNaughton had real reservations. They were eased by the obvious benefits of battle experience, a chance to examine the invasion plans for their military feasibility and an informal assurance that the Canadians would return once Sicily was captured.

As Farley Mowat has illustrated in his memoirs, the Sicily landing was precisely the kind of battle inoculation Canadian troops badly needed. An easy landing built gradually into a bitter series of engagements against tough, resourceful German troops. By the time the thirty-eight day campaign brought the Canadians to the Straits of Messina on August 6, 1943, they had become experienced, aggressive fighting men. The divisional commander, Major-General Guy Simonds, had begun to prove himself one of the army's best fighting generals. At Agira and Regalbuto, Canadians had won difficult and costly battles. Behind the lines, however, there were sour features of the campaign. General Dwight Eisenhower, the Allied commander of the invasion, had mentioned only American and British forces in his initial communique; Canadians were added only in an amended version. A Washington press leak robbed Mackenzie King of his chance to be the first to tell Canadians the news. General McNaughton, determined to visit his Canadians in the early days of the invasion, was denied permission by Montgomery on the grounds that Canadian commanders, fighting their first battles, did not need to be distracted. McNaughton returned to London in a fury.

Yet, even as a public relations exercise, Canada's overdue participation in the ground war was a triumph. King, who somehow believed that fighting in Italy would cost fewer casualties than in France, agreed to cabinet arguments that more soldiers be sent. Pressed by his eager generals in Ottawa, Ralston proposed that an extra armoured division and a corps headquarters be sent to Italy to gain experience and to increase the Canadian content of the operation. Allied commanders saw little need for more tanks in the hilly Italian terrain and none at all for an inexperienced corps headquarters. Under political pressure, they gave their consent. McNaughton did not. Instead of getting back a battle-hardened 1st Division and using its experience, he now saw the apparent destruction of his dream of a First Canadian Army with almost half its strength detached to a distant and subsidiary theatre. "The important thing for Canada at the end of the war," he argued with Ralston, "is to have her army together under the control of a Canadian." The Minister of National Defence and his cabinet colleagues were more impressed by newspaper editorials and excited letter writers. McNaughton was ignored. The headquarters of I Canadian Corps, the 5th Armoured Division and a host of ancillary troops set out on the long sea-borne route to Italy.

General McNaughton's outspoken opposition to the break-up of his army helped to undermine his position in England. Ottawa politicians, including Ralston, wanted agreement, not arguments, from generals. The British, too, found McNaughton a difficult and prickly associate. Both Ralston and the Chief of the Imperial General Staff, Sir Alan Brooke, had had strong differences with McNaughton long before the war. Yet the key strike against the Canadian commander was that he was too old, too set in his ways and too preoccupied with technology to keep an overall grip on an army on active service. In Exercise Spartan, held in 1943, McNaughton spent fascinated hours watching a bridging operation while his troops tangled themselves in a monumental traffic jam. That was enough evidence for Brooke but it was Ralston who took the bitter decision. An apparently lively and active-looking McNaughton returned to Canada at the end of December, 1943, recalled "on grounds of health." His successor, after a brief experience in command of I Corps in Italy, was Lieutenant-General H. D. G. Crerar.

King's faith that fighting in Italy would not be costly proved to be fantasy. Even in Sicily, a division and a tank brigade had suffered 2,310 casualties, 562 of them fatal. The Allies failed to exploit Italy's decision to switch sides and Churchill's image of the "soft underbelly" of Europe proved to be an ironic illusion. Experienced, well-trained German troops turned Italian mountains, rivers, vineyards and towns into traps for advancing armour and infantry. The Gustav Line, hastily created across Italy's narrow waist, halted the Allies well south of Rome in the winter of 1943–44. When General Crerar took over his new Canadian corps in February, conditions reminded him of his younger days at Passchendaele. In December, when Canadians began a fierce house-to-house battle for the coastal town of Ortona, medical officers encountered their first cases of battle fatigue. Rifle companies struggled at half-strength. Ortona cost Canada 1,372 dead.

Crerar stayed with his corps for only a matter of weeks before he and Simonds were summond back to England for D-Day preparations. His successor, Lieutenant-General E. L. M. Burns, was an intellectually accomplished soldier with a pervasively dour manner ill-adapted to either his Canadian subordinates or his British superior, General Sir Oliver Leese of the Eighth Army. In the spring, the Eighth Army was switched to Italy's western coast to punch a way north to the Anzio beachhead and Rome. Canadian tanks helped push through the gap in the Gustav Line and Burns's corps was given the job of penetrating the Hitler Line. The battle took four days and 900 casualties, mostly from the 1st Division. For the pursuit up the narrow Liri Valley, Leese launched both the Canadians and a British corps. The result was tangled traffic, confusion and fatal delay. The exasperated British general blamed Burns and his inexperienced headquarters and ordered the Free French forward to take up the pursuit. On June 4, Rome fell to the French and the Americans.

Within two days, Italy was the forgotten front. The D-Day invasion was the greatest combined operation in history. Five thousand ships moved into the Baie de la Seine, ready to unload 107,000 soldiers and 7,000 vehicles in a single day. Canadians shared in all three elements. RCAF squadrons were part of the Second Allied Tactical Air Force and Bomber Command. Canadian destroyers, frigates and minesweepers were part of the huge escort fleet and Canadians manned scores of landing craft. Juno, one of the five selected invasion beaches, was reserved for the 3rd Canadian Division and the 2nd Armoured Brigade. Beyond the beachhead, men of the 1st Canadian Parachute Battalion landed with the 6th British Airborne Division. Previewed at Dieppe, postponed through 1943, the Second Front had finally opened. Even McNaughton's dream of a Canadian Army was not utterly lost. Once the beachhead was clear and secure, Crerar would have his army, with British, Polish and other Allied formations to fill out its ranks.

Juno Beach was the toughest of the three assigned to British Commonwealth troops. Bombardment had not knocked out the German defences, and beach obstacles destroyed or damaged dozens of landing craft as they neared shore. Infantry, backed by armour, shook themselves out and kept moving despite heavy losses. Canada's price for the D-Day landing was 1,074 killed, wounded and missing. It was only the beginning. Pushing inland, the 9th Brigade ran into the 12th SS Panzer Division, a Hitler Youth formation that would wage a merciless battle with the Canadians throughout the Normandy campaign. Badly outnumbered by the invaders, the Germans outmatched them in veteran leadership and equipment. Panther and Tiger tanks and the ubiquitous 88mm gun proved far superior to the Allied equivalents. Only in the air were the Allies utterly in control; their dominance reduced German tank mobility and carved into the defenders' tactical advantages.

Crammed into the narrow beachhead, the Allies had little room to manoeuvre, or even to receive reinforcements. It was July 7 before the 2nd Canadian Division began to arrive and General Simonds's II Canadian Corps headquarters could become operational. Two days later, at the end of a series of costly, frustrating assaults by the British and Canadians, Caen fell. The pressure continued. In the struggle for Caen, the Canadians lost 1,194 men and 1,965 more in continued fighting from July 18 to 22. By holding the main German force, Montgomery's troops gave General George Patton's American Third Army a chance to break out at the other end of the beachhead, sweep around the German flank and catch them in an enormous pocket. Closing the pocket from the north would be the first big job for Simonds's corps.

Simonds's plan, Operation "Totalize," began with a night advance by the 2nd Division followed by a further daylight attack on August 8, with the Polish and 4th Armoured Divisions, backed by a weary 3rd Division. A key feature of the assault was "carpet" bombing by a huge force of American strategic bombers. Some of the "carpet" fell on the Canadians, with devastating and demoralizing consequences. The advance covered barely two miles and inexperienced crews harboured for the night as though a tactical exercise had gone wrong. An angry Simonds promptly ordered Operation "Tractable," a daylight version of the original night attack, using what remained of the 3rd and 4th Armoured Divisions. It should have been a disaster. Tanks and infantry lined up in two dense columns, the tanks covered with foot soldiers and their equipment. A Canadian officer carrying the complete operation plan blundered into the German lines. A smoke screen intended to blind the enemy blew back on the route of the advance. Dust clouds soared as tracked vehicles tore into the dirt. Yet what should have been a catastrophe rolled five miles through the German lines. Simonds's troops took 1,300 bewildered German prisoners and suffered mainly from yet another Allied bomber attack, this one including British and Canadian aircraft. Two days later, on August 16, Falaise was captured and the German main escape route was cut.

By the end of August, the Normandy battle was over. The remnants of the German army streamed eastward, offering only token resistance. They left behind 400,000 dead, wounded and prisoners, almost twice the Allied toll for the campaign. Yet the Canadians' losses were not light: 18,500 casualties, a third of them dead. It was almost twice the cost of Vimy Ridge in 1917. No division in the Allied forces had lost more than the Canadian 3rd. The 2nd Division came next.

High casualties were clear testimony to Canadian courage and determination against a skillful, well-equipped enemy. They were also the price of inexperience, a willingness to depend on self-confidence and raw valour rather than on brains and preparation. Operation "Tractable" had worked perhaps because it had been so incredible; on many other occasions, amateurism had resulted in costly failure. In "Totalize," two squadrons of tanks and two companies of infantry had been squandered simply because of an elementary error in map-reading. Tank-infantry co-operation, practised repeatedly in war games and exercises, broke down in Normandy simply because theory and reality often drifted apart. As in every other sector of the war, Canadians in Normandy had paid with their lives for inexperience, and for inferior equipment like their high-profile, under-gunned Sherman tanks or their infantry anti-tank weapons.

The Normandy casualties would have to be replaced. As Crerar's First Canadian Army moved up the Channel coast, under orders to capture the heavily fortified ports of Le Havre, Dieppe, Boulogne, Calais and Dunkirk, infantry battalions reported a fraction of their normal fighting strength. In Italy, too, heavy fighting left serious gaps. The fall of Rome had left the Canadian corps in reserve as the Allies bickered over strategy. The Americans insisted on a landing on the south coast of France; Churchill persisted in an attack through the Ljubliana Gap into Austria and the Balkans. The Canadians, waiting on the Volturno River, were not consulted. Instead, they rested, collected reinforcements and reorganized the 5th Armoured Division with the extra infantry brigade Italian campaigning demanded. Allied air supremacy allowed many of the men to be converted from anti-aicraft units. At the end of August, General Burns was ordered north to the Foglia River on the Adriatic, to attack the latest German defence system, the Gothic Line. Burns's own position was delicate. He had survived Leese's demand for his removal and for the break-up of his corps only after direct intervention by Generals Crerar and Stuart. The Gothic Line would be his final test.

Protected by mines, wire, 479 anti-tank guns, 2,375 machine gun nests and twenty-two tank turrets set in concrete, the Gothic Line was a murderous obstacle. After four days of fighting, the Canadians broke through. As ever, the Germans recovered promptly, fighting back desperately at each of a dozen river crossings so that Burns's advance could be held until the rains and winter arrived. A month of steady fighting cost the Canadians 4,000 casualties and 1,500 cases of battle fatigue. For Leese, it was not good enough. At the end of October, the Canadians returned to reserve and, on November 5, Burns was replaced by Lieutenant-General Charles Foulkes. "Though progress was not always as rapid as desirable," Burns argued later in his own defence, "nevertheless, during our period of action we went further and faster than any other Corps."

The combined impact of "Overlord" in Normandy and the Gothic Line offensive in Italy brought Canada suddenly face-to-face with the one crisis Mackenzie King had tried hardest to avoid. The facts were plain and inescapable: there were not enough trained infantry reinforcements to keep the army's fighting units even remotely up to strength. Moreover, the fact was public knowledge, proclaimed by Major Conn Smythe, owner of the Toronto Maple Leafs and an artillery officer, who had returned, wounded, to Canada. Reinforcements reaching Normandy, claimed Smythe, were "green, inexperienced and poorly trained." Cooks and clerks were forced to masquerade as trained soldiers. The solution was clear: the NRMA men must be sent overseas at once.

Word of the crisis persuaded Colonel Ralston to set off for France and Italy to see for himself. His investigation was characteristically painstaking. Systematically, he tracked down rumours of untrained reinforcements and proved most of them to be false. He took no claim at face value, whether from generals, war correspondents or veteran regimental sergeant-majors. The same painfully conscientious approach led him to his conclusion: "I regret to say that conditions and prospects of which I have learned," Ralston cabled King on October 13, "will I fear necessitate reassessment in light of the future probability particularly regarding infantry involving, I fear, grave responsibilities."

That was a verbose understatement. The prime minister was almost beside himself. The war was virtually over and won. It seemed incredible to him that an army of half a million men, half of them overseas, could not find 15,000 infantry reinforcements. Why had he been assured repeatedly by Ralston, Stuart, Crerar and other generals that each expansion of the army would not lead to conscription? Surely there must be some way out.

The questions were legitimate; the answers were complex. The war might well have ended in Europe in 1944 if, inexplicably, General Montgomery had not halted the British advance in Antwerp instead of clearing the Scheldt estuary or if rain had not stalled British armoured columns before they could reach embattled airborne troops at Arnhem, making it "the bridge too far." Canadian casualty totals might well have been lower if Crerar's soldiers had been better trained or if Burns's corps had not been hurried into the Gothic Line assault at a time when the Italian theatre had been drained of men. The crisis might never have developed if Ottawa itself had not insisted on splitting the Canadian army between two widely separated campaigns, entailing two administrative organizations and a long time in transit. If Canadians used more men than the Americans or British in administrative roles, it was partly because the King government had insisted on a two-front war. The manpower crisis in Canada might have been alleviated if inter-service jealousy had not allowed the RCAF to hoard highly qualified volunteers for its over-expanded aircrew training programme. The army's own reinforcement arrangements, as General Burns would later point out, had serious flaws. Working from British experience in North Africa, where the Luftwaffe had caused casualties in the rear areas as well as in the front lines, the army had kept too many reinforcements for the artillery, engineers, army service corps and other supporting arms and services and not enough, relatively speaking, for the infantry. General Stuart, now in command of the Canadian Military Headquarters in London, suppressed early warnings from his staff officers and hoped for the best. Only in August did Stuart acknowledge the problem. Men might still have been re-mustered or transferred from the RCAF but that would be demoralizing and, above all, there was no time. One might rage, condemn and mourn—King and his colleagues would do all three—but the army remained 15,000 short of the men it needed. When Canadian voters discovered what being under-strength meant to the men of an infantry company or platoon, they would not be put off with a soft political answer. That was something a veteran battalion commander like Ralston certainly knew.

King's response to the crisis was agile and desperate. His sense of outrage was understandable. He had triumphantly kept his Liberal party united to the eve of victory. He had placated pro-conscriptionists and anti-conscriptionists. He had bowed to the right wing in 1943 and to the left in 1944. Now his political resourcefulness faced an ultimate test. King's first ploy was to seek official assurance from Churchill that conscription would not be necessary at that stage of the war; the British leader's reply was dismayingly non-committal. General Stuart was excoriated; his successor in Ottawa, Lieutenant-General J. C. Murchie, was interrogated. There was no escape. Finally, the prime minister found his weapon. Earlier, he had contemplated resignation if conscription went through. Now, in a mind preoccupied with plots, he suddenly spied a conspiracy within his own cabinet. Was it a coincidence that Ralston, Ilsley, Macdonald, Howe and all the others who now supported conscription had also opposed his social reform measures? Was this really a device to drive him from power and to hand the Liberal party to reactionaries? A letter from a right wing Liberal backbencher, demanding that the NRMA men be sent overseas, was evidence enough. King would fight back. He had his means. General McNaughton had returned to Canada a bitter and unemployed hero. All three parties, even the CCF, had approached him as a potential candidate. King had considered him as a potential governor-general. Now he had another thought. McNaughton had always opposed conscription and the old general certainly detested Ralston.

On November 13, 1944, with only his new French-Canadian lieutenant, Louis St-Laurent, briefed, King prepared to spring his trap. McNaughton, the prime minister explained, was the man to make the voluntary system work. Ralston, he recalled, had never withdrawn his 1942 letter of resignation. As ministers sat stunned, Ralston rose, shook hands around the table, and quietly left. Not one of his cabinet allies rose to follow him. McNaughton, waiting in an anteroom, was now minister.

The new Minister of National Defence was utterly convinced that his personality and reputation would convert the NRMA men into volunteers. He met his generals on November 14, listened to their misgivings, and promptly issued a press statement that his discussions with them had only confirmed his conviction that "the continuation of the voluntary system will produce the reinforcements." Four of the officers promptly sent telegrams protesting that nothing at their meeting could possibly have justified such a conclusion. McNaughton had no magic beyond his name and that was a wasting asset. Major-General George Pearkes of Pacific Command, where most of the battle-ready NRMA men were still stationed, went farther. He collected his senior officers, summoned the press and had his colleagues explain the problems of getting the NRMA men to volunteer. The report infuriated King. "These men in uniform," he raged, "have no right to speak in ways which will turn the people against the civil power." On November 22, Murchie and other senior officers at Army Headquarters met formally with McNaughton and solemnly delivered their conclusions: "After a careful review of all the factors . . . I must now advise you that in my considered opinion the voluntary system of recruiting through Army channels cannot meet the immediate problem." A badly-shaken McNaughton promptly reported to the prime minister. It was, he confessed, "like a blow in the stomach." Already he had one resignation, from the military commander in Winnipeg. There would be others and the entire military machine would run down.

McNaughton's message was alarmist to the point of being unbalanced. Officers who resigned could be replaced. Murchie had given an opinion which, on the evidence available at the time and since, was irrefutable, but it was no act of mutiny for a soldier to give his honest views. Yet the notion of a "generals' revolt" was a godsend to King. It fitted his well-developed suspicion of soldiers. It would frighten his more timid anti-conscriptionist colleagues and switch their votes. Indeed, he had probably already come to his own conclusion that the NRMA men must go.

On the afternoon of November 22, instead of making a triumphal first appearance in the House of Commons, it was McNaughton's melancholy chore to go to the bar of the House (he was and would remain unelected) to announce that by order-in-council, the government proposed to send 16,000 NRMA men overseas. The decision would be upheld after a short but painful debate, by a vote of 143 to 70, with 34 French-Canadian Liberals among the dissenters. One of them, a victim of his principles and his 1939 promises to Quebec voters, was the former Minister of National Defence for Air, C. G. Power.

In the former war, conscription had been a desperate, divisive and, ultimately, an anticlimactic issue. So it proved again, though in a more muted form. Once again there were demonstrations in Montreal and Quebec. The most frightening challenge to the governmant came far away in Terrace, British Columbia, a remote camp in the mountains behind Prince Rupert. A brigade of NRMA men mounted anti-tank guns on the single railway line and announced that they had gone on strike. Their senior officers, summoned by Pearkes to the conference in Vancouver, returned to the camp, discipline was restored and most of the men dutifully boarded trains for the East. There were other abortive protests but claims that thousands of "Zombies" deserted or threw their rifles overboard when boarding transports at Halifax were largely fabrications. Almost 13,000 conscripts went overseas, 2,463 served in battlefield units and 69 died.

That was the anti-climax. As in 1918, a series of wholly unpredictable coincidences ensured that the anticipated battle losses did not occur. During the months that King and his colleagues debated the reinforcement crisis, Crerar's army certainly needed men. While the British and American forces raced across France, the Canadians were left with orders to capture coastal ports. Le Havre, Boulogne and Calais each fell after destructive, bloody sieges. Now Montgomery demanded speed. The Canadians were needed to repair his inexplicable mistake on September 3 when he allowed the British advance guard to rest at Antwerp. The Allied advance, supplied from distant Cherbourg, would be stalled until Antwerp's magnificent harbour facilities were open to the sea. The estuary of the Scheldt must be cleared of its deeply entrenched German garrisons.

The Scheldt battlefield was about as unpleasant as any that could be devised and the Germans had exploited its defensive potential with their usual skill. The polder land was flooded. Narrow dykes, sprayed by machine guns and registered for accurate artillery fire, provided the only access. Crerar, ill with dysentery, handed over command of his army to Simonds while General Foulkes came from Italy to take command of II Corps. Two Canadian divisions, the 3rd and the 4th Armoured, were ordered to squeeze out the Breskens pocket, south of the Scheldt; the 2nd Division pushed across the Beveland isthmus. It took three miserable weeks. Casualties were high. For the second time since D-Day, the Black Watch from Montreal was virtually wiped out—on Friday, October 13. When Beveland was cut off, Simonds ordered his infantry to take the long, narrow causeway across to Walcheren. After enormous losses, the deed was done but the bridgehead proved to be a hopeless base for attack. The island finally fell to a bloody amphibious assault by British troops and Royal Marines. The price for the Scheldt was 3,550 Canadian casualties, 2,000 of them from the 3rd Division.

For the generals in Ottawa, that was the grim accompaniment to the political manoeuvrings of the 1944 conscription crisis. Anyone transferred from among the cold, sodden Canadians on South Beveland might have felt that a genuine general's revolt would be justified. Yet, no sooner had the government acted than the need evaporated. When Canadians went into winter quarters along the Waal and Maas rivers, casualties, save from pneumonia and trench foot, were few. In Italy, too, Canadians settled down northwest of Ravenna to await a spring push into the Lombardy plains. In January, 1945, when British and American chiefs of staff met at Malta, they agreed that Eisenhower needed more troops for northwest Europe. The Canadian demand for reunification of its army, submitted as soon as McNaughton became minister, suddenly made sense. The move, from mid-February to mid-April, kept the Canadians largely out of harm's way. The same could not be said of the Canadians already in the Netherlands.

In early March, the 2nd and 3rd Canadian Divisions began a hard slogging advance into the Hochwald Forest. German paratroopers contested every inch of the advance. A Canadian Highland brigade, invited as a ceremonial honour to cross the Rhine with the famous 51st Highland Division, found itself engaged in a furious battle at Speldorp. Yet, all too plainly, the war was winding down. The divisions from Italy attacked the German line between Ijsselmeer and the Weser and resistance crumbled. By April 11, American troops had encountered the Soviet Army at the Elbe. On April 21, 1945, British troops entered a devastated Hamburg. The first sickening evidence of the German death camps gave a sudden, chilling significance to claims most soldiers had dismissed as mere propaganda.

For the reunited Canadian army, the last weeks of the war were spent liberating the northern Netherlands, meeting occasional resistance, particularly from units of the Dutch SS. The Polish and 4th Canadian armoured divisions fought their way into Germany. The caution of soldiers anxious not to be the last casualty of a victorious war was balanced by the urgent need to rescue the starving, flooded Dutch population and by the fear that, somehow, the Nazis would launch some fearful reprisal before their defeat. The newly arrived I Corps pushed into western Holland, avoided the destruction of Apeldoorn by waiting for it to be surrounded, and halted their advance by April 19. There was really no point in going farther and it made more sense to use the military transport to stockpile food for the starving population than to blast a few more miles into the flooded land. Besides, the advance had not been painless. Since crossing the Rhine, the Canadian divisions had lost 6,300 casualties, 1,482 of them forever. On May 5, at Wageningen, General Charles Foulkes accepted the surrender of the German armies in the Netherlands. For Canadians, the war against Hitler was over.

Cold
War
Canada

7

The war was not, of course, really over. For Canadians starving in Hong Kong prison camps or in Japanese coal mines, or for Japanese Canadians marking their fourth spring of internment, the Pacific War remained a terrible reality. Yet most Canadians believed that the real war was over. They met V.E. Day with wild rejoicing—in Halifax and some other cities, too wild. Anxious to protect businesses that had been hugely profitable during the war, Halifax merchants closed down the city and assumed that thousands of soldiers, sailors and airmen would do their celebrating elsewhere. The outcome, fuelled by 65,000 bottles of looted liquor and 100,000 quarts of stolen beer, was an orgy of vengeful destruction on May 8. A government investigation chose Admiral L. W. Murray as the scapegoat for his failure to provide adequate security or alternative entertainment. It was fair notice of the treatment wartime military leaders could expect.

Canadians celebrated victory, not the coming peace. Opinion surveys showed that people were convinced that the war would be followed by mass unemployment and a renewed depression. For Mackenzie King, it was an opportunity to promise the "New Social Order," reflected in the Marsh Report and in wartime economic management, as a Liberal alternative to going back to old ways. The federal election on June 11, 1945, found the Tories split between those who shouted "me too!" and those who complained that King was bribing Quebec with family allowances. As for the overconfident CCF, Canadians preferred social policies without socialism. For all the Liberal record of confusion and exhaustion, King won his party a narrow victory with 125 seats to an opposition combination of 120. The service vote, Conservative in 1940, switched to the Liberals, with the CCF a close second with 33 per cent, a contrast with the 15 per cent it won from civilian voters. Overseas, the vote was strongly CCF with a low turnout, suggesting that the NRMA men in Canada had favoured the Liberals. King himself felt the military vote when servicemen switched their official residence to Prince Albert to defeat the prime minister. Whatever the nuances of any electoral message, Canadians—and particularly those in the services—wanted an active, reforming postwar government.

Restored to power, King faced both the Pacific War and the problems of a postwar world with increasing weariness and indecision. Canada's role against Japan remained undefined because the prime minister could not decide whether to fight alongside the British, with their suspicious imperialism, or to switch to the dangerously possessive new American alliance. Whatever was done, Canada's Pacific commitment would certainly be limited: Bracken had hurt himself and his party by demanding conscription for the fight against Japan. The government's eventual decision was a compromise. A new division, the 6th, would be formed from overseas veterans who volunteered. It would be equipped and organized on American lines. A special RCAF force, composed mainly of bomber squadrons, was to join General Curtis LeMay's efforts to pulverize Japanese cities. Only the RCN would work with its British counterpart, using the chance to build up its big-ship fleet. The first of them, HMCS *Uganda,* was already off Okinawa when, to the navy's humiliation, crew members insisted on going home. They had never agreed to fight Japan and Ottawa had insisted that only volunteers would serve. The cruiser sailed for Canada. On the way, the crew learned that on August 6, a new and horrifying weapon had destroyed Hiroshima, and Nagasaki three days later. The atomic bomb had precipitated a peace movement already in progress in Tokyo. This time, the war was really over.

Canada had every reason to feel victorious and even a little grandiose. In numbers of fighting ships, she had the third largest navy in the world. The RCAF was the fourth largest air force. All three services had finally achieved an impressive level of efficiency. Even more significant was Canada's undoubted domestic prosperity. The war had cost Canada $18 billion, $10.5 billion of it added to the national debt. Yet the gross national product was $11,759 million in 1945 and rising. Canada's economic affairs were in order. The Hyde Park agreement had kept Canadian-American trade and financial settlements in balance while Britain had gone irreversibly into debt with both countries. In its postwar settlements, Canada simply wrote off almost $3.5 billion owed by Britain for everything from the BCATP to war loans.

Unlike the gloom of 1918, King's government could plan postwar reconstruction in a mood of strength and bullish confidence. Canada had shown that it could pay unimaginably high taxes and still prosper; the government cautiously decided to try a little of the same medicine in peacetime. Its programme, by past standards, was ambitious: a National Housing Act to spend a billion dollars on new construction, an Industrial Development Bank, an Export Credit Corporation, support for farm and fish prices. C. D. Howe, invited to head a vaguely consultative ministry of reconstruction, refused. He insisted instead on the kind of powerful, virtually unaccountable agency he had made of the Department of Munitions and Supply. Howe's device of accelerated depreciation had produced huge munitions plants in wartime. Colleagues were horrified when he set out just as aggressively to dispose of war assets, using double depreciation to persuade industrialists to convert to peacetime purposes as early as 1944 when munitions contracts began to run out. By 1947, Howe had sold off $107 million in war plants in return for guarantees that their new owners would keep them operating for at least five years. If foreign investors were first in line to buy, that was fine with Howe. As for warships, aircraft and other costly military equipment, they were ruthlessly scrapped. A field of Ansons was simply burned. RCAF bomber pilots cheerfully dumped their Lancasters in a field in Alberta. However costly to build, Howe argued, the equipment would now never be used. Storage cost money.

Some of Howe's corporate offspring received generous treatment. Trans-Canada Airlines, a special favourite, had ended the war with big financial reserves. Howe wanted the airline not merely as a flag carrier but as a showcase for Canada's aircraft industry. Using influential American contacts, Howe outmanoeuvred Lord Beaverbrook's plan for a British-run imperial air line. Other Howe favourites were Eldorado Nuclear, a major contributor to development of the atomic bomb through its uranium mining and smelting, and Polymer Corporation at Sarnia, whose artificial rubber production had exceeded American plants in efficiency. Howe saw his company as the foundation for an innovative Canadian chemical industry.

While C. D. Howe managed Canada's economic conversion to peace, other ministers handled the government's rich spending programmes. In 1919, the Union government insisted that able-bodied veterans must find their own way back to civil life with a little help in settling them on the land. In 1945, a more buoyant Canada behaved differently. A Veterans' Land Act provided much more generous incentives for ex-servicemen eager to establish themselves in farming or fishing. Programmes for wounded and disabled veterans built on the earlier experience and on research in rehabilitative medicine. Legislation now compelled employers to take back veterans; 200,000 wanted their old jobs back. Civil service rules accepted veterans' preference in hiring though not necessarily in promotion. War Service Gratuities, based on length of service, distributed $752 million in purchasing power. So did $100 per veteran in clothing allowances and a re-establishment credit allowed those who did not take advantage of training benefits or the Veterans' Land Act to spend money on a home or furniture. The training benefits sent 50,000 veterans to university and another 130,000 into vocational training programmes. This time, there was no temptation for an increasingly conservative Canadian Legion to launch a "cash bonus" campaign.

During ten years of Depression and six years of war, Canadians had been obliged to put off buying cars, refrigerators, even new kitchen tables. Returned veterans found themselves with money to buy whatever could be produced. Family allowances represented as much as an extra week's wages for a large, low-income family, lifting millions of Canadians out of poverty and into a new consumer society. Unemployment was high in 1945 but now there was unemployment insurance, with a quarter of a billion dollars in war-time premiums stacked away in reserve. The war had seen an explosion of adult education, from the Canadian Legion's courses for service personnel to training for RCAF radar technicians. Even Howe's munitions factories had been training grounds for a million industrial workers. The postwar training grants completed a dramatic enrichment of Canada's social capital. Mature veterans became some of the most hard-working, serious students Canadian universities and schools had ever seen.

Postwar Canada was no paradise. Returned servicemen experienced all the familiar problems with communities and families which could not or would not understand their problems. War brides, far more numerous than in 1914-19 because of the long time Canadians had spent in England, encountered cruelty and prejudice as well as kindness, cultural poverty as well as material abundance. As in 1919, unsatisfied demands brought turbulence. Unions and management struggled to test whether the wartime gains of P.C. 1003 would hold. In 1946, Canada experienced the worst year of strikes in her history. The outcome was the permanent unionization of most major industrial sectors and a more mature collective bargaining relationship on both sides. Workers would share in the postwar boom and, by their purchasing power, they would extend it. The boom, of course, depended on demand. Everything was needed. When the new government's housing programme floundered, Howe took it over. His new Central Mortgage and Housing Corporation promised 80,000 new homes a year; it delivered 71,000 in its first year. Not even C. D. Howe could deliver miracles in the midst of the postwar materials shortage. By 1948, Canada's gross national product had climbed far past its wartime record to reach $15.5 billion. Canadians had done well out of the war.

One consequence was that Canadians wanted to enjoy civilian life. The sailors of HMCS *Uganda* were not unique. In 1943, a Post-Hostilities Planning Committee, chaired by Hume Wrong of the Department of External Affairs, had invited the service chiefs to plan Canada's postwar armed forces and her commitment to the occupation of Germany. As a result, the government promised the Allies 25,000 soldiers and eleven RCAF squadrons as an occupying force but only until March 31, 1946. If Ottawa had any intention of extending the arrangement, sitdown strikes by homesick airmen and soldiers and a storm of domestic criticism changed its mind. Over strenuous British objections and on the argument that Canada had been excluded from the Allied Control Commission, Canada's occupying force came home in the spring of 1946.

Canada's military leaders still had optimistic postwar plans. On June 25, 1945, McNaughton and his two associate ministers, Douglas Abbott for the navy and Colin Gibson for the air force, listened to proposals that would have cost Canadian taxpayers about $190 million a year (plus $37 million to re-equip the army). The RCN wanted a task force with two aircraft carriers, four cruisers and 20,000 men. The Army's "Plan G" called for 55,788 regular soldiers, 155,396 in the reserves and a 48,500 "training force" based on compulsory service. The RCAF's demands, 30,000 in regular service,

15,000 in auxiliary squadrons and 50,000 in reserve, sounded comparatively modest. The government response was frosty. Abbott, who became minister after McNaughton had failed a second time to win a parliamentary seat, was a lukewarm advocate. Mackenzie King found the army's yearning for peacetime conscription "perfectly outrageous." Lieutenant-General Charles Foulkes, junior to Simonds but a more diplomatic peacetime soldier, was chosen as the army's postwar chief of staff and "Plan G" vanished. By the time the services had pruned their estimate, the RCN had to be content with 10,000 men, the army with 25,000 regulars and the RCAF with 16,000. By pre-war standards, this was an impressive force but any peacetime reduction was painful to admirals, generals and air marshals.

The pain was not eased when Brooke Claxton replaced Abbott as Minister of National Defence at the end of 1946. A Montreal corporation lawyer who enjoyed reminding generals that he had once served as a sergeant in the CEF, Claxton had used both experiences to devise a military law manual in 1939. He was better known as a progressive Liberal who had steered family allowances into operation in time for the 1945 election. Claxton was a minister with ideas. He promptly reorganized the rambling temporary buildings erected in wartime to house the three service staffs into an integrated headquarters. Operational staffs were housed in one building, personnel and pay staffs went to another and supply and equipment directorates to the third. Claxton also introduced a fourth service, the Defence Research Board. Conceived by the army's Colonel W. W. Goforth, vigorously opposed by the RCAF which had its own research activities, the Board came into being on April 3, 1947.

The government regarded its senior officers as political illiterates. Early postwar plans called for a Canadian Joint Services Staff College for middle-rank officers while their superiors broadened their minds at the Imperial Defence College in Britain or at the American National War College. Instead, on the urging of a British officer, Major-General J. F. M. Whiteley, backed by Lester Pearson from External Affairs and Dr. O. M. Solandt, first chairman of the Defence Research Board, Claxton overrode army and RCAF opposition and launched Canada's own National Defence College at Kingston on January 5, 1948. The student body included Canadian, British and American senior officers, civil servants and occasional defence-minded civilians. Studies ranged over the political, social and economic problems of Canada and the world. Claxton's choice of commandant, Lieutenant-General Guy Simonds, proved brilliantly successful. At a more junior level, Claxton's enthusiasm for tri-service integration became the lever for re-opening the Royal Military College, closed as an officer training school since 1942. Foulkes, who wanted officers to be university graduates, was out-flanked by the RMC's influential ex-cadet club and overruled by Claxton. The new college was designed to train officers for all three services and to educate them to a high academic standard.

Postwar adjustments were as hard for men in the ranks as they were for generals and admirals. When the government, alarmed at the first signs of a postwar recession, ordered establishments cut to 75 per cent, that still left more vacancies than recruiting depots could fill. Lagging pay scales, lack of quarters for families and the competition of a booming economy made the services unattractive. The RCAF had the most to offer. New jet aircraft gave pilots and ground crews a fresh challenge. The army also had a new role, at least for its three regular infantry battalions. As a Mobile Strike Force, soldiers received parachute training and new, air-portable equipment. Soldiers also won public recognition when they turned out to fight floods in the Fraser Valley in 1948 and virtually took charge of an inundated Winnipeg in the spring of 1950. The navy's problems were most acute and they became embarrassing public knowledge after minor mutinies on the new aircraft carrier *Magnificent* and on two destroyers, *Crescent* and *Athabaskan*, in 1949. An investigation headed by Rear-Admiral Rollo Mainguy revealed officers too prone to ape Royal Navy attitudes to discipline as well as problems of pay, leave and morale. It was part of the price of moving from the informality of a small ship navy of corvettes and frigates to much larger ships without thinking through a sensible approach to discipline and routine.

Canada's breakneck demobilization of wartime forces was by no means unique. Proportionate to its far greater strength, the United States probably surpassed Canada in the speed of its disarmament and the United Kingdom would certainly have done so but for colonial problems stretching from Palestine to Malaya. The illusion that Canadians had returned from another war to end war was short-lived. Even as Canada demobilized in 1946, politicians, service officers and officials of the Department of External Affairs grimly wrestled with an ugly postwar reality.

The Cold War really broke on the European and North American democracies with the Communist coup in Czechoslovakia in February, 1948 or perhaps with the Berlin blockade a month later. Until then, discretion, wishful thinking or war-engendered sympathy all conspired to make people overlook the fact that, alone among the major powers, the Soviet Union had not disarmed after 1945, had kept its captured territories and managed the nations of Eastern Europe as forcefully as the western powers managed occupied Germany. The Canadian attitude was illustrated by the plight of Igor Gouzenko, the Soviet cypher clerk who fled the Russian embassy in Ottawa with evidence of widespread Soviet espionage in Canada. King found his reports more embarrassing when they were proved to be true than when they were disbelieved. The indignation King felt at a trusted ally placing spies in his own office was more than countered by his concern lest Canada be responsible for breaking up the great wartime alliance.

Others were more cold-blooded. British post-hostilities planning as early as 1944 identified the Soviet Union as a great potential enemy though its threat was not seen as imminent before 1955-60. American planners agreed.

Guilt-ridden by the success of Japanese surprise attacks at Pearl Harbor and the Philippines in 1941, United States strategists assumed another war would start in the same way. The routes along which aircraft and supplies had been poured into Soviet hands could easily be reversed for a Soviet attack. The wartime agency for Canadian-American preparedness, the Permanent Joint Board on Defence, would continue not from inertia but necessity. Canadians were much slower to perceive the revolution in their defence system. The War of 1812 was finally over. So was the concept of imperial defence, with Canada secure behind the powerful Royal Navy. Field Marshal Lord Montgomery, Britain's postwar chief of the Imperial General staff, tried briefly to re-float the idea. By 1948, General Foulkes could return from a London conference to assure Claxton that: ". . . the day of Commonwealth Defence Policy is definitely finished and . . . the British are taking a much broader and realistic view of defence matters. . .". Realism was humbling.

The fading of British power left Canada alone with a very much more domineering defence partner. The war had taught Canadians how swiftly the Americans could move when their minds were made up and how little weight Ottawa's appeals really carried in Washington. Canadians also knew that whatever the United States wished to do for its own security, it would do whether or not Canada agreed. As the Cabinet War Committee gloomily reminded itself at the end of February, 1945, Americans would act "with an absence of the tact and restraint customarily employed by the United Kingdom in putting forward defence proposals." Canadians could, of course, sit back and let the Americans enjoy both the authority and the burden. Alternatively, Ottawa could have assumed the incredible cost and responsibility of making their country secure against both the Americans and the Russians. Neither was a serious alternative. Instead, defence planning from 1945 on was continued through the PJBD, with General McNaughton becoming Canada's representative when he left the cabinet in August, 1945. The government sadly concluded that, much as it had purchased useless American facilities in the North to preserve sovereignty, it would now have to do more than its own judgement deemed necessary. The effort was all the more vital because Canada's sovereignty over the vast Arctic region of ocean and islands was by no means universally acknowledged, even in Washington.

Canada's salvation must lie in multilateral associations. Mackenzie King had scorned the League of Nations and he had always suspected the British military connection but in his final years he grew increasingly alarmed that Canada might be trapped in the American nexus. With misgivings not generally shared by his two foreign policy lieutenants, St-Laurent and Pearson, King led Canada into the United Nations at San Francisco and promptly used its charter as an excuse not to join a Washington-inspired inter-American defence agreement signed at Chapultepec in 1945. Canadian service chiefs used the United Nations, not continental defence, as an argument for their post-1945 organizations. American pressure led Ottawa to develop

Fort Churchill as a research centre and proving ground but Ottawa insisted that the purpose was peaceful. When *Pravda* sneered at this sudden Canadian enthusiasm for Arctic geography, the government invited foreign military representatives to visit the base. The impressions of the Soviet attache, a young veteran of Stalingrad, are unknown.

Neither Ottawa nor Washington fully accepted the PJBD's Basic Security Plan, formally presented at the end of 1946. As General Omar Bradley noted, it was more useful in getting Congressional appropriations than in preparing for war. Canadian military leaders, in particular, suspected that any Soviet attack on North America would be a diversion, holding back United States and Canadian forces from the real war in Europe. The Mobile Strike Force's airborne battalions would be trained to attack small Soviet lodgements in the Arctic but the continent was really more seriously threatened by the kind of subversion Gouzenko had revealed than by an invasion of Soviet bombers or tanks. However, another PJBD proposal was completely accepted: Canadian forces must abandon their traditional British connection to become Americanized. All three services, with the RCAF leading, would convert to American weapons and equipment, training methods, tactical doctrines and communications. It was a logical development in an American-dominated defence system just as British arms and staff methods had seemed appropriate in the 1900s. Instead of struggling with obsolete wartime arms and vehicles, all three services had a powerful argument for re-equipment. American equipment might or might not be superior to British patterns; it would certainly be more easily available.

As an overall development, the Americanization of the Canadian forces should have been controversial. The issue was hardly raised. In 1947, St-Laurent, as Secretary of State for External Affairs, presented Parliament with a Visiting Forces bill, giving American as well as British officers power of command over their own forces on Canadian soil. Mild acrimony in the debate was subdued when he reminded members of Parliament that similar legislation for British Commonwealth forces had been adopted in 1933. Canadians would certainly have been happier if both Britain and the United States had joined in postwar standardization. Indeed, some progress was made, beginning with a humble but vital problem, a common screw thread. However, the Cold War soon gave Canada a broader multilateralism than she could ever have expected.

If defence spending was any barometer of world tensions, Canada looked out on the world of 1947-48 with profound optimism: Claxton's defence budget was only $195,561,641. Yet the world was visibly in crisis. In 1946, Churchill's speech at Fulton, Missouri, had given the democracies a new phrase: the Iron Curtain. From the perspective of Ottawa, Washington and London, the curtain was advancing. Greece and Italy were saved only by massive American military and economic aid. The overthrow of the Benes government in Czechoslovakia in February, 1948 recalled all the guilty memories of Munich. The blockade of Berlin was met immediately by a massive cargo airlift. On the other side of the world, Chiang Kai-shek's Kuomintang regime crumbled before the Communist advance. A Canadian destroyer, HMCS *Crescent,* stood by to rescue more than 800 Canadians. In western Europe, democratic and often socialist governments wrestled desperately with postwar reconstruction, but they had neither inherited defence forces after the war nor did they possess the means to build them. A collective protest against the Czech coup was more desperate than influential. Only the exhausted, bankrupt British had substantial armed forces. France, which had also attempted to re-arm, sent the best of its men and equipment to its hopeless colonial struggle in Indochina.

In the deepening crisis, Canada's response was cautious. King was personally appalled by news that Jan Masaryk, the Czech foreign minister, had jumped or been shoved to his death on February 10, 1948 but Canada took no action. Nor would the elderly prime minister, in his final months in office, approve Canadian participation in the Berlin airlift. Defence estimates for 1948-49 rose substantially and included the navy's first Arctic patrol ship—but King was horrified when President Harry Truman restored the draft in the United States. If Canada followed suit, King warned, Canadians would join the Communist party: "They will say if we are to risk our lives fighting Communism, we better save our heads by joining them." That August, King took his fears into retirement but his successor needed no guidance on conscription. Louis St-Laurent had not survived the 1944 crisis for nothing. Yet, far more than King and most Canadians, St-Laurent had a view of the world and of Canada's place in it. In domestic affairs, he was content to be chairman of the board in his cabinet room. Trusted colleagues like Howe, Claxton or Paul Martin, Minister of Health and Welfare (and soon of civil defence), could manage their departments without interference. In external affairs, he was a decisive force.

St-Laurent, the first French-speaking prime minister since Laurier, shared little of Quebec's traditional isolationism. Indeed, in a world where the Communist menace had replaced British imperialism as the gravest threat to Quebec's conservative Catholicism, foreign policy no longer cut so deeply across Canada's deepest national division. Maurice Duplessis, back in power since 1944, waged noisy battles with Ottawa but he also found it good politics to harry Quebec's remnant of Communists. Quebec isolationism was not dead but it would slowly become the monopoly of a new force in French the province's universities and its labour movement. It was characterized by younger men like Jean Marchand and Pierre Elliott Trudeau, or a chain-smoking television commentator named René Lévesque whose programmes in the 1950s taught Quebeckers much that they knew about the outside world.

St-Laurent, who identified with neither Duplessis nor the left, had inherited a suspicion of the British from both his French and his Irish ancestors, to say nothing of Mackenzie King. In Commonwealth affairs, his reactions gave him an unexpected empathy with leaders of the newer members like Jawaharlal Nehru of India. Such contacts persuaded him and his successor in External Affairs, Lester Pearson, that Canada's search for multilateral links should lead to the emerging, post-colonial nations. Was Canada not the first of them? Peacekeeping, the most obvious military expression of Canada's yearning to play a more idealistic role in the world, began with observer teams sent to Kashmir in 1948 to mediate a shaky truce between India and Pakistan.

Serious concerns came closer to home. By September, 1948, western European nations had nervously banded together in a European Defence Union with Britain's Lord Montgomery as chairman. The union would be helpless without the United States. On the contrary, American commitment would be the only effective deterrent to Soviet aggression. Achieving that commitment became a major Canadian goal. The result was a North Atlantic treaty of twelve nations with the United States fully involved. However, St-Laurent and Pearson had other concerns. As Canadians had feared, the United Nations had become as completely dominated by a few great powers as had wartime strategy. In the new North Atlantic Treaty Organization, each participant must have an equal voice. The point was accepted. Another Canadian goal, urged by Pearson to the annoyance and embarrassment of alliance partners, was the need for NATO to express shared political and moral values. Pearson's reward was Article II, a bland and sonorous piece of prose which did nothing to placate NATO critics.

NATO was, of course, a military alliance though one member, Iceland, had no military forces. It was based, St-Laurent assured Parliament, "on the common belief of the North Atlantic union in the values and virtues of Christian civilization." Out of deference to Dr. Antonio Salazar's Portugal, democracy was not mentioned. Yet if there were embarrassing anomalies in the Article II version of NATO—and even "Christian civilization" might be stretched a little when Turkey joined later—neither was the alliance the militaristic adventure depicted by Soviet propagandists and their Canadian echoes. NATO military goals of ninety divisions to match Soviet and East European strength were window-dressing. Rearmament was overdue and justified for a defenceless Europe. American military strength in Europe had fallen to a single under-strength division and a paramilitary constabulary. In itself, NATO planners believed, the alliance would be a deterrent to Soviet assault. The real benefit of the alliance was that, by pooling military strength, each member could actually do less.

Canada was typical in seeking cut-rate rearmament. Its 1949 defence budget amounted to only $360 million. Canada's major initial contribution to the alliance was the stockpile of British-pattern equipment stored since 1946 for its own forces. Handing over a division's worth of equipment to the Netherlands, with equal gifts later to Belgium and Italy and a regiment of field guns to Luxembourg, emptied Canada's inventory and put pressure on the

St-Laurent government to purchase replacements from the United States or from Canadian manufacturers. To their surprise, Canadian officers found that the United States could be as balky a supplier as Britain, with Congress first restricting American arms exports and then imposing a "Buy American" policy which kept Canadian suppliers out of the reviving United States arms market. Canada waited for more than a year for equipment and vitally needed spare parts before Congress passed the Mutual Defence Assistance Act in October, 1949. Canada was rewarded by special mention as a country where the United States could buy for sale offshore. Not until May 5, 1950, did the United States defence secretary agree to let Canada sell $15-25 million in defence supplies to American forces to offset its own much larger purchases.

NATO's leisurely rearmament was shaken out of phase on June 25, 1950. Virtually without warning, tanks and troops from North Korea struck across the UN-sanctioned demarcation line, the 38th Parallel, to push deep into the Republic of South Korea. An American-dominated UN Security Council, with the Soviet Union absent in a boycott, called on member nations to meet aggression. American ships and aircraft from the occupation forces in Japan were already in action. By July 5, American troops met the Communist forces and fell back. By mid-July the remnants of the South Korean army, the Americans and a British brigade from Hong Kong, were hemmed in around the port of Pusan. Then, with his remarkable strategic flair, General Douglas MacArthur unleashed an amphibious assault on Inchon, the port for the Korean capital of Seoul. The North Koreans, caught in the flank, reeled back. MacArthur ordered his army north across the 38th Parallel, swept into North Korea and promised that his troops would be home for Christmas.

For St-Laurent and Pearson, Korea was a test of the United Nations and collective security. Parliament, due to prorogue, learned that three RCN destroyers at Esquimalt would sail immediately. All parties welcomed the news. In August, with the UN's tiny army pinned at Pusan, the cabinet assigned the RCAF's only long-range transport squadron to join the American air bridge to the Far East. More reluctantly, the government agreed to send an infantry brigade group. When Parliament assembled to end a rail strike, members learned that the soldiers might be used for any United Nations operation, not merely Korea, but only with parliamentary consent. The truth was that Ottawa grew more uncomfortable as Korea became a U.S., not a UN operation. President Truman, for his part, wondered whether he or the redoubtable General MacArthur was really in charge.

Sending destroyers and a transport squadron merely redeployed members of the regular forces. NATO (and Canadian) defence planners anxiously pondered the significance of Korea, noting that MacArthur's campaign had required every mobilized division in the United States. If the Soviet Union had really plotted a diversion, it had succeeded. Yet, Foulkes reported from Washington, the Americans believed that their six divisions would win the war promptly. For its own ground force contribution, Canada could have sent its own Mobile Strike Force but it was under-strength by hundreds of men. Instead, the Korean contingent was recruited as a "Canadian Army Special Force," with a special appeal to Second World War veterans. Put on the spot by cabinet colleagues, Claxton took a deep breath and promised that the men could be found without conscription. He was right, though not by much. In 1949, Canada had skidded into a mild recession and the unemployed included thousands of veterans who had not adjusted easily to civilian life. Some would not have been ideal soldiers, either, but Claxton insisted that recruiting standards be cut to find the necessary ten thousand men. The result was an all-volunteer force with plenty of rough diamonds and a good deal of battle experience. Perhaps surprisingly, 3,134 of the 10,587 Special Force volunteers came from Quebec though opinion polls showed that only 21 per cent of Quebeckers approved of the Korean operation.

By November, the Canadian brigade was at Fort Lewis, Washington, training with American weapons squeezed out of the United States' own depleted stocks. In Korea, the war took a dramatic turn. MacArthur had ordered his men north to the Yalu River, Korea's border with China. Before the Americans arrived, Chinese troops poured into the war. As bitter winter weather swirled out of Manchuria, MacArthur's front line collapsed. A Marine division barely broke out of encirclement and escaped by sea. By the end of February, the UN forces halted forty miles south of Seoul. A fresh offensive carried them back to the 38th Parallel. When the American commander hinted that he would extend the war to achieve his promised victory, Truman finally intervened. After an epic civil-military confrontation, MacArthur was removed, received a hero's welcome in New York and Washington, and duly faded away. Even then, only a battalion of Canadians had reached Korea and the full Canadian brigade entered the line only on May 25, 1951, almost a year after the war had begun. Hard fighting continued. At Kapyong, where a British battalion was overrun by the Chinese the 2nd Princess Patricia's Canadian Light Infantry survived by calling artillery fire on its own positions and suffering only ten killed in an intense two-day battle. It was partly the reward of experience.

When it finally arrived, the Canadian brigade fitted naturally into a Commonwealth Division of British, Australian and New Zealand troops. A mixture of British and American weapons and vehicles would have created problems in a mobile war but the cease-fire negotiations which began on July 10, 1951, tied the war to a narrow, unmoving front reminiscent of 1914–18. The war dragged on, marked by patrol activity, occasional violent Chinese assaults and, despite total American command of the air, a growing volume of Chinese artillery and mortar fire. After a year, the original special force was replaced by a second brigade and, a year later, by a third, until 20,000 Canadians had served in Korea, suffering 1,557 casualties, 312 of them fatal. Most losses were suffered by the later brigades. For Canadians and, indeed, for most participants, Korea was a frustrating war. Seventeen United Nations members sent contingents, but the Americans were in charge. Never before had Americans fought a war without hope of a decisive conclusion and allies feared that the United States' fury at the Communist triumph in China would add pressure to use the atomic bomb in a bid for victory. Truman's admission at a press conference soon after the Chinese troops entered the conflict that the use of the bomb was "under active consideration" by General MacArthur, brought a shocked British prime minister to Washington. The Americans huffily insisted that the UN had given them responsibility for the war and that the president must not be asked even to consult his allies. The UN allies, who had deplored even the earlier MacArthur decision to cross the 38th Parallel, wondered where their influence lay.

MacArthur's replacement by a less flamboyant General Matthew B. Ridgeway cooled fears that a septuagenarian general would launch an American crusade into Asia. It could not make Americans conscientious about consulting allies. Canada's own grievance came late in the war when a company of Canadian soldiers was ordered to join in the unpleasant task of quelling prison camp riots. Ottawa was deeply annoyed. It had not been consulted about involving Canadians as apparent oppressors in a clever Communist propaganda ploy. Indeed, its own liaison officer in Tokyo had not thought the episode worth reporting. The errant officer was removed but the American commander, General Mark Clark, never did understand why Canada was offended. A British general would not have been so mystified.

Understandably, the excitement and drama of the Korean War occupied whatever attention Canadians could spare for military matters. Like Americans, they grew bored and disillusioned with the interminable ceasefire negotiations, orchestrated, as they apparently were, to serve some inscrutable Communist propaganda purpose. The war and accompanying American rearmament cured the shallow recession, created a demand for manpower and materials and spurred the inflation which had already begun with the end of wartime price and wage controls. As Minister of Finance, Douglas Abbott refused to implement controls but, like J. L. Ilsley, he insisted that Canada's new defence effort be financed from taxes, and accordingly curbed consumer spending and turned down the Canadian housing programme. Canadians, who had earlier given St-Laurent the most lopsided Liberal majority in history in the 1949 election, gave little evidence of suffering.

Not everyone was preoccupied with the Far East in 1950. China's involvement in the Korean War frightened NATO leaders and enraged them against the foolhardy general who had provoked it. Those who still believed that Moscow orchestrated the entire Communist world, believed that the USSR had indicated an unexpected eagerness to engage in a general war. Korea was no mere brushfire war but part of a clever global strategy. Moreover, Soviet nuclear tests in 1949 showed that the American monopoly of the atomic bomb had ended. Instead of the cautious, economical rebuilding of forces envisaged at the end of 1948, NATO planners took the Chinese intervention as a warning that the West had as little as eighteen months to prepare for a major war. General Dwight D. Eisenhower, the soft-spoken commander of the wartime Allies in Europe, was summoned from the presidency of Columbia University to become Supreme Allied Commander. To provide him with a tactical instrument, NATO members agreed to create an "Integrated Force," free to be moved as needs dictated. On January 26, 1951, Eisenhower landed in Ottawa. His message was blunt: immediate con-tributions would be far more valuable than much larger aid in a year's time. His nervous and defeatist European partners desperately needed reas-surance.

Ottawa dutifully responded. To the delight of generals, shipments of obsolete British-style equipment to Europe increased. The RCAF, mindful of the BCATP, proposed to expand facilities to train NATO jet pilots and navigators. Eventually, it would graduate 1,400 a year. The navy, reverting to its escort and convoy role as part of a NATO Atlantic command, asked for new destroyer escorts and fast refits of older warships as well as a strength of 23,000 regulars. The RCAF had already begun to take delivery of the F-86 Sabre, an American-designed fighter built at Canadair in Montreal. It asked for 350 more. On February 5, 1951, Claxton announced the dramatic scale of Canada's rearmament: a hundred ships for the RCN, forty squadrons for the RCAF, an entire infantry division for the army. The total cost, over three years, was to be $5 billion. Canada would immediately recruit an additional brigade group, 10,000 men, for service in Europe. The RCAF would send an air division of twelve F-86 squadrons.

If Eisenhower wanted a dramatic commitment, by Canadian standards, he had one. By the standards of an alliance facing imminent Soviet attack, the response was, of course, distinctly modest. The army's 27th Brigade, this time recruited from reserve regiments, was in Europe before the end of 1951 but the first two RCAF squadrons joined NATO's ranks only in mid-1952 and the entire twelve squadrons were not ready until the summer of 1953. Canada agreed to deliver a full infantry division three months after the fighting began and a second division three months later. General Simonds, now the army's chief of staff, noted that a lack of shipping dictated that any Canadians planning to fight in Europe had better be there when the fighting broke out. His observation brought no response.

Simonds and General Foulkes, now promoted to be chairman of the Chiefs of Staff Committee, differed sharply over the destination of the new Canadian brigade. To Foulkes, a proponent of the American defence con-nection, it was obvious that the Canadians might as well start getting used to working with the American army. Equipment, weapons and supplies would, in any case, come up the American pipeline. Simonds fought back, insisting that Canadians had far more confidence in British organization and leadership and far more faith that their separate identity would be respected. Switching to political arguments, Simonds also insisted that Canada should throw its weight behind the non-American wing of NATO: ". . . the US with relatively limited experience in world affairs and because her policies were at times subject to unpredictable and emotional influences, could conceivably, without some balancing restraint, carry the democratic nations into a Third World War." With Canada's experience in Korea to back him up and support from Arnold Heeney of External Affairs, Simonds won the argument. The RCAF air division went to Europe under American auspices but the 27th Canadian Infantry Brigade joined the British Army of the Rhine.

Rearmament involved more than armed forces. To equip itself with authority for a crisis without using the full weight of the War Measures Act, the St-Laurent government pushed through an Emergency Powers Bill. Only the CCF overtly condemned its vague and sweeping powers. The Conservatives, caught by their previous insistence that the government act decisively, now grumbled that the government might have gone too far. C. D. Howe, who had managed Canada's postwar economy from the Department of Trade and Commerce, regained much of his vast wartime authority through a new Department of Defence Production, able to "control and regulate the production, processing, distribution, acquisition, disposition or use of materials or the supply and use of services deemed essential for war purposes." Again the Conservatives were trapped between their fervour as Cold Warriors and their hostility to government economic management. What they did learn from the acrimonious debate was that an angry, embattled Howe could be made to embarrass his own party. The benefits of Howe-baiting would be remembered in 1955 when the Defence Production Act was renewed.

Military expansion also revived Canada's most durable military problem, manpower. From 1950 to 1953, armed forces strength rose from 47,000 to 104,000. All three services faced recruiting problems. The RCN, still troubled by difficulties uncovered in 1949 by the Mainguy report, needed to find and retain skilled tradesmen and technicians for its modern ships. It did not reach its recruiting target until the end of the 1950s. The RCAF was still the most attractive service for young Canadians and it was the first to revive its Women's Division in peacetime, but like the navy, it had to train most of its own technicians. As usual, it was the army which presented the most critical problems. The NATO crisis revived talk of conscription. Simonds favoured it; Claxton firmly cut him off but even the defence minister admitted to a discreet Press Gallery confidant that conscription would come the moment war with Russia began. "With this Prime Minister," he claimed, "we can do anything in Quebec." That might be an illusion. Opinion polls showed that 37 per cent of Quebeckers had favoured the NATO commitment but 83 per cent still opposed any form of conscription. Unemployment, not anti-communism, had brought French Canadians to the Special Force in 1950; by 1952, the brigade was short 374 infantry and most of them were missing from the battalion of the Royal 22e Regiment.

The army as a whole reached 49,278 men, but short-term enlistments for the two brigades overseas led to a rapid turnover. By early 1953, the army's adjutant-general warned that Canada might not be able to meet her commitments in Europe and the Far East. The problem eased when the Korean conflict finally ended in an armistice in July, 1953. General Simonds's faith that armies and recruiting could be built on *esprit de corps* led to revival of the 1st Canadian Division with its historic red patch insignia, the transfer of historic regiments like the Queen's Own Rifles, the Black Watch, the 8th Hussars and the Fort Garry Horse from the militia and the creation of a Regiment of Canadian Guards, complete with scarlet tunics and bearskins. A more practical step for morale and discipline was the decision, opposed by Simonds, to allow wives and families to join Canadian service personnel in Europe. It was also evidence that Canada now saw her NATO undertaking not as a crisis response but as a continuing burden.

To manage a defence budget which had more than quadrupled from 1950 to the 1953 level of $1,907 million, Claxton added five new assistant deputy ministers to manage proliferating administrative tasks. Widely publicized scandals in the army's engineering services in 1953, including headlines reporting horses on the payroll, persuaded the prime minister to add an Associate Minister of National Defence. True to Claxton's dream of service integration, the new minister was not assigned a specific service but took on a miscellany of chores. Foulkes's appointment as chairman of the Chiefs of Staff Committee, the agency which had really supplanted the Defence Council as a policy-making body, was another of the minister's steps toward integration. Claxton's interest in military law led, on June 30, 1950, to final passage of a new National Defence Act. As a further step away from Britain, the act supplanted British statutes like the Army Act by providing a common discipline code for the three services. The Canadian Forces Act and the Defence Services Pension Act replaced a welter of different service pay and pension arrangements with a single set of remuneration and benefit policies. In 1954, when a tired Claxton retired to the board of Metropolitan Life, his goals of a single defence budget, increased defence research, tri-service personnel policies and a Canadian system of military law had all been achieved.

The older interservice rivalries had not, of course, been resolved. Despite a vigorous claim from the RCAF, the navy retained and developed its own Naval Air Service. A bitter contest over rival research and development budgets was not really resolved by inviting the chairman of the Defence Research Board to serve as judge. He merely restored each service's traditional share and called for more money. A dispute about training new officers revealed real differences in service philosophies. The re-opened Royal

Military College, fed by graduates from the two-year programme at the former naval college at Royal Roads in Victoria, produced four-year graduates strong in science and engineering. That satisfied the RCAF, which wanted a few highly-qualified officers for long service and a great many short-service officers as aircrew. Both the army and the RCN needed more officers to cope with rapid expansion and the RCAF mixture of long-service and short-service commissions did not suit their needs. The problem was complicated when Claxton's concern about the shortage of French Canadian officers in all three services led to the opening of the Collège Militaire Royal de St-Jean in 1952. The RCAF balked at taking over the new college as an administrative responsibility. In any future reversion to single-service colleges, the air force might find itself saddled with an ill-equipped institution committed to a bilingualism the RCAF itself was most reluctant to espouse. The wrangle over officer training continued unresolved until the belated discovery that the shortage had solved itself. With 17,283 officers by 1955, the armed forces could no longer claim a crisis.

Most inter-service disputes seemed transient or trivial. One was not. Canada's wholesale commitment to NATO's Integrated Force in 1951 reflected more than a judgement about where the threat seemed greatest. Like its later UN peacekeeping operations, Canada looked on NATO as a way of broadening its options outside the unequal continental partnership with the United States. The election of General Eisenhower as president in 1952 and the advent of a Republican administration in Washington disturbed many Canadians. John Foster Dulles, the new Secretary of State, sought to fulfil the new government's tax-cutting goals by switching the emphasis in defence from costly and unpopular conventional forces to the cheaper but more frightening emphasis on a prompt use of the nuclear deterrent. The switch was concealed behind an apparently more defiant and inflexible assertion of the Cold War principles. In the circumstances, the Canadian government and particularly Lester Pearson strained to persuade the world that Canada was more than a "squeaky second fiddle to the United States." Yet the Dulles policy also emphasized continental defence against the growing threat of a Soviet nuclear attack. The RCAF's share in North American defence began as a debate in the Chiefs of Staff Committee; it would eventually topple a Canadian government.

In 1952, that seemed utterly improbable. A year later, the Liberals won another easy election victory. Canada was prosperous, even booming. Perhaps many Canadians would have preferred a Democratic government in Washington. More were repelled by Senator Joe McCarthy's red-baiting of prominent Americans. Canadians could afford to be tolerant. Their own Communists were at liberty but they had been driven into insignficance. In the universities and the CCF, the old liberal traditions of pacifism and isolationism survived but some of the pillars of its earlier age, like Frank Underhill and Professor Arthur Lower, had enlisted in the Cold War. Canada's few defence analysts were rarely critics. Defence, for those who accept its carnivorous assumptions, usually justifies its ends, whatever the argument about the means. Canadians in the 1950s could apparently afford both guns and butter. Indeed, believers in Keynes could insist that spending on guns put butter on the table.

The postwar RCAF had given little emphasis to air defence. A few auxiliary squadrons, flying Mustangs and Vampire jet fighters on weekends, and reserve anti-aircraft batteries practising with aged 3.7 inch guns, satisfied a remote threat. Yet, with its eye on the future and with C. D. Howe's warm blessing, the RCAF had already embarked on building Canada's first fighter aircraft. The need was clear. Canada's distances and scarce navigational aids required a long-range aircraft with the security of two engines and a second crew member to navigate. The new plane would have Canadian-designed Orenda engines, also fitted in the thousands of F-86 Sabres turned out by Canadair. A. V. Roe at Malton, successor to Howe's Federal Aircraft, would build the CF-100. In 1951, Brooke Claxton announced an air defence force of nine squadrons of CF-100s, nine radar stations and a new ground observer corps to spot incoming enemy aircraft.

It was not enough. The Soviet atomic bomb was swiftly followed by a test of the vastly more powerful hydrogen bomb. May Day displays of air power confirmed that the Russians could deliver their thermonuclear weapons to the heart of America. Fifty hydrogen bombs, Foulkes told his colleagues after a trip to Washington, could wipe out the American war-making capacity. Only fifty Soviet bombers in a thousand-plane raid had to get through and the Russians had won the war. Luftwaffe pilots over Germany had been triumphant when they knocked down one bomber in five. Continental air defence was no longer for weekend warriors; it was a huge, costly priority in which Canada must either play its part or be taken over. By 1954, Canada's scattered radar installations had become a Pinetree Line of thirty stations straggling across the continent and costing $450 million. Canada paid a third of the price and split the annual cost of manning and operation with the United States. Already, more warning time was needed for faster Soviet bombers. An electronic scanning device devised at McGill University provided the basis for a Canadian-financed Mid-Canada Line, begun in January, 1955. The line not only combined Canadian technology and resources; it left the Americans with no excuse for not providing the far more costly sea and air "wings" along the 55th Parallel which prevented the Mid-Canada Line from being outflanked.

Canadians could take a legitimate pride in their air defence contribution. Within the secret sessions of the chiefs of staff, General Simonds, like Foulkes before him, protested the distorting effect on defence priorities of the costly radar lines and the extravagance of designing aircraft like the CF-100 and its proposed successor, the CF-105 Arrow. The aircraft industry, Simonds grumbled, seemed to have great difficulty in estimating its costs. The admirals kept their complaints to themselves. The navy's attempt to build *St. Laurent* class destroyer escorts, the biggest job Canadian shipyards had ever tackled, also proved costly and troublesome before the seventh ship was delivered in 1957. Only the army, still the Cinderella service, did much complaining. Its only serious development project, an armoured personnel carrier called the Bobcat, was chronically stalled by conflicting design requirements and shortage of funds.

By American standards, such inter-service quarrels were minor. In the early 1950s, American policy on air defence was complicated by bitter public battles among advocates of carriers, missiles and strategic bombing, with the United States Congress as financial arbiter. When the United States Air Force triumphed, its own ranks were split between supporters of the powerful Strategic Air Command under General Curtis LeMay and those who wanted to rebuild American air power in Europe and the Far East. The change of administration in 1952 caught key decisions in mid-flight. During the summer of 1952, scientists at the Massachusetts Institute of Technology, working on a USAF contract, had proclaimed the benefits of an Arctic line of radar stations. Their report was thrown into the inter-service battle.

Throughout the controversies, Canadian defence officials had the unedifying experience of watching top-secret defence information and wild allegations hurled about the Congress and the American press as ammunition for the contending forces. At least some of the claims about a defenceless North America were designed to pressure Ottawa into bearing a bigger financial burden. Claxton had approved the Mid-Canada line because of his shrewd judgement that such evidence of Canadian exertion might forestall American pressure to participate in the enormously costly Arctic radar line. He was right. Canadian contractors helped construct the Distant Early Warning line between 1955 and 1957 but American taxpayers paid the bill. Moreover, part of Ottawa's price for permitting construction was an explicit American statement of Canada's sovereignty over the Arctic.

Three radar lines, offshore picket ships and flying radar patrols might detect invading aircraft. Only other aircraft could identify and, if necessary, destroy them. Even by 1956, the CF-100 was too slow to out-run a jet bomber. At best, radar controllers could vector the fighter to intersect the incoming flight path, giving the pilot one chance to sight and destroy a target. The CF-105 Arrow would solve that problem with its supersonic scheme and phenomenal fire control system—if it were ever built. C. D. Howe had boasted that Canada could manufacture anything. In fact, the Arrow was to be a mixture of Canadian and American systems and the mix was constantly changing. When the J-67 engine ran into development troubles, Avro switched to the Canadian-designed Iroquois. When the Hughes Corporation would not adapt its fire control system for the Arrow, the order was switched to RCA until its ASTRA system proved a failure. A Canadian-designed missile system was abandoned as already obsolete and then revived when the U.S. Navy's Sparrow II was scrapped. A worried Howe confessed to the House of Commons in 1955: "I can say now that we have started a programme of development that gives me the shudders." The RCAF concluded that auxiliary squadrons could not handle the new plane and cut its orders from 400 to 100. Frantic sales efforts overseas produced no foreign buyers. Price estimates fluctuated wildly, depending on the case anyone wanted to make, but by 1957 values, they were enormous—from $2.5 million to $6 million per aircraft, or even $12.5 million if each plane bore its full share of all the abortive development costs.

The Avro Arrow was only part of keeping up to date in air defence. A supersonic defence battle needed a complex, foolproof communications system and a computer-like mechanism to absorb complex data and spit out directions to fighters, anti-aircraft missiles, governments and civil defence authorities. In Europe, NATO air defences were undermined when France refused to surrender air sovereignty to an alliance-wide air control system. In North America, Washington wanted a bilateral North American Air Defence Command. Ottawa was willing but efforts to link the arrangement to NATO got a frosty response from the Americans. In February of 1957, Ralph Campney, Claxton's successor, argued the case for the proposed NORAD arrangement in the cabinet. With an election pending, ministers sniffed trouble and postponed a decision until they were safely back in office.

Air defence was hardly an issue when Canadians voted on June 10, 1957, but another military excursion distinctly was. Canada's cultivation of what soon would be called the Third World had begun at San Francisco in 1945 with the birth of the United Nations. Canada's postwar self-image as a "middle power," rich enough to be idealistic, free of superpower arrogance, immune from the taint of colonialism, persuaded Canadians that they could be honest brokers in a crooked world. Mackenzie King had rejected a UN request for Canadian observers in Korea in 1948 but St-Laurent had no hesitation in sending Canadians to Kashmir or in joining India and Poland in an International Control Commission to cover France's retreat from Indochina in 1954. Canadians served on the UN Truce Supervisory Organization, keeping a shaky peace between Israel and her bitter Arab neighbours. In 1954, Lieutenant-General E. L. M. Burns served as chief of staff of the UN's Palestine operation.

Burns was closer than he wanted to be when, on October 29, 1956, a badly provoked Israel sent her forces deep into neighbouring Egypt. By prior arrangement, Britain and France joined the war to avenge the Egyptian seizure of the Suez Canal earlier that year. Washington was furious at its allies. The Soviet Union threatened to flatten London and Paris (while its own forces busily crushed a popular anti-Soviet uprising in Hungary). The Egyptian government stubbornly refused to collapse as Britain's Anthony Eden had confidently expected. At the United Nations, it was Lester Pearson's chance and he took it. As chairman of the Security Council, he proposed that a UN police force would separate the warring parties and enforce the old borders. The belligerents resentfully agreed to be separated. As Canada's share of the force, the Queen's Own Rifles left Calgary for Halifax. There was a hitch. Colonel Nasser was displeased. Soldiers of the Queen were not wanted on Egyptian soil. General Burns, summoned from his supervisory duties to take charge of the new UN operation, discreetly pointed out that his real need was for competent administrative units and signallers. In due course, HMCS *Magnificent* left Halifax laden with vehicles, equipment, stores and a thousand Canadian soldiers, most of them from supporting arms and services. The Queen's Own went back to Calgary.

Pearson's initiative won him the Nobel Peace Prize. Many Canadians were delighted to have played a role in the world. Others were not. For the first time, Britain had entered a conflict and Canada had not only stood on the sidelines but opposed her. Even the rejection of the Queen's Own rankled. In June of 1957, Canadian voters had plenty to think about—an aging prime minister, the arrogance of C. D. Howe during the debate on the trans-Canada pipeline and the first symptoms of a new recession. The pride in Canada's peace-keeping initiative faded; resentments remained. They hardly mattered. Everyone knew that on June 10 the Liberals would be returned. Many Canadians voted against them anyway. To their amazement, the Progressive Conservatives emerged with the most seats. Moreover, when the Tories produced not only a prime minister in John Diefenbaker but an entire new cabinet, Canadians were almost exhilarated to discover that the nation did not depend on the familiar grey figures of the past twenty-two years. The Liberals, fresh from choosing Lester Pearson as their new leader, grossly miscalculated when they prematurely toppled the minority Diefenbaker government. On March 31, 1958, the electorate promptly gave the Conservatives the biggest majority in history, 208 seats to a mere 45 for the Liberals and 8 for the CCF.

To Canadians, merely for an inexperienced government to cope seemed a triumph. A minority government could legitimately put off tough decisions, show its generosity to the voters and, on April 1, 1958, return with power to do anything it felt necessary. The new prime minister was no military expert. A former CEF lieutenant, Diefenbaker's military career ended honourably but without distinction in a training accident. The military experience came with his new Minister of National Defence. Almost since his resignation from Pacific Command in the wake of the 1944 conscription crisis George Pearkes had served as Tory defence critic. He was also a shrewd enough politician to nominate Diefenbaker for the Progressive Conservative leadership in 1956. Pearkes's weakness was that of any presumed expert in his own field: he knew too many answers to bother asking enough questions.

Diefenbaker, on the other hand, had the self-assurance of ignorance. Acting as his own external affairs minister, he blithely signed the controversial NORAD agreement when Pearkes brought it to him, ignoring his own officials and other cabinet colleagues. General Foulkes, for one, was acutely embarrassed. Diefenbaker's consent created a tightly organized, centralized defence system. The NORAD commander at Colorado Springs could, in a crisis, order American and Canadian forces into action. So too, in his absence, could his Canadian deputy, Air Marshall Roy Slemon. Such a prompt response was the inevitable consequence of air warfare technology but the serious implications for Canadian sovereignty seem to have struck the prime minister only when he faced the jeers of his Liberal critics. Diefenbaker, characteristically, did not defend the arrangement or clarify the safeguards or the consultation built into the agreement. Instead, with some justice, he merely denounced the Liberals for condemning a deal they themselves had negotiated and which they would certainly have signed. That might be smart politics but it left ordinary Canadians with the suspicion that both parties had been equally bent on doing something wrong.

Diefenbaker also faced a much tougher problem: the Arrow. Like the NORAD agreement, it was a decision the Liberals had gratefully postponed. On the very day that the first prototype Arrow rolled out of its Malton hangar, October 4, 1957, a Soviet missile carried Sputnik I into orbit around the earth. In the race for a new generation of air weapons, intercontinental ballistic missiles, the USSR had suddenly registered an impressive lead. The very threat for which the Arrow was designed, the manned jet bomber, might suddenly be superseded by the missile age. Bewildered by competing advice, complex technology and undoubtedly soaring costs, the Conservative cabinet finally issued a statement on the Arrow on September 23, 1958. Development of the aircraft would continue for a further six months. Canadian commitment to ASTRA and the Sparrow missile was over. Instead, Canada would acquire new radar equipment, the Bomarc missile and the SAGE control system to meet the new missile threat. The statement revealed more ignorance than decisiveness. Avro and its huge workforce would get the first Arrow test flight into the air but no more. Mention of the Bomarc was absurd. It was, to be true, a missile, but its only use, if it ever worked, would be against bombers.

For six months, the Arrow programme wandered on, with General Pearkes making desperate bids for foreign sales but to no avail. On February 20, 1959, it was all over. Within minutes, Avro's Crawford Gordon had fired 14,000 employees. For reasons as yet unfathomed, the Conservative government ordered all thirty-seven pre-production models destroyed. Contractors ripped each machine apart and carted away the wreckage as scrap. A prime minister who boasted of his Canadian nationalism had administered the most bitter single blow to Canadian pride. Yet even the Liberal opposition, by condemning the manner, not the substance, of the Arrow decision showed that they too would have cancelled the project. As though fatally bound to prevaricate, Diefenbaker and Pearkes insisted that the decision was purely strategic—that the Arrow was useless in a missile age—and then confused the issue by mentioning the Bomarc. The real reason, as Pearkes would later confess, was economic. Canada, General Foulkes had insisted, could not afford an $8 million fighter. Even with a hundred Arrows in service, most of Canada's air space would still be defended by the USAF. If Britain, which had abandoned its own major missile programmes in despair at their cost, was willing to turn to the United States as a supplier, Canadians could also abandon to the superpowers the costly privilege of designing weapon systems.

Yet no defence decision is purely economic. Part of the Arrow's development problem had been the need to shop among a welter of competing major corporations for its weapons, guidance system and engines. Each change entailed costly alterations to the airframe. To Americans, competition was the lifeblood of a market economy. It was also incredibly wasteful. The Arrow died because of strategic confusion, beginning with commanders preoccupied with service concerns, compounded by political leaders who felt no obligation to penetrate to the hard core of defence issues. Excluded from serious defence information while they were merely opposition members, Diefenbaker, Pearkes and their colleagues had neither the time nor the inclination to make themselves thoroughly informed once they were in office. Finally, the Arrow was killed not because Canada could not afford it but because it felt no need to. National priorities lay elsewhere. The country's postwar economic strength and its attendant opportunities had been frittered away. Concerned about rising unemployment and persistent budget deficits, the Diefenbaker government concluded that the Arrow, for all its brilliant design team and its 14,000 workers, was too costly for a country in economic decline. After his defeat, Diefenbaker would be celebrated as the last hope for Canada's economic independence. In office, he had taken one hard look at the costs and risks of technological independence, had quailed and fled.

His government promptly began to pay the price. Willing to help a troubled ally, the United States agreed to waive its Buy America Act and a tangle of customs and fiscal regulations by approving a formal Defence Production Sharing Program. Since the United States continued to modernize while Canada's major research and development programmes had stalled, most of the initial advantages flowed north. Between 1959 and 1969, Canada acquired a favourable balance of defence business of over half a billion dollars. The defence industries developed under Howe's careful tending, became branch plants, importing some advanced American technology, doing business worth an average of $600 million during the 1960s and moving modestly into the world export trade in arms and military equipment. In return, Canada would import its major defence items from the United States.

During the Arrow controversy, the prime minister had proclaimed that the age of the manned fighter was over and that only missiles were needed for a modern defence force. To show its determination, the government purchased two squadrons of Bomarc missiles to be based at La Macaza, Quebec and at North Bay, Ontario, to shield population centres around Montreal and Toronto. For good measure, a battery of Honest John surface-to-surface missiles was purchased for the army's brigade in Europe. The trouble started at once. Conceived by a University of Michigan research team and developed by the powerful Boeing Corporation, the first version of the Bomarc, with liquid fuel and a conventional warhead, was scrapped as a failure. Boeing tried again with the Bomarc-B, built for solid fuel and a nuclear warhead. Only Boeing's powerful influence in Congress and a lucky test flight saved the weapon from oblivion in April, 1960. One powerful argument for sceptics in Washington was the heavy dependence of Diefenbaker on the Bomarc. Diefenbaker's dependence was mixed with ignorance. To the end, the prime minister insisted that the Bomarc had non-nuclear warheads. Perhaps no one told him that none was even considered for the Bomarc-B. Militarily, it would have been absurd to launch a million-dollar rocket with only a fair chance of hitting a single bomber. Some scientists also insisted that a high-altitude nuclear explosion could even "cook" the bomb load on an enemy plane, rendering it harmless.

Whatever Diefenbaker had told Parliament, manned interceptors were still needed. Only a pilot could check that a radar blip really meant the Third World War and not a tight formation of geese or an errant airliner. From the start, the Canadian chiefs of staff had said so. Diefenbaker had ignored them. Now, with the CF-100s and the F-86s long past their working life, replacement had become urgent. The Americans generously offered sixty-six F-101 Voodoo fighters, sitting idle at a Nevada storage depot. The USAF had relegated the Voodoo to the Air National Guard; it would do to equip three RCAF squadrons. Since Canada's pride forbade an outright gift, a complicated barter deal developed. The Pentagon reluctantly agreed to swap the Voodoos for CL-44 Yukon transport aircraft produced at Canadair. Ottawa balked. Tory MPs from ridings hurt by the Arrow cancellation rebelled at a Montreal factory profiting from Malton's loss. In the end, Canadair got an even better deal. It would produce the F-104 Starfighter, deliver enough for a shrunken eight-squadron RCAF contribution to NATO and send another $50 million worth of fighters to other NATO members. In addition, Canada took over American-manned radar stations on the Pinetree Line.

Between them, the Voodoo and the Bomarc represented a humiliation which not even the Diefenbaker talent for bluster could hide. The government had scrapped a half-billion dollar development programme and emerged with sixty-six explicitly second-rank American fighters and a small collection of dubious anti-bomber missiles. The ICBM threat, dragged in as a justification for the Arrow decision, remained unanswered and, perhaps, unanswerable. As they followed his twists and turns, Canadians might wonder whether their prime minister could tell the truth or, more probably, whether he understood what he was saying. The confusion was soon compounded.

Throughout the 1950s, most Canadians were probably not much better informed than their prime minister about the horrifying implications of continental air defence. The potential of thermonuclear holocaust seemed appropriate only for science fiction. Disarmament negotiations, a passionate preoccupation for liberal idealists in the late-1940s, had degenerated into another cold war ritual, generating more suspicion of covert advantage-seeking than hope. Yet, the defence policies of the Eisenhower and Dulles era made thermonuclear weapons the only real American deterrent to Soviet power. Not even German rearmament could produce sufficient conventional strength to resist a serious Soviet invasion of western Europe. First the British and then the French developed their own small independent nuclear arsenal. The Americans had christened their defence strategy the "New Look" and had appointed Admiral Charles Radford, whose wartime motto had been "kill the bastards scientifically," to head the Joint Chiefs of Staff. Publicly, John Foster Dulles promised "massive retaliation" for any Soviet aggression and journalists expanded on his mixture of Presbyterian rectitude and devotion to capitalism.

In a nuclear age, strategy was no longer designed by generals on horseback but by academics and mathematicians. A Harvard professor, Henry Kissinger, argued persuasively that limited wars might still be possible in a nuclear age and that they might well be necessary to keep an enemy from nibbling for gains that could not possibly justify nuclear retaliation. A Canadian, R. J. Sutherland, was credited with formulating the "first strike, second strike" concept, as vital to nuclear strategy as Newton's law of gravitational forces had been for physics. Victory, the Defence Research Board scientist argued, was not a matter of who made the first strike but how much retaliatory strength survived for the victim to strike back. Suddenly, Sutherland's doctrine gave a new dimension to total air defence. Protecting Strategic Air Command had always been a major NORAD task. American airmen needed no reminder of what had happened to bombers at Clark and Hickam fields in 1941. Intelligence experts noted that the Soviet Union was devoting enormous energy to building shelters and promoting civil defence. In a nuclear holocaust, millions would die but millions more might be saved if food, water and medical supplies were stockpiled and if people took shelter from radioactive fallout. Suddenly, it was no longer a handful of Communist sympathizers or the modest community of pacifists who were busy making people's flesh creep at nuclear horrors: it had become the business of governments.

In Canada, civil defence had frequently bordered on the absurd. In 1948, Ottawa had appointed the veteran enthusiast for armoured warfare, Major-General Frank Worthington, as Civil Defence Co-ordinator. Worthington had done his best, crusading chiefly for standardized hose couplings for Canadian fire departments. In 1951, the defence department had passed civil defence to the Department of Health and Welfare. Now it returned with a vengeance.

In the postwar years, the role of the Canadian militia had undergone a painful transformation. In peace or war, it had always been the front line of Canadian defence. In 1946, that role apparently survived as the reserve army units were built into six divisions and four armoured brigades. By pre-war standards, training, equipment and financial support seemed almost lavish. Then, without official acknowledgement, the proud role evaporated. After Korea and NATO, Canada's real front line troops were men of the regular army. In a Third World War, experts broadly hinted, only the forces in being on "D-Day" would count. Costly new equipment was reserved for the regular brigades. Very little trickled down to the reserves. Interest and recruits faded. The social prestige of a militia commission, devalued after 1919, mattered very little after 1945. In 1953, units of the Reserve Army mustered barely a fifth of their authorized strength and only 15,000 men and women went to camp. Brooke Claxton responded with a commission headed by Major-General Howard Kennedy. The old name returned when the reserve army became the Canadian Army (Militia). General Kennedy's advice was clear; the militia must be reorganized as the nucleus for units to be formed in an emergency; its personnel must be trained in peacetime for wartime duties. It was a brave idea and popular at the annual meetings of defence associations organized by reserve officers. Carefully camouflaged, even in the mid-1950s, was another notion: the militia would be a nucleus for a civil defence organization.

General Simonds and other senior army officers fought the conversion of the militia to civil defence, adding it to their list of grievances against the RCAF and its overweening influence. A civil defence role, they believed, would end recruiting and utterly demoralize the loyal core of officers and men who had kept the reserve force alive. Kennedy's report brought a militia revival: more militia trained in 1955 than in any postwar year. The generals lost their battle. In 1956, Ralph Campney announced that the army would henceforth be trained for civil defence. The generals, trying to cushion the blow, hid the full implications from militia units. As with other tough defence decisions, the painful task of adjusting the militia to its new role fell to the new government. General Pearkes was a gloomy and reluctant messenger. No one knew better than he did that militia morale had been tied to the vicarious excitement of war and to contact with modern weapons. "You can't serve two masters," Major-General W. H. S. Macklin had warned militia officers, "and if you are going to divert your efforts to civil defence, you might as well turn in your tanks." That was more or less what Conservative defence policy entailed. Summer camps ended after 1957. On May 28, 1959, civil defence responsibilities were formally laid on the Canadian Army. Artillery, armoured and infantry militia regiments abandoned corps training to learn the skills of finding and treating casualties in bombed-out buildings. Militia and regular units across Canada were reorganized in sixty-six mobile support columns and assigned to likely target areas. As the generals had foreseen, members left the militia in droves.

Their resentment was matched by the Canadian public. For the first time since the Second World War, the government set out to involve every Canadian in a defence problem. Citizens were urged to build fall-out shelters for themselves and their families and to stock them with food and water. To match the army's National Survival responsibilities, a national Emergency Measures Organization, with provincial and municipal components, was established. Spokesmen insisted on its potential value for natural disasters like floods, forest fires or violent storms like Hurricane Hazel but there was no effort to conceal its real purpose. Sirens appeared on roofs of public buildings. Newspaper articles explained the signficance of heat, light and blast in a nuclear explosion. Classroom teachers were instructed to train their students to crawl under their desks and to look away from windows at the moment of detonation. Civil defence exercises tested readiness and found appalling gaps. The CBC was ordered to broadcast around the clock and to be available as the anchor of a National Survival network.

The theory of civil defence was that a prepared population would not only be more likely to survive the catastrophe but that it would also be willing to endure the prospect with greater fortitude. Reality was quite different. Soviet propaganda experts could hardly have devised a more ingenious way to alarm or divide a population. The absurdity and amateurism of the precautions played counterpoint to the horrifying consequences of thermonuclear attack, emphasized and underlined by the government and the communications media. An American report from the Hudson Institute, written by Dr. Herman Kahn, argued cheerfully that the United States really could survive the annihilation of its major cities and most of its people because the real strength of the nation lay in its rural and small-town hinterland. Kahn became the model for *Dr. Strangelove*, an influential anti-war film of the era. Canadians responded to Kahn and his Canadian counterparts with horror, not appreciation.

In Britain, the United States and Canada, peace movements and demands for unilateral nuclear disarmament were not new but the government's openness about the hazard and the fatuous means to cope with it gave such movements life, enthusiasm and a host of well-documented arguments. The Liberal Party in 1960 proclaimed its uncompromising opposition to the acquisition of nuclear weapons for Canada. Its leader's wife, Maryon Pearson, joined the Voice of Women, a new and vocal peace organization. The CCF, transforming itself with labour union backing into the New Democratic Party, fervently endorsed nuclear disarmament. Cards, letters and petitions poured into the offices of the prime minister and his colleagues.

John Diefenbaker was no half-hearted cold warrior. He and the Conservatives had often berated the Liberals for faint-heartedness in the anti-communist crusade. In an election speech to a predominantly East-European audience, Diefenbaker had even spoken of rolling back the Iron Curtain. In power, the stridency was somehow muted. The defence budget, $1.8 billion in 1957, fell to $1.5 billion in 1960. In a world tour, Diefenbaker attempted to retain the Third World friendships acquired by his predecessors. He had begun by retaining the External Affairs portfolio, made a tragic error by appointing Dr. Sidney Smith, the former president of the University of Toronto, and finally, on Smith's death, turned to his old ally, Howard Green. A CEF veteran better known as a former crusader against oriental Canadians, Green had seemed suitably cast as Minister of Public Works. At External Affairs, he emerged in the unexpected guise of a naive idealist, convinced of the wickedness of nuclear weapons and profoundly suspicious of their closest producer, the United States.

More than a year after Green's appointment, on October 10, 1960, General Pearkes discreetly withdrew to the lieutenant-governorship of British Columbia. His successor, Douglas Harkness, was a wartime lieutenant-colonel in the artillery and a former Calgary history teacher. With none of Pearkes's seniority or influence, but with substantially more respect from his subordinates, Harkness set out to fight his department's battles in the cabinet. It was a nearly impossible chore. Green's influence was predominant. Having made one incredibly tough decision on the Arrow, Diefenbaker had retreated into chronic indecision, barely camouflaged by strident denunciations of enemies public and conspiratorial. Only one policy line had become clear: Canada would not acquire nuclear weapons.

The truth was that, under Diefenbaker, she had acquired little else. Though Diefenbaker seemed unable to admit it, the sole alternative to a nuclear warhead for the Bomarc-B was a load of sand. The Voodoo fighters could fly but to hit an enemy they needed nuclear-tipped rockets. So did the F-104 Starfighter, the light tactical bombers the RCAF had acquired to replace its Sabres. So did the Honest John missiles purchased for the army. Nuclear opponents in the cabinet added another argument: since the nuclear warheads, at Congressional insistence, remained exclusively under American guard and control, Canada's sovereignty would be infringed by such an American presence on Canadian soil. Since a healthy contingent of Americans could already be found at bases like Gander and North Bay, the argument was far-fetched. Conservative ministers, reading their mail or watching knots of nuclear protesters on the lawns of Parliament Hill, needed no rational arguments.

As the Cold War edged into its greatest crisis, most of Canada's newest weapons sat helpless on the ground.

Unification
and
Detente

8

On October 25, 1962, American networks broke into normal programming and switched audiences to the White House. John F. Kennedy had decided to confront the Kremlin. Barely a hundred miles from the American mainland, the Soviet Union had secretly established missile bases in Cuba. The president, in his hard New England accent, proclaimed an immediate naval blockade of the island until the bases were removed. Immediately, NORAD's commander-in-chief ordered DEFCON 3, the state of alert just prior to actual war. Americans, their allies and much of the world waited breathlessly for the next development. Then, melodramatically, Soviet ships carrying missiles to Cuba altered course. Aerial reconnaissance showed dismantling of the missile sites. The hottest crisis of the Cold War passed into history. President Kennedy had become, for many, the last American hero.

For Canadians, the Cuban missile crisis was no such triumph. Like other major American allies, she had received a sudden emissary, bearing a package of fuzzy air photos, but from Canada, as a NORAD partner, much more was demanded. Her Bomarcs and Voodoo squadrons protected not only Toronto and Montreal but the heavily populated northeastern United States. In the crisis, they remained unarmed, their nuclear warheads still barred from Canadian soil. For two days, the prime minister and his divided cabinet debated proclaiming the alert before allowing American fighters and air-tankers to come to their Canadian dispersal points.

Unofficially, Canadians had been more dependable allies than John Diefenbaker knew. Without authority, Douglas Harkness had quietly put the forces on alert though without cancelling leaves. The RCN sent its ships to sea and, within thirty-six hours they had relieved American warships needed for the Cuban blockade. It was the prime minister who believed that he reflected the true Canadian public opinion. For two years, his daily mail had run heavily in favour of nuclear disarmament. In the cabinet, Howard Green and his allies could point to a burgeoning of peace organizations in universities and churches, to the growth of the Voice of Women and to newspaper editorials, some of them from comfortably conservative sources. Canadians were obviously tired of the Cold War and of Washington's leadership. James M. Minifie, widely known as the CBC's Washington correspondent, published *Peacemaker or Powdermonkey*, an eloquent argument for Canadian neutralism. Lesser tracts on the same theme poured from the presses.

Spokesmen like Minifie lifted the Canadian peace movement into spheres which campus radicals and its own venerable leaders could never have attained. When veteran CCFers and trade unionists met in Ottawa in August, 1961, to form the New Democratic Party, the convention was awash in nuclear disarmament buttons. The NDP platform promised an immediate end to the NORAD agreement and party leaders had to argue vigorously even to retain an equivocal commitment to NATO. Since 1960, the Liberals were on record as opposing nuclear weapons for Canada and, in the circumstances, there seemed to be no reason for the Diefenbaker government to jeopardize any of its fading popularity by defying the anti-nuclear mood. The armed forces might be humiliated by the impotence of their new weapons but that was a trifling political concern.

The electoral problems of his government had surprised even the prime minister. Hurt by high unemployment and a mid-campaign balance of payments crisis, the Conservatives on June 12, 1962 lost 92 of the 208 seats they had won in 1958. Diefenbaker's 116 supporters faced 100 Liberals, 19 New Democrats and a wholly unexpected contingent of 30 Social Crediters from Quebec. Apart from those Toronto ridings that remembered the Arrow, defence policy was barely a campaign issue.

The Cuban missile crisis of October, 1962, changed everything. Opponents of nuclear weapons might argue that the episode vindicated their warnings about the dangers of Cold War confrontation. Nationalists might rejoice that Diefenbaker had finally asserted Canadian independence at the moment of crisis. A far larger group of Canadians, generally indifferent to the complexities of defence and foreign policy, felt deep disquiet. Even before the missile crisis, the Gallup Poll had detected a surprising shift of public opinion in favour of nuclear arms, an ironic commentary on the clamorous disarmament crusade. After the Cuban crisis, a torrent of media coverage of defence issues made more Canadians aware of their government's confusion and public equivocation.

On January 4, 1963, NATO's retiring supreme commander in Europe, General Lauris Norstad, stopped in Ottawa as part of his farewell tour and, at an airport press conference, made it undiplomatically clear that Canada had committed itself to a nuclear role in the alliance. An American general on Canadian soil declaring that the Canadian government had not told the truth caused a sensation. Six days later, home from a Nobel Prize-winners' dinner in Washington, armed with a report from the Liberal defence critic, Paul Hellyer, on sagging service morale, Lester Pearson exploded his own bomb. At a nomination meeting in Scarborough, the Liberal leader reversed his party's stand: a Liberal government would, after all, accept nuclear weapons and then negotiate non-nuclear roles for the armed forces. Though Pearson immediately drew stinging abuse from the nuclear disarmers, he knew from the polls that he now commanded public opinion and that his statement would split open the minority Tory government. Diefenbaker realized his danger. On January 25, he delivered a virtuoso performance in the House of Commons, lengthy, confusing, savagely denunciatory. Canada, the prime minister insisted, had no nuclear commitment to NATO, whatever General Norstad claimed. It was all to be decided at the next NATO Council meeting.

Five days later, on January 30, 1963, in an almost unprecedented intervention, the American State Department issued a statement bluntly presenting as facts what Diefenbaker had denied or concealed: the Bomarc-B had never had a conventional warhead; the Voodoo could never perform effectively without nuclear-tipped missiles; Canada's choice of weapons for NATO had already confirmed her intended nuclear role.

Twice in a month, Americans had called the Canadian prime minister a liar. It was insensitive, tactless and true. No one knew it better than Douglas Harkness and on Sunday, February 3, he resigned. Pearson and his advisers carefully framed a motion of non-confidence based not on defence policy but on the government's self-evident disarray. Both the New Democrats, who might well have favoured Diefenbaker's defence stand, and the Social Crediters, whose Quebec members had inherited the traditional isolationism of their region, found themselves swept up in the rush to defeat the Progressive Conservative regime. On the evening of February 5, Diefenbaker's government was defeated. Only the defection of two more ministers, George Hees and Pierre Sevigny, the associate minister of national defence, remained to confirm the Tory downfall.

The election called for April 8, 1963 should have been about defence. Certainly the NDP insisted that nuclear arms were at stake and Diefenbaker announced that he would issue a formal, unequivocal statement on Conservative defence policy. It never appeared. Instead, like other politicians, the prime minister set out to prove that a party leader is never more free from searching questions than when he is engaged in the democratic give-and-take of an election campaign. Wattles quivering, forefinger stabbing, Diefenbaker rallied his shattered followers with denunciations of American meddling and scorn for Liberal opportunism. The response varied, from those who saw the Tory chieftain as a regional messiah to those who dismissed him as a deceitful windbag. The latter were fewer than they imagined. As confident of victory as Diefenbaker himself had been in 1962, Pearson emerged from the election with only 129 Liberals to 95 Conservatives. Once again, slightly reduced contingents of New Democrats and Social Crediters shared the balance of power. Not even the Liberals, bleary-eyed on the morrow of a flawed victory, could have predicted that Canada would be theirs for another full generation.

Despite Pearson's denunciations of Tory indecision, Liberal defence policy in 1963 was scarcely crystalline. An honest observer would have noted that the Conservatives had merely carried pre-1957 policies to their logical conclusion. A Liberal government would also have scrapped the Arrow, joined NORAD and accepted NATO roles suited to a highly professional and technologically advanced force. Members of that force had done their best to restore that kind of Liberal government. Service voters, counted separately since 1940, had been strongly pro-Liberal since 1945 but in the wake of the nuclear arms debate, they voted 70 per cent Liberal, 20 per cent Conservative and a mere 4 per cent for the NDP.

The services had voted for the expansionary days of the past. Times had changed. Opinion polls supported Pearson's qualified rejection of the peace movement but its forces remained strong in his own party, among Conservatives and especially in the NDP. In 1951, Canada's commitment to the NATO "Integrated Force" had seemed vital to encourage a bankrupt, demoralized Europe; by 1963, NATO's European members appeared to be in booming economic health and well able to look after their own defence needs. NORAD, designed to meet a Soviet bomber threat, would have to change out of recognition to cope with intercontinental ballistic missiles—even if that was ever technologically feasible. It was easy to blame politicians for the confusion of the Diefenbaker government but when ministers look bad, departments share the responsibility. Within the Department of National Defence, the RCAF had suffered most of the humiliation, as first the dream of a Canadian-built supersonic fighter vanished and then its pride as a fighting service was bruised by cast-off Voodoos and unarmed Starfighters. The humiliation had not forestalled the waste of millions of dollars and the denial to the lower priority army and navy of equipment and programmes they wanted very badly.

As part of a general probe of Liberal waste and maladministration, the Conservatives had appointed a Royal Commission on Government Organization headed by J. Grant Glassco. The report on the Department of National Defence was unflattering. Despite Claxton's apparent reforms, the Commission could not understand the triplication of arrangements for pay, recruiting, public relations or intelligence. It found that more than two hundred inter-service committees had become bottlenecks, not facilitators. It detected the administrative confusion that had contributed to the costly collapse of development programmes like the Arrow or the army's Bobcat armoured personnel carrier. It condemned the lack of civilian control in the department and complained that each of the three service chiefs had independent access to the minister. The chairman of the Chiefs of Staff Committee had the prestige of rank but no power and neither he nor the minister had an independent staff, capable of evaluating each service's demands. The consequence of these weaknesses, the Commission argued, was a disturbing shift in the defence budget away from new equipment and toward pay, allowances and current maintenance. In 1954, capital spending had captured 42.4 per cent of the budget; by 1962, the share was 18.9 per cent and falling.

In their programme, the Liberals had promised a searching review of Canadian defence policy—a political codeword for wait and see. Pearson's choice for the Department of National Defence was Paul Hellyer, a 40-year-old Toronto businessman, an MP since 1949, an aggressive man with few of the gentler political graces. An associate defence minister at the end of the St-Laurent years and Liberal defence critic in opposition, Hellyer had done more than anyone to switch Pearson's nuclear stand. His appointment seemed logical. Yet Hellyer was ambitious. For most politicians, the Department of National Defence was a graveyard. Even Brooke Claxton, the ablest of the postwar ministers, had retired exhausted and besmirched by criticism. The 1960s would be no easier, with a new government committed to spending no more on defence and the opposition parties already insisting on spending far less. The new minister was determined that his time in the department would not interfere with fulfilling his ultimate ambition, the leadership of his party. In a few years he would make his achievements a by-word not just in Canada but in the world. Though he did not initially plan the outcome, Hellyer would create the first completely unified, single-uniform armed force anywhere.

Integration was nothing new in Canada. Liberal ministers had traditionally espoused it as the one defence reform that appealed to their anti-military colleagues. By 1963, dental, medical, legal and chaplains' services had all been integrated though the economies were less conspicuous than the fact that each reform had produced more senior officers. The Glassco Report was a ready-made blueprint for more integration, particularly at National Defence Headquarters. Hellyer was not satisfied. Integration from the bottom up had failed; he would impose it, in proper hierarchical fashion, from the top down. Instead of a weak chairman of the chiefs of staff, there would be a single Chief of the Defence Staff. Instead of three powerful service heads, he would create four heads of branches, each managing an integrated function: operations, personnel, logistics and finance. Each of the services had such a branch; Hellyer would combine them. The new minister did not stop there. As his diary shows, service resistance propelled him onward. Even without their heads, the three services, with their tiresome rivalries and inefficiencies, might somehow survive. Few Canadians outside the military community would ever grasp the significance of a headquarters reshuffling. To Hellyer, armed forces unification may initially have been only an ultimate step; it soon became an integral part of both an institutional reform and his personal campaign.

The promised Liberal defence review took the form of a white paper released in March, 1964 and compiled with only a little reflection of the report of a special parliamentary committee on defence which had been meeting frequently since the previous June. The white paper was a long document, sometimes vague, often rhetorical and rarely original. Canada's strategic problems had not changed with a new government nor would they alter much over the ensuing generation. Canada would remain in NATO and NORAD though peacekeeping was proclaimed as the highest priority and continental defence dropped to third place. The navy would continue to hunt submarines; Bomarcs, Voodoos, Starfighters and Honest Johns would all need their nuclear tips. Strategic doctrine now referred to "flexible response" instead of the "masssive retaliation" of the Dulles era but the change was modest. No scenario for World War III promised a leisurely mobilization; battles would be fought with the forces and equipment in being. The reiteration of old realities could not be made to sparkle by adjectives like "flexible," "mobile" and "imaginative." If Hellyer suspected that even a thorough integration of headquarters would win him little fame, he was right. Tucked away in the white paper was an explicit statement of the minister's radical plan. There was little comment. If the government wanted to shuffle staff officers to find money for new equipment in a steady-state defence budget, there would be no complaints—except from those who demanded that the savings be bigger and spent on peaceful purposes. Very few critics saw to the heart of the country's real defence problem. One of them was Andrew Brewin, the NDP's defence commentator and, unlike some of his colleagues, an informed and prudent critic of the defence establishment. "There is only one effective way of cutting Canada's defence expenditures," Brewin concluded, "and that is to reduce the role or the attempted functions to be performed by the Canadian services. This, of course, the White Paper does not recommend." Instead, almost to illustrate the Liberal commitment to peacekeeping, an infantry battalion and a scout car squadron had left for Cyprus in mid-March, 1964 to attempt to separate warring Greeks and Turks. As if to illustrate Hellyer's concern for global mobility, the RCAF delivered the troops and HMCS *Bonaventure*, the navy's aircraft carrier, loaded its decks with their vehicles and supplies. Instead of cutting commitments, as Brewin had suggested, Canada had assumed another thankless and endless military responsibility.

Within the forces, Hellyer's promise of a "single unified defence force" was met with bewilderment. This was not what the services had expected from a restored Liberal government. The needs were obvious: tanks and armoured personnel carriers for the army, replacements for the RCN's aging destroyers and a new long-range patrol plane to replace the Argus. Hellyer admitted the needs but he also insisted that the forces themselves must be drastically reorganized so that equipment costs could be met from an existing budget. At the special parliamentary committee, General Simonds had suggested that Canada needed a tri-service force like the United States marines. The image was clever if misleading; like other tough, disciplined professionals, the marines were useful but their basic role as an amphibious landing force was highly specialized. To Hellyer, the concept remained persuasive. In a modern world, he insisted, technology had wiped out the distinctions among land, sea and air warfare. Personnel must be adaptable. A demand for qualified signallers for the Congo peacekeeping operation in 1960 had been partially frustrated because neither RCAF nor RCN communications technicians could be switched to an army task. Why not make trades and specialties interchangeable? The reward would be more varied careers and broader promotion prospects.

The new minister moved quickly. A month after the white paper appeared, Bill C-90 was introduced on April 10, 1964, creating a single Chief of Defence Staff and a functional structure for National Defence Headquarters. In a year preoccupied by debating a national flag and unearthing Liberal scandals, Hellyer's legislation passed close parliamentary scrutiny but escaped public fanfare or media attention. The parliamentary committee ignored criticism from three retired officers and the bill passed without amendment on July 7, 1964. As the three service headquarters shuffled into their new organizations, Hellyer turned to a more difficult problem: the command structure. While the navy sat calmly, confident that its maritime role was assured, the army argued for regional commands while the RCAF insisted on a functional system. The outcome was an awkward compromise—six functional commands, most of them with regional responsibilities: Maritime Command for the navy and the air force's anti-submarine squadrons; Mobile Command for the army's brigade groups and the RCAF's ground support squadrons; Training Command; Material Command and two absorbed unaltered from the RCAF, Air Defence Command and Air Transport Command. Communications Command became a seventh while Canadian forces in Europe would report directly to Ottawa. The new commands were proudly announced on June 7, 1965 and, on May 1, 1966, the former camps, stations and land-based "ships" of the navy became thirty-nine Canadian Forces Bases. A single recruit training system, integrated technical schools and messes and an automated pay system went into effect.

Senior officers felt entitled to a breathing space to resolve problems, establish jurisdictions and adjust to the most drastic organizational changes in their experience. Their advice had been brusquely ignored by the minister but they had worked their dutiful best to support him. Hellyer had no such intention. Years before, as an eager aircrew trainee, he had been suddenly transferred to the army as part of the RCAF's token solution to the 1944 manpower crisis. The memory still rankled. So did the opposition he was encountering from senior officers. More and more his achievements were being acclaimed. Experts from abroad demanded details. "He has earned the nation's gratitude and its continued support" intoned the *Winnipeg Free Press* in a New Year's Day salute for 1966. The *Vancouver Sun* offered an even more useful comment for a would-be leadership contender: "young Mr. Hellyer seems to be quietly pulling off what may in time be recorded as this government's greatest achievement." Unification would proceed.

Few of Hellyer's senior officers had accepted his major premises for unification, whatever their view of integration. For all the talk of "marines," the Canadian services had had remarkably little to do with each other except when the RCN and the RCAF co-operated in anti-submarine warfare. Canada's postwar military experience had seen the army in Korea and Germany while the air force worked with NORAD and provided a NATO air division which had very little to do with the army's brigade group. The 1964 white paper offered little evidence that the roles would change. Apart from peacekeeping, primarily an army role, the hunt for non-nuclear tasks had led to a vague commitment to NATO's northern flank where Norway not only banned nuclear weapons but foreign soldiers from its soil. Unification may not have imperilled the bonds of regimental, squadron or ship loyalty, as its critics proclaimed, but Hellyer took few pains to say so. A subsidiary purpose was certainly to "Canadianize" the services by eliminating British-style uniforms, badges and customs though some could claim that such elements had been themselves "Canadianized" by service in two world wars. The new green uniforms and the badges of the unified armed forces were designed instead to be compatible with those of Canada's new imperial protector, the United States.

The most serious issue of unification should have been whether the operational challenges of three different fighting environments, land, sea and air, could be met by a single service. The Glassco Commission had concluded that the demands were incompatible. In his own argument against the change, General Simonds had illustrated how each environment influenced a junior officer's fundamental decision to fight or flee. An air force pilot decided for himself whether or not to attack an enemy. The decision for a junior naval officer was made for him by his captain. An infantry lieutenant had to persuade not only himself but a couple of dozen others to share the hazards of an attack. There was a logical reason for some services to stress technical or professional skill as a basis for promotion while others emphasized qualities of leadership. Common uniforms and ranks might be bureaucratically neat but they concealed real differences of role and responsibility.

Hellyer and perhaps most Canadians could dismiss such arguments as vague, feeble or nostalgic relics from old officers fighting past wars. Opposition struck the minister and some of his advisers as tantamount to mutiny. Service tradition dictated that the only course open to officers with principled objections to a policy was to resign. Two senior generals had done so in 1964; they were followed in the summer of 1966 by seven admirals. One of them, Rear Admiral William Landymore of Maritime Command, forced the minister to dismiss him. The others went quietly. They were followed by Hellyer's first Chief of Defence Staff, Air Chief Marshal Frank Miller, and the Chief of Technical Services, Air Marshal Clare Annis. As a protest movement, the resignations proved an utter failure. Vacancies were quickly filled by ambitious subordinates. Hellyer's staff reminded journalists of the generous service pensions for senior officers. Admirals, generals and air marshals proved inept as political lobbyists, and their efforts inspired more cartoons than editorials. Not even proof that Hellyer had censored Admiral Landymore's testimony to a House of Commons committee stirred politicians and journalists for long. Canadians had long boasted of their indifference to military affairs; they now proved the point. A country which had never really felt threatened felt no obligation to those who had defended it in the past and who now pleaded for their advice on its future security to be accepted.

Not all senior officers agreed with the critics. Even if unification was misguided, the professional code of obedience dictated that orders be obeyed. Air Chief Marshal Miller's successor was shrewdly chosen. General Jean-Victor Allard had been a gallant fighting soldier in Italy and an able Canadian brigade commander in Korea. Allard treated unification as a political directive and as an opportunity. A chronic optimist, he determined to find virtues which fellow officers had overlooked. As a French Canadian, he was less wedded to traditions which primarily satisfied Canadians of a British background.

In Centennial Year, 1967, Canadians were urged to achieve some special project. Paul Hellyer's was pre-determined. Whatever else fell apart that year, a commentator noted, it would not be the armed forces. The Conservatives decided not to co-operate. When Hellyer introduced Bill C-243 on December 7, 1966 with a rambling sixty-five-page speech, the opposition answered in kind, concluding with a filibuster on third reading. Hellyer was utterly frustrated. Pearson's resignation could not be long delayed and the ambitious minister wanted a turn in a less controversial department before the succession contest. The government proposed closure. The NDP consented. So did Real Caouette, the Social Credit leader; despite Liberal denials, he insisted that unification would release funds for a higher milk subsidy. On April 25, 1967, a tired House of Commons passed the Canadian Forces Reorganization Bill. That summer the three services commemorated their vanishing traditions in a huge Centennial tattoo. Even unmilitary Canadians found it the most exciting spectacle of the year.

Integration and unification, however, had really concealed a more fundamental weakening of the armed forces. Critics blamed Hellyer's reforms for the departure of 26,300 service personnel during the first eighteen months of integration, 13,142 of them prematurely. Most had been attracted by jobs and wages in a booming economy, Hellyer answered; others represented a bulge of Second World War veterans reaching the official age limit. Morale, he insisted, was high and getting higher because more funds would be available for new equipment. The minister was probably right; morale was more closely related to equipment than to staff structures or even the green uniform. The army still drove Centurion tanks long after European allies had abandoned them. Not until 1967 were armoured personnel carriers purchased for the infantry. Until then, they pretended that their 1952-vintage trucks were tracked vehicles. Hellyer's air force advisers favoured purchase of the American F-4 Phantom jet fighter; the minister insisted on the Northrop F-5 Freedom Fighter, a cheaper aircraft developed primarily for Third World and technologically unsophisticated air forces. When the price of building the new plane at the Canadair plant in Montreal rose above $215 million, Hellyer cut the order from 125 to 115 aircraft. The navy's anti-submarine role was even more costly. In 1963, Vice-Admiral H. S. Rayner had met the new government with a list of worries, ranging from his concern for Arctic sovereignty to a growing menace from Soviet missile-carrying submarines. Hellyer's response was to cancel eight general-purpose frigates approved by his predecessors and to insist on the anti-submarine role. The RCN purchased three submarines from British shipyards and won approval for four "Tribal" class gas-turbine powered helicopter destroyers and refits for its destroyer escorts and the big, aging *Bonaventure*.

By the time he left the defence department in 1967, Hellyer could feel proud of his achievements. He had out-wrestled the admirals and generals, devised a defence organization the rest of the world could envy, imposed his "global and mobile" theory on equipment purchases and stayed close to his budget ceiling of $1.5 billion a year. Only inflation had kept him from spending a quarter of every defence dollar on capital and equipment needs. A destroyer worth $20 million in 1960 cost $50 million by 1968.

Critics would also complain that two of those destroyers cost as much as Canada's entire foreign aid to India for a year. Hellyer had annoyed the military without placating an anti-military and increasingly isolationist electorate. He had stayed within his budget mainly by attrition in uniformed manpower, from 120,781 in 1963 to 110,000 by 1967. In NATO, Canada's air contribution had dropped to six squadrons and it would go lower if the Star-fighter was not soon replaced. In NORAD, the Mid-Canada line was abandoned and both the DEW line and many Pinetree line stations would follow. Far from shifting funds to equipment, Hellyer's term had seen a shrinking in capital spending from $251 million in 1963-64 to only $212 million in 1966-67. Brewin's 1964 warning that real economies could come only from fewer roles had been ignored; Hellyer had added roles in Cyprus and NATO's northern flank and his main purchase, the CF-5 fighter, proved valueless before it left the assembly line. It was little to show for so much re-forming zeal. After their brief preoccupation with defence in 1962-63, most Canadians lost interest. Military spending was not so much a menace as a waste. Canadians felt very secure in the 1960s. Walter Gordon, once Pearson's political conscience and still a cabinet minister, wondered publicly in 1967 whether Canada had any business belonging to NATO or NORAD. Gordon's welcoming echo came not from the NDP but from Dalton Camp, president of the Progressive Conservative party.

The Canadian sense of security was apparent in rising anti-Americanism. The distant, dirty war in Vietnam allowed Canadians a sense of moral superiority over their embattled neighbours. A government eager to distance itself from an unpopular war offered sanctuary to a tide of American deserters and draft-dodgers. The sight of American technology employed to blast a seemingly helpless Third World nation justified neutralists and opponents of defence. Such people remained, of course, a minority isolated in universities and the radical community. Most Canadians in 1968 wore a hangover from the Centennial euphoria. Old preoccupations had returned. A mild recession and rising inflation underlined the vulnerability of a branch-plant economy. In a technological age, Canada had fallen behind in research and development. Civic moralists pondered the consequences of a permissive age, the price of easy contraception and the inroads of the drug culture. Above all, there was Quebec. The Centennial mood had been lifted by the glittering triumph of Montreal's Expo 67; it had been shattered by the acclaim for Charles de Gaulle's cry of "vive le Québec libre."

In the spring of 1968, the resolution of every problem seemed to be bound up in the enigmatic, compelling personality of Pierre Elliott Trudeau. On December 14, 1967, Lester Pearson announced his impending resignation. On April 6, 1968, Liberals chose a successor. Hellyer, who had run so tirelessly for the job, lasted to the third ballot. Trudeau, an MP only since 1965, was the winner from the outset. By April 20, he was prime minister. Before the convention aura had faded or the hard questions could be posed, Trudeau dissolved Parliament and escaped into the image-ridden immunity of an election campaign. On the night of June 26, his party emerged with 155 seats, its first clear majority since the summer election of 1953.

The Trudeau enigma remained. Friends and enemies claimed that he had dressed in Nazi uniforms as a prank in wartime Montreal. A few fatuous souls accused him of Communism because he had once rowed to Castro's Cuba. In 1963 he had certainly voted NDP to protest Pearson's nuclear change-of-heart. Commentators compared his acerbic intellect to Arthur Meighen's; others noted a three-part name and a Scottish grandmother and recalled Mackenzie King. Trudeau certainly shared King's distaste for the military mind but he admired such military qualities as courage and fitness. The new prime minister admired clear, precise formulations of problems but he proved to be endlessly indecisive. He promised new leadership but tolerated cabinet mediocrities and did nothing to retain a dwindling stock of talent. He gave little attention to military matters but when he chose to deploy troops in the October crisis of 1970, he did so with drastic ferocity.

The services, formally unified from January 1, 1968, may have quietly rejoiced at the discomfiture of "Corporal Hellyer" but they had little to expect from his successful rival. Trudeau's "new leadership" depended less on his cabinet colleagues than on rapid expansion of his own office and on a ruthlessly systematic analysis of each major government policy and priority. Defence was an obvious target for the new approach to rational decision-making and the prime minister's own staff set out to make the hard choices Liberals had promised and failed to deliver five years before. Defence analysts like John Gellner had always complained that Canadian government had made defence policy from the wrong end, choosing weapons and personalities, when the first step should be to determine goals. The Trudeau government would make no such elementary error. On April 3, 1969, the prime minister issued the defence priorities of the new Liberal regime:

(a) the surveillance of our territory and coastline—i.e., the protection of our sovereignty;

(b) the defence of North America in co-operation with United States forces;

(c) the fulfilment of such NATO commitments as may be agreed upon;

(d) the performance of such international peacekeeping roles as we may from time to time assume.

While most Canadians probably dismissed the statement as a typical delphic evasion, Trudeau had in fact turned the Hellyer priorities of 1964 upside down. Hellyer's least concern had been "providing for certain aspects of security and protection within Canada"; as "surveillance," it had surged to the top. Peacekeeping, the primary role for Hellyer's unified organization, had fallen to the bottom. NATO and NORAD had traded places in significance. The real importance of the changed priorities trickled into view during 1969. Leo Cadieux, Hellyer's successor as Minister of National Defence, went to Brussels in May to warn NATO leaders that Canada might be cutting its contribution. On June 23, he told Parliament that Canada would henceforth need only 80-85,000 men for her defence roles. Three months later, the NATO allies learned the meaning of Cadieux's visit. Canada's NATO contingent of 10,000 men was cut in half, leaving a weak combat group of 2,800 soldiers and three squadrons of obsolete Starfighters. As part of the cut, the entire NATO contingent would concentrate at Lahr under American command. The last British connection was severed. The navy's *Bonaventure,* fresh from a $12 million refit, was scrapped. Five regular regiments, the Fort Garry Horse, the Canadian Guards, the Queen's Own Rifles, the Black Watch and the 4th Royal Canadian Horse Artillery, would vanish from the active list. Reserves would be cut from 23,000 to 19,000 members, mostly at the expense of supporting arms and service units. Bases would close.

Once they were convinced that both shoes had dropped, the services surveyed the damage and concluded that without Cadieux as their advocate it would have been worse. Prince Edward Island's Liberal government reminded Ottawa that Summerside was its second largest industry and won a reprieve. Other communities had no such influence. The prime minister, weathering his first blasts of unpopularity from other quarters, could conclude that defence cuts were popular. Yet cuts, save by omission, did not make a defence policy. Trudeau's 1969 statement merely added a responsibility called surveillance and then cut strength by almost a fifth. Cadieux went to his reward as ambassador to France and his department passed to another minister with leadership ambitions. Donald S. Macdonald made no claim to military experience nor was he prepared to spend his career in the defence department but he was willing to add prose to the stark outline of Trudeau's defence priorities. *Defence in the Seventies,* published in 1970, sought, dip-lomatically, to explain the military role in ensuring sovereignty, not merely in the Arctic and on the oceans but in aid to the civil power and in contributing to "the social and economic development of Canada." Civilian defence critics, who had always hoped that peacetime forces could somehow find themselves more peaceful roles, were pleased. Colin Gray, an academic observer, welcomed "a sensible redirection of attention to those domestic missions that have often been slighted in the past in the face of more glamorous big league 'real soldiering' alliance duties."

Macdonald's *Defence in the Seventies* remains the clearest rationale of Liberal defence for the decade. Its suggestion of a conflict between the military and civil function of the services hinted at another reform imposed from Trudeau's powerful Privy Council Office in 1972 when the service heads of branches at National Defence Headquarters became Assistant Deputy Ministers and, in some cases, were replaced by civil servants. The change was a penalty for bad decisions which senior officers themselves had often op-posed.

The penalty for service commanders who had not foreseen the Trudeau defence policy was civilian management of their departments, not just civilian control. Civil servants without military experience could not understand why armed forces needed operational medical or supply organizations as much as they needed infantry or fighter pilots. Lessons taught as long ago as the Crimean War meant nothing to an ambitious bureaucrat waiting for promo-tion to the Treasury Board or the Department of Health and Welfare. Hellyer's vision of a "global mobile" peacekeeping force had left with him: his 115 CF-5 fighters had not. Some equipped a new French-speaking squadron at Bagotville; most went into storage. The military took the blame. The *Bonaventure's* costly refit, due to government insistence on political patronage, was blamed on admirals. Four superb "Tribal" class anti-submarine destroyers, perhaps the best of their kind in the world, joined the navy only after the Trudeau government announced its support for a general-purpose role. The navy's experimental hydrofoil, *Bras d'Or,* after $52 million in development costs, was put in storage by government order though its pro-ponents argued that it and sister-ships would be ideal for Maritime Command's new task of watching over coastal waters and off-shore fisheries.

Sovereignty was a role the Canadian forces might have relished. Gray's sneer about "real soldiering" ignored the enthusiasm more adventurous of-ficers had always felt for the Arctic. In 1970, when a northern headquarters was finally opened at Yellowknife, Brigadier-General Ramsay Withers's com-mand was limited to thirty-five men. While Canada's interest in its oceans revived in the 1970s with a crisis of over-fishing and the discovery of badly-needed oil and gas reserves, Maritime Command was left ill-equipped and often grounded by budget restrictions on fuel and by the maintenance prob-lems of its decrepit aircraft. In 1977, Canadians and the world sneered when a Polish schooner sailed undetected into the eastern Arctic because Maritime Command lacked the means to find her. With only 10,000 men, the command drafted reservists and even sea cadets to find crews for its ships.

Defending sovereignty was not limited to fishery patrols or Arctic outposts. *Defence in the Seventies* cautiously included internal security in the role. Aid to the civil power was no novelty though its practices and procedures had faded from popular memory since the 1930s. Canadian television viewers became familiar with steel-helmeted American soldiers and national guardsmen playing their role in the "long hot summers" of the sixties. British troops were dragged into the pitiless communal violence of Northern Ireland and French troops and paramilitary police recaptured Paris's Left Bank in the violent May Days of 1968. Canada could not be immune. The peacekeeping role turned out to be a fair cover to allow soldiers to practise riot control. The prime minister warned a Queen's University audience that violence in the United States could conceivably spill over into Canada.

In fact, violence was perfectly indigenous. In 1969, Montreal youths, chanting the fashionable slogans of revolution, razed an English-owned bus garage after city police went on strike. While provincial police and troops rushed to Montreal, crowds looted downtown stores. A year later, on October 5, 1970, the British trade commissioner in Montreal, James Cross, was seized by a group proclaiming itself the Quebec Liberation Front. Five days later, another FLQ cell kidnapped Quebec's labour minister, Pierre Laporte. While Front communiques demanded ransoms, publicity for the FLQ manifesto and free passage to Cuba, Montreal's artists, students and connoisseurs of radical chic lionized the kidnappers. Leading critics of the inexperienced provincial government of Robert Bourassa met, debated the crisis, and offered their services as a more competent substitute administration.

On October 14, two days after Laporte was seized, Trudeau ordered troops into Ottawa to guard public buildings and prominent politicians. On the fifteenth, the Quebec prime minister formally requisitioned aid to the civil power. The battalions of the Royal 22e Regiment, already posted just north of Montreal, responded at once. Next morning, at 4 a.m., "after consideration of all the facts and particularly letters received from the Prime Minister of Quebec and the authorities of the city of Montreal, reporting a state of apprehended insurrection," Trudeau invoked the War Measures Act.

It was unprecedented. On the basis of facts then and later revealed, it was unjustified. It was also overwhelmingly popular at the time and, in terms of the crisis itself, a brilliant success. Military doctrine on riot control prescribed that all possible force be displayed at the outset, not dribbled piecemeal into the contest. Shock was the best safeguard against bloodshed. Trudeau's target was not two frightened little bands of terrorists, one of which very soon strangled its helpless victim; it was the affluent dilettantes of revolutionary violence, joyously cheering on the anonymous heroes in the FLQ cells. The War Measures Act and the thousands of helmeted soldiers pouring into

Montreal chilled the enthusiasm, dispersed the coffee table revolutionaries and left them isolated and frightened when police arrested hundreds whose guilt, if any, was limited to dreaming of blood in the streets.

For the Canadian armed forces, the Quebec crisis was an ambiguous experience. It was an exhilarating test for staff officers, communications systems and troops. Few had ever shared in an operation of such magnitude. The failures were minor. It was also fortunate that the troops could withdraw as early as November 12 without suffering or inflicting casualties. The episode brought a surge of recruits and short-lived hopes that the government might reconsider its 1969 cuts. Thoughtful officers also knew that "Priority One," as aid to the civil power was termed, posed greater dangers for the armed forces than any other. The prime minister had staked his own prestige on the proclamation of emergency powers but he had also thrown the prestige of the armed forces into a potential civil war. In 1972, when the Liberal government claimed that it was ready to use the forces again, Michael Forrestal, the Conservative defence critic, warned: "the deliberate use of the military to enforce the will of one group of Canadians over the will of another group of Canadians is detrimental to the credibility of the armed forces." No party was willing to propose an alternative.

The October crisis had sent the predominantly English-speaking armed forces into a tense French-speaking milieu. Unification had not altered the fact that the working language of Canada's defenders was English. Instead, the army's painfully-developed awareness of the needs of both national groups had been diluted by the predominantly unilingual navy and air force. The problem's dimensions had not really changed in a century. Language is not merely a means of communication; it is a reflection of culture and an instrument of power. Because the two national languages had rarely co-existed outside Quebec, northeastern Ontario and the Acadian regions of the Maritimes, few English-speaking Canadians and a diminishing number of Quebecois bothered to learn a second language. The dominance of English, consciously affirmed in the RCN and the RCAF and guaranteed by strength of numbers in the army, had been powerfully reinforced by close relations with first the British and then the American armed forces.

By the 1960s, the problem would not wait. Having belatedly discovered the potential of government, Quebecois would either share fully in federal power or establish their own provincial state. The Pearson government had temporized with the problem. A Royal Commission on Bilingualism and Biculturalism had lavished unprecedented sums on studies and reports, recording a discontent the English-speaking majority had usually ignored. Trudeau had come to Ottawa in 1965 to demonstrate his conviction that French Canadians could establish full equality for themselves in a federal Canada; as prime minister, he was in a powerful position to make his expectation come true. Bilingualism in federal institutions was one of the priorities his staff of policy-makers was charged with implementing. The Canadian armed forces were an obvious place to start. They were a model of most of the problems French Canadians experienced in relating to federal institutions. A resulting reluctance to enlist had contributed to the divisive conscription crisis of two world wars. Even in the postwar period, when more francophone Canadians enlisted, few reached the higher ranks. There were some good reasons. The services had provided technical training and experience at a time when these were scarce in Quebec. A career in the armed forces led inevitably to service outside Quebec and serious problems for servicemen and their families in adjusting to unfamiliar and sometimes inhospitable surroundings. The heart of the problem was that, outside a single infantry regiment, the Royal 22e Regiment, and some units stationed in Quebec, French-Canadian personnel had no choice but to work mainly in English.

There might have been other ways to reduce linguistic discrimination in the Canadian forces but it was almost inevitable that the Royal 22e Regiment would provide the model. In 1968, Leo Cadieux announced that other French-language units would be created. HMCS *Ottawa*, a destroyer-escort at Halifax, would be the first. The CF-5 squadron at Bagotville was another. Other units followed. The 5e Groupement de combat was formed at Valcartier. To provide it with armour and artillery, the 14e Regiment blindé, based on the Regiment de Trois-Rivières, and a light artillery regiment were created. Smaller French-language units, from engineers to military police, guaranteed a French-speaking representation for every branch of the unified forces. A "Francotrain" programme established separate French-language training schools for recruits and for many of the three hundred specialist skills. The third report of the Royal Commission on Bilingualism and Biculturalism demanded more and the government agreed. Both French and English gained equal status in the forces. French-language units in Mobile Command outside Quebec and at National Defence Headquarters were created. The new policy dictated that bilingualism be demanded of officers in the higher ranks and that promotion policies achieve a closer proportional representation of French and English throughout the rank structure.

Like other Canadians, English-speaking members of the armed forces might welcome bilingualism in theory but the practice provoked sharp resentments. Members of disbanded units were bitter when new French-speaking regiments were authorized in their place. A defence budget too weak to afford new aircraft or trucks had to bear the high costs of duplicating training facilities and translating complex technical manuals. Interference with merit and seniority principles in promotions provoked the harshest reaction. Rumours fed on resentment. Even the periodic honours list for the new Order of Military Merit was allegedly inflated to guarantee a 28 per cent quota of francophones. Highly-qualified English-speaking applicants for the forces joined waiting lists until the trickle of francophone recruits filled their share of vacancies. The forces were not, of course, exceptional. The Trudeau government's official languages programme contributed a good deal to the bilious discontent of much of the federal public service in the seventies. The armed forces, once a virtual English-speaking monopoly, came to resemble the country they served, even if the result was two mutually resentful solitudes. Despite Cadieux's hopeful promise that he would not "divide the force on a unilingual or geographical basis," the French-language units were hardly more integrated in the country than was Quebec itself. Yet a century and more of evolutionary change had demonstrated that evolutionary change would never be fast enough. Canadians, inside and outside the armed forces could hope, as with Canada itself, that patience and a more mature understanding of the value of representative military institutions would make the pain worthwhile.

By dropping peacekeeping into fourth priority, *Defence in the Seventies* had made one modest concession to realism. Canadian enthusiasm had faded since the dramatic days of the Suez crisis of 1956. The Congo expedition of 1960 had done most to cure both the UN and Canada of illusions about the value of intervention. The four-year operation cost the UN secretary-general his life and the organization its financial solvency. Canadians, who had virtually insisted that their government make a contribution, were lucky to escape with a few officers brutally beaten and much tropical experience. The problem with peacekeeping was that opportunities arose unpredictably and the pressure to act ignored the priorities of white papers. Abruptly expelled from the Sinai on the eve of the Six Days War of 1967, Canadians returned to the Middle East six years later to provide administrative support for a UN force on Israel's northern border with Syria and Lebanon. In Cyprus, NATO and Commonwealth pressure locked up a peacekeeping force which seemed to become an indispensable part of the island's fragile economy.

Experience, costly and sometimes painful, had taught Canadians when peacekeeping might work. They had no illusions, therefore, when Canada was named with Poland, Hungary and Indonesia to a grandly-titled International Commission of Control and Supervision to watch over the end of the war in Vietnam. The circumstances gave every warning of failure: there was no independent agency to back the commission, there was no independent arrangement for transportation, communication or protection of supervisory teams; above all, there was not much desire, except on the part of the Americans, even to stop fighting. Canada initially contemplated a peacekeeping army of 20,000: in the end, North Vietnam accepted an observer force of a thousand, a quarter of them Canadians. Under American pressure, Ottawa consented to participate for sixty days. Within the first forty days, teams reported 6,060 violations of the truce. Canadian observers stayed for their sixty days, continued reluctantly for sixty more days and finally left after one of their number had been shot down in a helicopter. They had covered the American retreat, the exchange of prisoners and little more. Even the Americans were annoyed at them. The open-mouthed diplomacy of Michel Gauvin, head of the Canadian mission, had almost deliberately exposed the futility of the settlement President Richard Nixon claimed to have extorted from Hanoi by his Christmas bombing offensive of 1972.

In 1969, Trudeau and his advisers had wanted to reduce Canada's involvement in defence alliances almost as much as they had wanted to discount the Hellyer commitment to peacekeeping. Events refused to fit in with their expectations. The strategic threats that both NATO and NORAD had been designed to face stubbornly refused to go away. As the Soviet bomber fleet grew older, even the Americans sharply cut back on NORAD. Washington's anti-missile defence systems remained off Canadian soil and firmly in American hands. Neither the bomber threat nor the need to check on intruding aircraft disappeared. President Jimmy Carter cancelled plans for an American supersonic bomber in 1977 but the Soviet Union grimly proceeded with its own Backfire bomber. In 1975, as part of a renegotiated NORAD agreement, Canada accepted responsibility for her entire air space. Instead of simply scrapping the wornout Voodoos, the Trudeau government discovered that its gesture of national confidence would have to be backed by a new fighter aircraft and elaborate radar and communications systems.

NATO also failed to fade away. The prime minister discovered that there was a price to pay for his bold decision to halve the Canadian forces in Europe. European leaders could discount the military value of even 10,000 ill-equipped Canadians but Trudeau's sudden reduction of the Canadian contribution might well have encouraged President Richard Nixon, hard-pressed in Vietnam, to follow suit. While Trudeau's defence review damaged relations with NATO partners, his simultaneous foreign policy review had called for greater emphasis on European relations. Diplomats, dutifully seeking new trading arrangements, discovered that Ottawa's defence policy had damaged their bargaining power. No one had explained to Trudeau's picked team of policy analysts that defence, trade and diplomatic influence might be tightly related nor that European politicians tended to be sceptical about Soviet offers of detente or disarmament.

Second thoughts about NATO led to Canadian reassurances at Brussels, not to re-equipment. Starfighters, converted to a ground attack role, sucked in birds and debris at low levels but Ottawa offered no replacement. Even politicians were embarrassed by the 1945-vintage Centurion tanks. A proposal to replace them with 100 British-made Scorpion reconnaissance vehicles faded when NATO commanders bluntly warned that they would be death traps on a European battlefield. Only in 1976, fifteen years late, did the cabinet agree to buy 128 German-made Leopard tanks at a cost of $137 million—a little less than two CF-5s. When they were delivered, British, German and Soviet armies had already adopted a superior battle tank. Even the belated tank purchase owed little to demands from defence associations. The prime minister had discovered that a NATO military contribution was Canada's ticket of admission to major disarmament negotiations, to the European Security Conference finally held at Helsinki in 1976 and, above all, to serious trade negotiations with the growing European Economic Community. Leopard tanks might not frighten the Russians but they pleased Canada's German allies and potential trading partners.

The most important military development of the 1970s was not the dramatic growth of Soviet tank armies in eastern Europe or the one-sided Soviet victory at the Helsinki talks. It was the emergence of Soviet naval power into warm water. By the end of the decade, Soviet fleets could challenge American naval dominance in almost every area of the world including the Mediterranean and the Red Sea. Soviet submarines, using new routes under the polar ice cap, could proceed safely to undersea locations off North America already surveyed by Soviet fishing fleets. Russian hunter-killer submarines could blockade the Atlantic as Hitler's U-Boats never had. Canada was immediately involved. When NATO planners realized that only Norwegian bases would allow it to cope with the Soviet Northern Fleet, Canada's vague northern flank commitment became more precise. By 1978, Canadian defence planners finally had to think hard about how they would deliver their promised forces to northern Norway. Canada's own claim to 5,800,000 square miles of ocean bed could also be challenged, though apparently not sufficiently to persuade Ottawa to expand its fleet. Instead, it approved a leisurely building programme for six patrol frigates, to be delivered late in the 1980s, and purchased eighteen Lockheed patrol planes for $1,042 million.

Purchasing the long range patrol aircraft showed how painfully little had changed after a decade of integration, unification, "civilianization," two conflicting white papers and the grandly titled 1974 Defence Structure Review. From 1972, when Lockheed offered twenty-three off-the-shelf Orion patrol planes for $300 million, the purchase decision had been reviewed by the cabinet, countermanded by the Department of Industry, Trade and Commerce, lobbied by Canadian electronics firms and their American head offices, switched to Boeing and back again, delayed when Lockheed was accused of bribery, reinstated, cancelled when the American company could not borrow money to start production, and then reconfirmed. For its billion-dollar deal, Canada purchased highly sophisticated electronic gear packed into a middle-aged aircraft. Armed forces planners insisted that they had performed their tasks well: no one dared criticize the rest of the process. Other equipment purchases were no more impressive. For $171 million, the government contracted with a Swiss firm to manufacture 441 wheeled armoured vehicles for purposes politely described as peacekeeping. The deal was delayed while the Department of Industry, Trade and Commerce tried to win friends in Brazil's military junta by arguing hard for the Brazilian "Urutu." The Swiss won by promising to build the machines at Thunder Bay, close to constituents of the President of the Treasury Board. The biggest defence contract allowed the overdue replacement of the Voodoo and Starfighter. Four of the six original contractors were eliminated simply because they cost too much. One of them, the Panavia Toronado, was the result of an earlier Canadian proposal to meet dual specifications for a high-altitude interceptor and a low-level fighter bomber. Trudeau had ended Canadian participation. The competition winner, the McDonnell-Douglas F-18D, still essentially unproven, emerged as the best of two poor choices. The ultimate loser, General Dynamics, spilled its bile in Quebec's 1980 referendum campaign by proclaiming in large advertisements that Ottawa had spurned Quebec's industrial interests.

Hellyer had promised that integration of National Defence Headquarters would usher in an age of efficiency, co-operation and economy. Experience had done little to prove him right. "Civilianization" of the headquarters had allegedly been a punishment for high cost overruns in construction of the "Tribal" class destroyers. The history of purchasing the Aurora and the new fighter aircraft suggested that few real gains had been made. Perhaps the real blame lay not with the structure of the Department of National Defence nor with its procession of rapidly changing ministers but with the centralization of power in the prime minister's office, under a man more brilliant in debate than in decision-making. The structure of the department also had nothing to do with continuing inflation nor with the government's attempts to control its total spending by recurrent but variously titled "freezes," "squeezes" and "cutbacks." Ministers could extract cabinet promises to add seven and even twelve per cent to defence budgets for equipment purchases but well-publicized general spending curbs regularly delayed purchasing decisions and, inevitably, added to their cost.

The world was not as comfortable for Canadians in the seventies as it had been in the sixties but their government resisted any temptation to relieve their anxieties by defence spending. After Health and Welfare and the Department of Finance, National Defence remained the third largest federal spending department, but its cabinet status remained humble. In a decade, it saw seven ministers, three of them in a single year. Some of them, like Cadieux and Edgar Benson, waited only for comfortable retirement appointments. Others, like James Richardson and Barnett Danson, were cabinet novices without influence or, in both cases, political prospects. In a cabinet where disagreement usually meant delay, ministers without the prestige to carry their arguments became a costly luxury.

Over the decade, even unification was eroded. By 1975, each of the old services had reappeared in the guise of a command—Maritime for the navy, Mobile for the army, and an Air Command, uniting Air Defence and Air Transport Commands and the squadrons and bases once associated with Mobile and Maritime Commands. If the changes began to revive separate identities and service pride, they did not bring that influence to Ottawa. The terms "navy," "army" and "air force" became permissible in 1975 but their respective commanders remained in Halifax, Montreal and Winnipeg, to fume at policy and equipment decisions that made sense chiefly to politicians and civil servants. Fifteen years of experience suggested that unification was better suited to routine administration than to the operational purposes armed forces exist to perform. It was still as hard for civilian officials to understand an army's need for operationally-available supply and medical services as it had been for the British War Office before the Crimean War. It was always cheaper to replace uniformed cooks and mechanics with civil servants or to require army service battalions to perform routine chores at the expense of field training. To Hellyer, it had seemed logical that anyone who flew belonged in a single service. Experience on the navy's helicopter-equipped destroyers might have led him to a different conclusion. To civilians, the special concerns and experiences which had led the three services in different and sometimes incompatible directions were evidence of the rigid military mind. Arguments pressed too hard became insubordination or even an intolerable challenge to civil supremacy.

Late in the 1970s, the Liberal government showed symptoms of relenting. Before the 1979 election, sensing that even the public had come to share some concern about Canadian defences, the government announced a cautious programme to add 4,700 men and women to a uniformed strength of less than 78,000 and a capital spending programme that would aim to reach at least 20 per cent of the defence budget. It was a programme endorsed by the Progressive Conservatives and confirmed when Joe Clark led his party into a minority government in June, 1979. Clark's choice for Minister of National Defence, Allan McKinnon, had been a career army officer and an able critic of confusion in defence budgeting and purchasing. By September, 1979, McKinnon had also established his own task force to advise how far unification could be unscrambled.

The task force was fated to report to a new minister in a Liberal government. By February 22, 1980, the Conservatives had sealed their political fate for at least four years and their interim government represented little more than an extra nine months' delay in purchasing programmes. The new minister, a wartime RCAF pilot, brought more prestige and a little more cabinet experience to the department than his recent predecessors. Within weeks, Gilles Lamontagne had confirmed the new fighter aircraft contract, the design contract for replacement warships and a miscellany of acronymic purchases ranging from ADLIPs (Automatic Data-Link Plotting Systems) to TARP (Terminal Aids Replacement Programme). Despite the pleas of McKinnon's task force, Lamontagne would not restore separate uniforms or undo the Trudeau government's "civilianization"; he would unscramble the separate means by which navies, armies and air forces organize and train for active service.

Yet, like all his peacetime predecessors, Lamontagne and his colleagues would live with a phenomenon that runs closer to the heart of Canadian defence policy than weapons or uniforms. Not for more than a century and a half have most Canadians sensed a genuine military threat to their country and its institutions. War itself, as an experience, has receded to the memories not of fathers but of grandfathers. That is no crime. It is, after all, evidence of a highly successful defence and foreign policy that Canadians have enjoyed such a unique and durable immunity from fear.

The immunity has never been purchased without sacrifice. Other nations have purchased time with lives and treasure so that Canadians could overcome peacetime neglect and prepare themselves in equipment and training. Once prepared, Canadians have gone to war and a hundred thousand have not come back. Their sacrifice has been part of Canada's immunity.

Neither sacrifices nor immunity can be depended upon forever. Canada's allies no longer dominate even their share of the world. Canada's claim to Arctic and ocean resources is no longer a matter of indifference to a world in desperate shortage of resources and of virgin territory in which to seek them. Canada's retreat from the industrial and technological competence she could claim at the end of the Second World War has left her militarily as well as economically close to the status of an underdeveloped nation.

In military affairs as in economics, underdevelopment means dependency. For most of its first century, Canada's armed forces had depended on Great Britain for their doctrines, weapons, values and structure. British military liabilities in technology and tactics had cost Canadians heavily. Because the British had learned from experience, Canadians had benefited from the lessons. Underlying the relationship was mutual respect for fighting qualities and a shared political and military tradition. In the new relationship with the United States, there was much less comfort. Canadians might admire American technological prowess but they had no comparable confidence in American fighting skill or tactical competence. The American armed forces in the wake of the Vietnam conflict did little to inspire confidence. Unlike the British after South Africa, the Americans gave little sign of accepting the military reforms demanded by a military setback.

In peacetime, few Canadians would worry about the consequences of the new military dependency for their country. Many would cling to the neutralist fantasy of the sixties; more would continue to believe that they lived in Raoul Dandurand's "fire-proof house." Old certainties persist until, one morning, they utterly vanish. Only then will experts press forward to explain how long ago the circumstances altered.

Canada's military immunity is a vanished certainty. It would be sad if Canadians were the last to discover it.

Further Reading

Of all the branches of historical writing in Canada, according to the prominent British historian, H. J. Hanham, military history appears to be the most advanced. This may only reflect the fact that old soldiers have usually found leisure to write, and readers find battles more interesting than the growth of the grain trade. A more solid reason is probably early official sponsorship of military history and the superb professional guidance of the Canadian Army's historical section by Colonel Charles Stacey. He and his successors have provided a vital core for military historians, both professional and amateur, across Canada. Much of the work recommended here reflects their influence.

Among the general introductions to Canadian military institutions and problems, the Stacey influence is apparent. G. F.G. Stanley was a deputy director of the historical section before he wrote *Canada's Soldiers: A Military History of an Unmilitary People*, rev. ed. (Toronto: Macmillan, 1967). D. J. Goodspeed produced the best overall history of the three services, *The Armed Forces of Canada, 1867-1967: A Century of Achievement* (Ottawa: Queen's Printer, 1967). J. L. Granatstein and the late J. M. Hitsman were both members of Stacey's historical organization. Their book, *Broken Promises: A History of Conscription in Canada* (Toronto: Oxford, 1977) deals in a partisan but highly informed way with a continuing issue. So do articles collected by Jean-Yves Gravel, *Le Québec et la guerre* (Montreal: Boréal Express, 1974). Canadian naval history has been somewhat overshadowed by the energy and productivity of the army's historians but G. N. Tucker, *The Naval Service of Canada: Its Official History*, 2 vols. (Ottawa: King's Printer, 1952) provides a substantial coverage from the origins to the end of the Second World War although it was written with perhaps more concern for detail than entertainment. The Royal Military College has been another centre for Canadian military history. Richard A. Preston, a former professor at the RMC, offers a comprehensive history of Canadian-American defence relations in *The Defence of the Undefended Border: Planning for War in North America, 1867-1939* (Montreal: McGill-Queen's, 1977).

Chapter 1

A number of books have dealt authoritatively with the problems of defence at Confederation. The pioneer was Charles Stacey's *Canada and the British Army, 1846-1871: A Study in the Practice of Responsible Government*, rev. ed. (Toronto: University of Toronto Press, 1963). Other important books are Kenneth Bourne's *Britain and the Balance of Power in North America, 1815-1908* (London: Longman's, 1967) and J. M. Hitsman's *Safeguarding Canada, 1763-1871* (Toronto: University of Toronto Press, 1968).

On the Canadian militia, two lively and opinionated contemporary accounts may be found in some libraries, George T. Denison's *Soldiering in Canada* (Toronto: George Morang, 1900) and R. H. Davis's *The Canadian Militia: Its Organization and Present Condition* (Caledonia: Wm. T. Sawle, 1873). For a more academic study, see Desmond Morton, *Ministers and Generals: Politics and the Canadian Militia, 1868-1904* (Toronto: University of Toronto Press, 1970) and *The Canadian General: Sir William Otter* (Toronto: Hakkert, 1974). Jean-Yves Gravel, *L'Armée au Québec (1868-1900)* (Montreal: Boréal Express, 1974) reflects a close social study of the 9th Voltigeurs. See also R. A. Preston's *Canada's R.M.C.* (Toronto: University of Toronto Press, 1979) for more than an institutional history.

The militia in the Northwest has often been left to play the role of chorus. The volunteers and their descendants have nonetheless left many accounts of their exploits. The most valuable, because of his central role in both 1870 and 1885 is C. A. Boulton's *Reminiscences of the North-West Rebellions* (Toronto: Grip, 1886). R. C. MacLeod's *The North West Mounted Police and Law Enforcement* (Toronto: University of Toronto Press, 1976) extracts truth from fiction and establishes the military as well as the police role of the force. C. P. Stacey's article, "The Military Aspect of Canada's Winning of the West 1870-1885," *Canadian Historical Review*, XXI, 1 (March 1960) remains relevant. The best single history of the troubles of 1870 and 1885 remains George Stanley's *The Birth of Western Canada: A History of the Riel Rebellions* (Toronto: University of Toronto Press, 1961) supplemented by his biography, *Louis Riel* (Toronto: Ryerson, 1963). Desmond Morton deals primarily with the military campaign of 1885 in *The Last War Drum: The North-West Campaign of 1885* (Toronto: Hakkert, 1972).

Chapter 2

The most important single book on Canada's involvement in the frequently vague and absent-minded imperial defence arrangement is R. A. Preston's *Canada and "Imperial Defence": A Study of the Origins of the British Commonwealth Defense Organization, 1867-1919* (Toronto: University of Toronto Press, 1967) supplemented by Bourne's *Britain and the Balance of Power* and Morton's *Ministers and Generals*. Norman Penlington looks at a brief but significant period in *Canada and Imperialism, 1896-1899* (Toronto: University of Toronto Press, 1965). Carl Berger's chapter on militarism in *The Sense of Power: Studies in the Ideas of Canadian Imperialism, 1867-1914* (Toronto: University of Toronto Press, 1970) introduces an important but unconsidered aspect of Canadian military attitudes. Carmen Miller's article, "Sir Frederick William Borden and Military Reform, 1896-1911," *Canadian Historical Review*, L, 3 (September 1969), does some overdue justice to a man less favourably seen by Lord Dundonald in *My Army Life* (London: Arnold, 1926). On Canadians abroad in imperial service see C. P. Stacey,

"Canada and the Nile Expedition of 1884-85," *Canadian Historical Review,* XXXIII, 4 (December 1952), expanded in more popular form in Roy McLaren's *Canadians on the Nile, 1882-1898: Being the Adventures of the Voyageurs on the Khartoum Relief Expedition and Other Exploits* (Vancouver: University of British Columbia Press, 1978). An outspoken Canadian in South Africa was W. H. McHarg, *From Quebec to Pretoria with the Royal Canadian Regiment* (Toronto: Briggs, 1902). A more kindly view of his commanding officer is in Morton's *The Canadian General* or in his "Colonel Otter and the First Canadian Contingent in South Africa, 1899-1900" in Michael Cross and Robert Bothwell, eds., *Policy by Other Means* (Toronto: Clarke, Irwin, 1972).

Chapter 3

A great deal has been written about Canada and the First World War although, beyond a narrowly military focus, a great deal remains to be said about an event which left so few aspects of Canadian life untouched. G. W. L. Nicholson's *The Official History of the Canadian Army in the First World War: Canadian Expeditionary Force, 1914-1919* (Ottawa: Queen's Printer, 1962) remains the central source though it may be supplemented, particularly from the appendices of A. F. Duguid's incomplete *Official History of the Canadian Forces in the Great War, 1914-19, General Series,* vol. I (Ottawa: King's Printer, 1938). Another official history, Sir Andrew Macphail's *Medical Services, 1914-1919* (Ottawa: King's Printer, 1925) was really a rebuttal in a stormy controversy with Herbert A. Bruce, *Politics and the C.A.M.C.* (Toronto: Briggs, 1919).

A number of biographies and autobiographies have broadened our understanding of the war and its impact. W. R. Bird's *Ghosts Have Warm Hands* (Toronto: Clarke, Irwin, 1960) is probably the best single memoir from any Canadian soldier in the war. E. L. M. Burns's *General Mud* (Toronto: Clarke, Irwin, 1970) recalls the experience of a highly intelligent Canadian officer in both world wars. J. A. Swettenham's *To Seize the Victory: The Canadian Corps in World War I* (Toronto: McGraw-Hill Ryerson, 1965) recognizes the contribution of Sir Arthur Currie while his three-volume biography, *McNaughton,* 3 vols. (Toronto: McGraw-Hill Ryerson, 1968-69) is a full account of probably the most fascinating Canadian soldier. Currie's contribution would be better appreciated by the revision and publication of A. M. J. Hyatt's doctoral dissertation on his career. At home, the role of Sir Joseph Flavelle has been brilliantly depicted by Michael Bliss in *A Canadian Millionaire* (Toronto: Macmillan, 1978), while the wartime prime minister finally has an objective treatment by Craig Brown in *Robert Laird Borden: a Biography* (Toronto, Macmillan, 1980, vol. 2).

While the regional significance of conscription was capably presented years ago by Elizabeth Armstrong's *The Crisis of Quebec, 1914-1918,* rev.

ed. (Toronto: McClelland and Stewart, 1974), the kind of comprehensive regional history which should be written is illustrated by Barbara Wilson, *Ontario and the First World War* (Toronto: University of Toronto Press, 1977) and by John Thompson, *The Harvests of War: The Prairie West, 1914-1918* (Toronto: McClelland and Stewart, 1979). A more modest but highly creditable project was produced by Daphne Read and a group of university students, *The Great War and Canadian Society: An Oral History* (Toronto: New Hogtown Press, 1975). Myer Siemiatcki, "Munitions and Labour Militancy: The 1916 Hamilton Machinists' Strike," *Labour/le Travailleur*, III, 1978, illustrates the potential of another kind of historical study of the war in Canada. J. A. Corry's "The Growth of Government Activities in Canada, 1914-1921," *Historical Papers*, 1940, has still not been superseded although it should have inspired dozens of detailed studies. An example is David Smith's article, "Emergency Government in Canada," *Canadian Historical Review*, L, 4 (December 1969). Wartime politics have been explored by John English in *The Decline of Politics* (Toronto: University of Toronto Press, 1977).

Chapter 4

The history of Canadian defence between the wars has been virtually defined by the two excellent volumes of James Eayrs, *In Defence of Canada: From the Great War to the Great Depression* and *Appeasement and Rearmament* (Toronto: University of Toronto Press, 1964-1965). The memoirs and biographies of soldiers and politicians add something to understanding of the period, particularly Swettenham's *McNaughton* vol. I and M. A. Pope, *Soldiers and Politicians: The Memoirs of Lieutenant-General Maurice Pope* (Toronto: University of Toronto Press, 1962).

Surprisingly little has been written about the hundreds of thousands of returned soldiers beyond the predictable denunciations and *apologiae* of the time. Desmond Morton's "Kicking and Complaining: Postwar Demobilization Riots in the Canadian Expeditionary Force, 1918-19," *Canadian Historical Review*, LXI, 3 (September 1980), marks a small beginning.

A variety of books deal with Canada's reluctant approach to the Second World War, notably the introductory lecture by C. P. Stacey in *Mackenzie King and the Atlantic Triangle* (Toronto: Macmillan, 1976) and J. L. Granatstein, *Canada's War: The Politics of the Mackenzie King Government, 1939-1945* (Toronto: Oxford, 1975). Stacey's *The Military Problems of Canada* (Toronto: Ryerson, 1940) attempted to set Canada's war effort in historical context. Victor Hoar's *The Mackenzie-Papineau Battalion* (Toronto: Copp Clark, 1968) is a sensitive and ingeniously researched account of some very brave but unofficial Canadian soldiers. Ronald Liversedge's *The On-to-Ottawa Trek and Other Recollections*

(Toronto: McClelland and Stewart, 1973) reflects a sturdily unofficial view of the experience of being a Royal Twenty Center.

Chapter 5

As with the First World War, Canadians have been slower to write the history of the home front than of fighting in 1939-45, although the balance is slowly being rectified. The official record is dominated by Charles Stacey's massive *Arms, Men and Governments: The War Policies of Canada, 1939-1945* (Ottawa: Information Canada, 1970) although there are huge areas of activity which he understandably by-passed. J. W. Pickersgill and D. F. Forster's *The Mackenzie King Record*, vol. I, 1939-44 and vol. II, 1944-45 (Toronto: University of Toronto Press, 1960, 1968) provide an important documentary record. Granatstein's *Canada's War* provides a further account from King's perspective.

Canadian-American relations in the war are dealt with by Eayrs in *Appeasement and Rearmament*, by Colonel Stanley Dzuiban, *Military Relations Between the United States and Canada 1939-1945* (Washington: Office of the Chief of Military History, 1959) from an American perspective and, from a more Canadian viewpoint, in R. D. Cuff and J. L. Granatstein, *Ties that Bind: Canadian-American Relations in Wartime from the Great War to the Cold War* (Toronto: Hakkert, 1977).

Granatstein's *The Politics of Survival: The Conservative Party, 1939-1945* (Toronto: University of Toronto Press, 1967), Norman Ward's edited *Memoirs of Chubby Power: A Party Politician* (Toronto: Macmillan, 1966) and Andre Laurendeau, "The Conscription Crisis" in Philip Stratford ed. *Witness for Quebec* (Toronto, Macmillan, 1973) all provide important sidelights on wartime politics in Canada. So does Roger Graham's *Arthur Meighen*, vol. 3; *No Surrender* (Toronto, Clarke, Irwin, 1965). Both the 1942 and the 1945 conscription crises are discussed at length in Granatstein and Hitsman, *Broken Promises*.

Treatment of the Japanese Canadians has been recorded by Ken Adachi, *The Enemy That Never Was: A History of the Japanese-Canadians* (Toronto: McClelland and Stewart, 1976), and more anecdotally by Barry Broadfoot, *Years of Sorrow, Years of Shame: The Story of the Japanese Canadians in World War II* (Toronto: Doubleday, 1977). Broadfoot's technique of editing interviews infuriates historians but it conveys many authentic messages, particularly in *Six War Years, 1939-1945: Memories of Canadians at Home and Abroad* (Toronto: Doubleday, 1977). A more conventional but solidly informative historical account is Robert Bothwell and William Kilbourn's *C. D. Howe: A Biography* (Toronto: McClelland and Stewart, 1979).

The role of women in the war has been briefly explored in articles by

Ruth Pierson, "Women's Emancipation and the Recruitment of Women into The Canadian Labour Force in World War II," *Historical Papers,* 1976 and "Jill Canuck: CWAC of All Trades but no Pistol-Packing Momma," *ibid.,* 1978. Wartime reforms in labour relations are described by Laurel MacDowell, "The Formation of the Canadian Industrial Relations System During World War II," *Labour* III, 1978.

Chapter 6

The history of Canadians overseas has been adequately dealt with for the navy by Tucker's *The Naval Service of Canada,* vol. 2 and comprehensively for the army in Charles Stacey's *The Official History of the Canadian Army in the Second World War,* vol. I, *Six Years of War* and vol. 3, *The Victory Campaign* (Ottawa: Queen's Printer, 1955, 1960) and by G. W. L. Nicholson's, *The Canadians in Italy,* vol. 2 (Ottawa: Queen's Printer, 1956). An official history of the RCAF fell victim to that service's postwar priorities and has become the belated and somewhat leisurely preoccupation of the now-unified Directorate of History. W. A. B. Douglas and Brereton Greenhous of the directorate have published an unofficial and outspoken one-volume history, *Out of the Shadows: Canada in the Second World War* (Toronto: Oxford, 1977) which, despite too many minor editing errors, provides a lively and sometimes controversial account of the war.

The navy shrewdly provided itself with a popular history soon after the war, Joseph Schull's *The Far Distant Ships* (Ottawa: King's Printer, 1950), before many of the problems and technological developments of the convoy war could be publicized. More recent accounts include John Swettenham's *Canada's Atlantic War* (Toronto: Samuel-Stevens, 1979), Alan Easton's *50 North: An Atlantic Battleground* (Toronto: Ryerson, 1969), James B. Lamb, *The Corvette Navy* (Toronto: Macmillan, 1977) and perhaps the best of the personal memoirs, Hal Lawrence, *A Bloody War: One Man's Memories of the Canadian Navy, 1939-45* (Toronto: Macmillan, 1978). Hugh Garner's novel, *Storm Below* (Toronto: Simon and Schuster, 1971) captures much of the atmosphere of lower deck life on a corvette, an experience the author shared.

In personal memoirs, the RCAF has been as ill-served as in its official history and the army has generally matched the lead established by its official histories. Ross Munro's *Gauntlet to Overlord: The Story of the Canadian Army,* (Edmonton: Hurtig, 1973, rev. ed.) was a journalist's account, to match Joseph Schull's work for the RCN. Farley Mowat's evocative history of *The Regiment* (Toronto: McClelland and Stewart, 1973) was more than that dreary genre normally allows and the first volume of his personal war memoirs, *And No Birds Sang (ibid.,* 1979) matches Will Bird's account of the earlier war. Swettenham's biography of *McNaughton,* vol. 2, establishes that soldier's place in the war while Burns's *General Mud* offers an autobiographical defence of a commander his subordinates ironically called "Smiling Sunray."

Burns's *Manpower in the Canadian Army* (Toronto: Clarke, Irwin, 1956) provides important factual background to the 1944 conscription crisis, largely supporting the criticisms of the generals which are heavily apparent in R. M. Dawson's *The Conscription Crisis of 1944* (Toronto: University of Toronto Press, 1961), originally a research note for Dawson's planned biography of Mackenzie King. King's position is also defended by Granatstein in *Canada's War* and *Broken Promises*. Stacey's *Arms, Men and Governments* attempts to right the balance a little. So does R. H. Roy's biography of General Pearkes, *For Most Conspicuous Bravery* (Vancouver: University of British Columbia Press, 1977).

Chapter 7

Canadian veterans and their postwar experiences have again been neglected after the Second World War, with the exception of an enterprising little book by Joyce Hibbert, *The War Brides* (Toronto: Peter Martin, 1978). Postwar defence policy is again dominated by the writing of James Eayrs, with two more volumes of *In Defence of Canada*, vol. 3, *Peacemaking and Deterrence* and vol. 4, *Growing Up Allied* (Toronto: University of Toronto Press, 1972, 1980) carrying the story into the 1950s. Canadian foreign policy became a more studied phenomenon, particularly as earlier members of the Department of External Affairs brought their wisdom and experience back to the universities. John Holmes, *The Shaping of Peace: Canada and the Search for World Order, 1943-57* (Toronto: University of Toronto Press, 1979) is typical of the benefits of the cross-fertilization.

Canada's role in Korea was given official study by H. F. Wood, *Strange Battleground, Official History of the Canadian Army in Korea* (Ottawa: Queen's Printer, 1964) and Thor Thorgrimmson and E. C. Russell, *Canadian Naval Operations in Korean Waters, 1950-1955* (Ottawa: Queen's Printer, 1965). A comprehensive study of the diplomatic aspects of Canada's participation is that of Denis Stairs, *The Diplomacy of Constraint: Canada, the Korean War and the United States* (Toronto: University of Toronto Press, 1974). Canadian peacekeeping activities were explored by Alastair Taylor, David Cox and J. L. Granatstein in *Peacekeeping: International Challenge and Canadian Response* (Toronto: Canadian Institute of International Affairs, 1968). General E. L. M. Burns, as a direct participant, recorded his experiences in *Between Arab and Israeli* (Toronto: Clarke, Irwin, 1962). See also James Eayrs, *The Commonwealth and Suez* (Toronto: Oxford, 1964).

The unhappy history of Canada's involvement in continental air defence is best recorded by Jon B. McLin, *Canada's Changing Defence Policy, 1957-1963* (Baltimore: Johns Hopkins, 1967) although possibly more might now be said from a greater perspective. The fate of the Arrow has been recorded by many embittered victims. The best recent account is probably James Dow, *The Arrow* (Toronto: James Lorimer, 1979). The polemics about Canadian defence policy in the nuclear age range from J. M. Minifie's witty and sometimes persuasive *Peacemaker or Powdermonkey: Canada's Role in a Revolutionary World* (Toronto: McClelland and Stewart, 1960) to John Warnock's *Partner to Behemoth, The Military Policy of a Satellite Canada* (Toronto: New Press, 1970). No history of the great National Survival escapade has yet been written.

Chapter 8

Modern defence policy understandably has much analysis, endless polemic and virtually no history. Andrew Brewin's *Stand on Guard: The Search for a Canadian Defence Policy* (Toronto: McClelland and Stewart, 1964) reflects a shrewd and realistic appraisal of the 1964 white paper within the obvious constraints of the NDP's rather other-worldly defence policies. Paul Hellyer's onward march from integration to unification is described and offered a sympathetic preliminary evaluation by W. J. Kronenberg, *All Together Now: The Organization of National Defence in Canada, 1964-1972* (Toronto: Canadian Institute of International Affairs, 1973).

Foreign policy and defence advice for the new Trudeau government is reflected in Stephen Clarkson, ed., *An Independent Foreign Policy for Canada* (Toronto: McClelland and Stewart, 1968) and by Lewis Hertzman, John Warnock and Tom Hocken, *Alliances or Illusions: Canada and the NATO-NORAD Question* (Edmonton: Hurtig, 1969). James Eayrs even offered an ingenious rationale for the total abolition of the armed forces in "The Military Policies of Contemporary Canada: Principles, Problems, Precepts, Practices," in Richard Leach, ed., *Contemporary Canada* (Durham: Duke University Press, 1967).

The Trudeau government's response, the 1969 white paper, generated a number of books both critical and sympathetic. A collection of essays in Hector Massey's *The Canadian Military: A Profile* (Toronto: Copp Clark, 1972) includes some valuable analyses among much dross. Colin S. Gray's *Canadian Defence Priorities: A Question of Relevance* (Toronto: Clarke, Irwin, 1972) struggled, not always successfully, to make sense out of a contradictory situation. John Gellner's *Bayonets in the Streets: Urban Guerillas at Home and Abroad* (Toronto: Collier-Macmillan, 1974) urged in the aftermath of the Quebec crisis that the army stay out of counter-insurgency operations in Canada although his alternative of a paramilitary police was not well received.

In the seventies, some of the optimism underlying Trudeau's early defence and foreign policies has withered. The change is illustrated by books like Brian Cuthbertson's *Canadian Military Independence in the Age of the Superpowers* (Toronto: Fitzhenry and Whiteside, 1977) and Gerald Porter's mildly alarmist *In Retreat: The Canadian Forces in the Trudeau Years* (Ottawa: Deneau & Greenberg, 1978). A valuable summary of the problems and dangers of modern defence policy, disarmament and other unfashionable concerns for an unmilitary people is General E. L. M Burns's *Defence in the Nuclear Age: An Introduction for Canadians* (Toronto: Clarke, Irwin, 1976). Like this chapter, books on the recent past must depend on limited public sources. Future revision is inevitable and to be welcomed.

Index